Penguin Books

Death in the Afternoon

Ernest Miller Hemingway was born in 1899 at Oak Park, a
highly respectable suburb of Chicago, where his father, a
keen sportsman, was a doctor. He was the second of six
children. The family spent holidays in a lakeside hunting
lodge in Michigan, near Indian settlements. Although
energetic and successful in all school activities, Ernest twice
ran away from home before joining the Kansas City *Star* as a
cub reporter in 1917. Next year he volunteered as an
ambulance driver on the Italian front and was badly
wounded. Returning to America he began to write features
for the Toronto *Star Weekly* in 1919 and was married in
1921. That year he came to Europe as a roving correspondent
and covered several large conferences. In France he came into
contact with Gertrude Stein – later they quarrelled –
Ezra Pound, and James Joyce. He covered the Greco-Turkish
war in 1922. *Three Stories and Ten Poems* was given a
limited publication in Paris in 1923. Thereafter he gradually
took to a life of bull-fighting, big-game hunting, and
deep-sea fishing. He visited Spain during the Civil War.
Latterly he lived mostly in Cuba and died in July 1961.

He early established himself as the master of a new,
tough, and peculiarly American style of writing and became
a legend during his lifetime. But, as John Wain wrote in the
Observer after his death, 'Though there were many
imitators there was never truly a "School of Hemingway",
because the standard he set was too severe.'

His best known novels include *A Farewell to Arms* (1929),
For Whom the Bell Tolls (1940) and *The Old Man and The
Sea* (1952). In 1954 he was awarded a Nobel Prize for
Literature. Ernest Hemingway had three sons.

Death in the Afternoon

Ernest Hemingway

 Penguin Books
in association with Jonathan Cape

Penguin Books Ltd, Harmondsworth,
Middlesex, England
Penguin Books Australia Ltd, Ringwood,
Victoria, Australia
Penguin Books (N.Z.) Ltd,
182–190 Wairau Road,
Auckland 10, New Zealand

First published in the U.S.A. in 1932
Published in Great Britain by Jonathan Cape in 1932
Published in Penguin Books 1966
Reprinted 1971, 1972, 1973, 1974, 1976
Copyright © Ernest Hemingway Ltd, 1932

Made and printed in Great Britain by
Cox & Wyman Ltd,
London, Reading and Fakenham
Set in Monotype Bembo

Chapter 1

At the first bullfight I ever went to I expected to be horrified and perhaps sickened by what I had been told would happen to the horses. Everything I had read about the bull ring insisted on that point; most people who wrote of it condemned bullfighting outright as a stupid brutal business, but even those that spoke well of it as an exhibition of skill and as a spectacle deplored the use of the horses and were apologetic about the whole thing. The killing of the horses in the ring was considered indefensible. I suppose, from a modern moral point of view, that is, a Christian point of view, the whole bullfight is indefensible; there is certainly much cruelty, there is always danger, either sought or unlooked for, and there is always death, and I should not try to defend it now, only to tell honestly the things I have found true about it. To do this I must be altogether frank, or try to be, and if those who read this decide with disgust that it is written by someone who lacks their, the readers', fineness of feeling I can only plead that this may be true. But whoever reads this can truly make such a judgement when he, or she, has seen the things that are spoken of and knows truly what their reactions to them would be.

Once I remember Gertrude Stein talking of bullfights spoke of her admiration for Joselito and showed me some pictures of him in the ring and of herself and Alice Toklas sitting in the first row of the wooden barreras at the bull ring at Valencia with Joselito and his brother Gallo below, and I had just come from the Near East, where the Greeks broke the legs of their baggage and transport animals and drove and shoved them off the quay into the shallow water when they abandoned the city of Smyrna, and I remember saying that I did not like the bullfights because of the poor horses. I was trying to write then and I found the greatest difficulty, aside from knowing truly what you really felt, rather than what you were supposed to feel, and had been taught to feel, was to put down what really happened in action; what the actual things were which produced the emotion that you experienced. In writing for a newspaper you told what happened and, with one trick and another, you communicated the emotion aided by the element of timeliness which gives a certain emotion to any account of something that has happened on that day; but the real thing, the sequence of motion and fact which made the emotion and which would be as valid in a year or in ten years or, with luck and if you stated it purely enough, always, was beyond me and I was working very hard to try to get it. The only place where you could see life and death, i.e. violent death now that the wars were over, was in the bull ring and I wanted very much to go to Spain where I could study it. I was trying to learn to write, commencing with the simplest things, and one of the simplest things of all and the most fundamental is violent death. It has none of the complications of death by disease, or so-called natural death, or the death of a friend or someone you have loved or have hated, but it is death nevertheless, one of the subjects that a man may write of. I had read many books in which, when the author tried to convey it, he only produced a blur, and I decided that this was because either the author had never seen it clearly or at the moment of it, he had physically or mentally shut his eyes, as one might do if he saw a child that he could not possibly reach or aid, about to be struck by a train. In such a case I suppose he would probably be justified in shutting his eyes as the mere fact of the child being about to be struck by the train was all that he could convey, the actual striking would be an anti-climax, so that the moment before striking might be as far as he could represent. But in the case of an execution by a firing squad, or a hanging, this is not true, and if these very simple things were to be made permanent, as, say, Goya tried to make them in *Los Desastres de la Guerra*, it could not be done with any shutting of the eyes. I had seen certain things, certain simple things of this sort that I remembered, but through taking part in them, or, in other cases, having to write of them immediately after and consequently noticing the things I needed for instant recording, I had never been able to study them as a man might, for instance, study the death of his father or the hanging of someone, say, that he did not know and would not have to write of immediately after for the first edition of an afternoon newspaper.

So I went to Spain to see bullfights and to try to write about them for myself. I thought they would be simple and barbarous and cruel and that I would not like them, but that I could see certain definite action which would give me the feeling of life and death that I was working for. I found the definite action; but the bullfight was so far from simple, and I liked it so much, that it was much too complicated for my then equipment for writing to deal with and, aside from four very short sketches, I was not able to write anything about it for five years – and I wish I could have waited ten. However, if I had waited long enough I probably never would have written anything at all since there is a tendency when you really begin to learn something about a thing not to want to write about it but rather to keep on learning about it always and at no time, unless you are very egotistical, which, of course, accounts for many books, will you be able to say: now I know all about this and will write about it. Certainly I do not say that now; every year I know there is more to learn, but I know some things which may be interesting now, and I may be away from the bullfights for a long time and I might as well write what I know about them now. Also it might be good to have a book about bullfighting in English and a serious book on such an unmoral subject may have some value.

So far, about morals, I know only that what is moral is what you feel good after and what is immoral is what you feel bad after and judged by these moral standards, which I do not defend, the bullfight is very moral to me because I feel very fine while it is going on and have a feeling of life and death and mortality and immortality, and after it is over I feel very sad but very fine. Also, I do not mind the horses; not in principle, but in fact I do not mind them. I was very surprised at this since I cannot see a horse down in the street without having it make me feel a necessity for helping the horse, and I have spread sacking, unbuckled harness and dodged shod hoofs many times and will again if they have horses on city streets in wet and icy weather, but in the bull ring I do not feel any horror or disgust whatever at what happens to the horses. I have taken many people, both men and women, to bullfights and have seen their reactions to the death and goring of horses in the ring and their reactions are quite unpredictable. Women that I felt sure would enjoy the bullfights with the exception of the goring of the horses were quite unaffected by it; I mean really unaffected, that is, something that they disapproved of and that they expected would horrify and disgust them did not disgust them or horrify them at all. Other people, both men and women, were so affected that they were made physically ill. I will go into the way some of these people acted in detail later but let me say now that there was no difference, or line of difference, so that these people could be divided by any standard of civilization or experience into those that were affected and those that were not affected.

From observation I would say that people may possibly be divided into two general groups; those who, to use one of the terms of the jargon of psychology, identify themselves with, that is, place themselves in the position of, animals, and those who identify themselves with human beings. I believe, after experience and observation, that those people who identify themselves with animals, that is, the almost professional lovers of dogs, and other beasts, are capable of greater cruelty to human beings than those who do not identify themselves readily with animals. It seems as though there were a fundamental cleavage between people on this basis although people who do not identify themselves with animals may, while not loving animals in general, be capable of great affection for an individual animal, a dog, a cat, or a horse for instance. But they will base this affection on some quality of, or some association with, this individual animal rather than on the fact that it is an animal and hence worthy of love. For myself, I have felt profound affection for three different cats, four dogs, that I remember, and only two horses; that is horses that I have owned, ridden or driven. As for horses that I have followed, watched race and betted on, I have had profound admiration and, when I had betted money on them, almost affection for a number of these animals; the ones that I remember best being Man of War, Exterminator (I believe I honestly had affection for him), Epinard, Kzar, Heros XII, Master Bob, and a half-bred horse, a steeple-chaser like the last two, named Uncas. I had great, great admiration for all of those animals, but how much of my affection was due to the sums I staked I do not know. Uncas, when he won a classic steeplechase race at Auteuil at odds of better than ten to one, carrying my money on him, I felt profound affection for. But if you should ask me what eventually happened to this animal that I was so fond of that Evan Shipman and I were nearly moved to tears when speaking of the noble beast, I would have to answer that I do not know.* I do know that I do not love dogs as dogs, horses as horses, or cats as cats.

The question of why the death of the horse in the bull ring is not moving, not moving to some people that is, is complicated; but the fundamental reason may be that the death of the horse tends to be comic while that of the bull is tragic. In the tragedy

* Mr Shipman having read this informs me that Uncas after having broken down is now used as a hack by Mr Victor Emanuel. This news does not move me one way or another.

of the bullfight the horse is the comic character. This may be shocking, but it is true. Therefore the worse the horses are, provided they are high enough off the ground and solid enough so that the picador can perform his mission with the spiked pole, or vara, the more they are a comic element. You should be horrified and disgusted at these parodies of horses and what happens to them, but there is no way to be sure that you will be unless you make up your mind to be, no matter what your feelings. They are so unlike horses; in some ways they are like birds, any of the awkward birds such as the adjutants or the wide-billed storks, and when, lifted by the thrust of the bull's neck and shoulder muscles their legs hang, big hoofs dangling, neck drooping, the worn-out body lifted on the horn, they are not comic; but I swear they are not tragic. The tragedy is all centred in the bull and in the man. The tragic climax of the horse's career has occurred off stage at an earlier time; when he was bought by the horse contractor for use in the bull ring. The end in the ring, somehow, seems not unfitting to the structure of the animal and when the canvases are stretched over the horses, the long legs, and necks, the strange-shaped heads and the canvas covering the body to make a sort of wing, they are more like birds than ever. They look a little as a dead pelican does. A live pelican is an interesting, amusing, and sympathetic bird, though if you handle him he will give you lice; but a dead pelican looks very silly.

This is not being written as an apology for bullfights, but to try to present the bullfight integrally, and to do this a number of things must be admitted which an apologist, making a case, would slide over or avoid. The comic that happens to these horses is not their death then; death is not comic, and gives a temporary dignity to the most comic characters, although this dignity passes once death has occurred; but the strange and burlesque visceral accidents which occur. There is certainly nothing comic by our standards in seeing an animal emptied of its visceral content, but if this animal instead of doing something tragic, that is, dignified, gallops in a stiff old-maidish fashion around a ring trailing the opposite of clouds of glory, it is as comic when what it is trailing is real as when the Fratellinis give a burlesque of it in which the viscera are represented by rolls of bandages, sausages and other things. If one is comic the other is; the humour comes from the same principle. I have seen it, people running, horse emptying, one dignity after another being destroyed in the spattering, and trailing of its innermost values, in a complete burlesque of tragedy. I have seen these, call them disembowellings, that is the worst word, when, due to their timing, they were very funny. This is the sort of thing you should not admit, but it is because such things have not been admitted that the bullfight has never been explained.

These visceral accidents, as I write this, are no longer a part of the Spanish bullfight, as under the government of Primo de Rivera it was decided to protect the abdomens of the horses with a sort of quilted mattress designed in the terms of the decree 'to avoid those horrible sights which so disgust foreigners and tourists'. These protectors avoid these sights and greatly decrease the number of horses killed in the bull ring, but they in no way decrease the pain suffered by the horses; they take away much of the bravery from the bull, this to be dealt with in a later chapter, and they are the first step toward the suppression of the bullfight. The bullfight is a Spanish institution; it has not existed because of the foreigners and tourists, but always in spite of them, and any step to modify it to secure their approval, which it will never have, is a step towards its complete suppression.

This that has been written about one person's reaction to the horses in the bull ring is not put in because of a desire of the author to write about himself and his own reactions, considering them as important and taking delight in them because they are his, but rather to establish the fact that the reactions were instant and unexpected. I did not become indifferent to the fate of the horses through the callousness of seeing a thing many times so that the emotions are no longer touched. It was not a matter of the emotions becoming insulated through familiarity. However I feel about the horses emotionally, I felt the first time I saw a bullfight. It might be argued that I had become callous through having observed war, or through journalism, but this would not explain other people who had never seen war, nor, literally, physical horror of any sort, nor ever even worked on, say, a morning newspaper, having exactly the same reactions.

I believe that the tragedy of the bullfight is so well ordered and so strongly disciplined by ritual that a person feeling the whole tragedy cannot separate the minor comic-tragedy of the horse so as to feel it emotionally. If they sense the meaning and end of the whole thing even when they know nothing about it; feel that this thing they do not understand is going on, the business of the horses is nothing more than an incident. If they get no feeling of the whole tragedy naturally they will react emotionally to the most picturesque incident. Naturally, too, if they are humanitarians or animalarians (what a word!) they will get no feeling of the tragedy but only a reaction on humanitarian or animalarian grounds, and the most obviously abused thing is the horse. If they sincerely identify themselves with animals they will suffer terribly, more so perhaps than the horse; since a man who has been wounded knows that the pain of a wound does not commence until about half an hour after it has been received and there is no proportional relation in pain to the horrible aspect of the wound; the pain of an abdominal wound does not come at the time but later with the gas pains and the beginnings of peritonitis; a pulled ligament or a broken bone, though, hurts at once and terribly; but these things are not known or they are ignored by the person who has identified himself with the animal and he will suffer genuinely and terribly, seeing only this aspect of the bullfight, while, when a horse pulls up lame in a steeplechase, he will not suffer at all and consider it merely regrettable.

The aficionado, or lover of the bullfight, may be said, broadly, then, to be one who has this sense of the tragedy and ritual of the fight so that the minor aspects are not important except as they relate to the whole. Either you have this or you have not, just as, without implying any comparison, you have or have not an ear for music. Without an ear for music the principal impression of an auditor at a symphony concert might be the motions of the players of the double bass, just as the spectator at the bullfight might remember only the obvious grotesqueness of a picador. The movements of a player of the double bass are grotesque and the sounds produced are many times, if heard by themselves, meaningless. If the auditor at a symphony concert were a humanitarian as he might be at the bullfight he would probably find as much scope for his good work in ameliorating the wages and living conditions of the players of the double bass in symphony orchestras as in doing something about the poor horses. However, being, let us suppose, a man of culture and knowing that symphony orchestras are wholly good and to be accepted in their entirety he probably has no reactions at all except pleasure and approval. He does not think of the double bass as separated from the whole of the orchestra or as being played by a human being.

As in all arts the enjoyment increases with the knowledge of the art, but people will know the first time they go, if they go open-mindedly and only feel those things they actually feel and not the things they think they should feel, whether they will care for the bullfights or not. They may not care for them at all, no matter whether the fight should be good or bad, and all explanation will be meaningless beside the obvious moral wrongness of the bullfight, just as people could refuse to drink wine which they might enjoy because they did not believe it right to do so.

The comparison with wine drinking is not so far-fetched as it might seem. Wine is one of the most civilized things in the world and one of the natural things of the world that has been

DEATH IN THE AFTERNOON

brought to the greatest perfection, and it offers a greater range for enjoyment and appreciation than, possibly, any other purely sensory thing which may be purchased. One can learn about wines and pursue the education of one's palate with great enjoyment all of a lifetime, the palate becoming more educated and capable of appreciation and you having constantly increasing enjoyment and appreciation of wine even though the kidneys may weaken, the big toe become painful, the finger joints stiffen, until finally, just when you love it the most you are finally forbidden wine entirely. Just as the eye, which is only a good healthy instrument to start with becomes, even though it is no longer so strong and is weakened and worn by excesses, capable of transmitting constantly greater enjoyment to the brain because of the knowledge or ability to see that it has acquired. Our bodies all wear out in some way and we die, and I would rather have a palate that will give me the pleasure of enjoying completely a Château Margaux or a Haut Brion, even though excesses indulged in in the acquiring of it have brought a liver that will not allow me to drink Richebourg, Corton, or Chambertin, than to have the corrugated iron internals of my boyhood when all red wines were bitter except port and drinking was the process of getting down enough of anything to make you feel reckless. The thing, of course, is to avoid having to give up wine entirely just as, with the eye, it is to avoid going blind. But there seems to be much luck in all these things and no man can avoid death by honest effort nor say what use any part of his body will bear until he tries it.

This seems to have gotten away from bullfighting, but the point was that a person with increasing knowledge and sensory education may derive infinite enjoyment from wine, as a man's enjoyment of the bullfight might grow to become one of his greatest minor passions, yet a person drinking, not tasting or savouring but *drinking*, wine for the first time will know, although he may not care to taste or be able to taste, whether he likes the effect or not and whether or not it is good for him. In wine, most people at the start prefer sweet vintages, Sauternes, Graves, Barsac, and sparkling wines, such as not too dry champagne and sparkling Burgundy, because of their picturesque quality while later they would trade all these for a light but full and fine example of the Grandes cruses of Médoc though it may be in a plain bottle without label, dust, or cobwebs, with nothing picturesque, but only its honesty and delicacy and the light body of it on your tongue, cool in your mouth and warm when you have drunk it. So in bullfighting, at the start it is the picturesqueness of the paseo, the colour, the scene, the picturesqueness of farols and molinetes, the bullfighter putting his hand on the muzzle of the bull, stroking the horns, and all such useless and romantic things that the spectators like. They are glad to see the horses protected if it saves them from awkward sights and they applaud all such moves. Finally, when they have learned to appreciate values through experience, what they seek is honesty and true, not tricked, emotion and always classicism and the purity of execution of all the suertes, and, as in the change in taste for wines, they want no sweetening but prefer to see the horses with no protection worn so that all wounds may be seen and death given rather than suffering caused by something designed to allow the horses to suffer while their suffering is spared the spectator. But, as with wine, you will know when you first try it whether you like it as a thing or not from the effect it will have on you. There are forms of it to appeal to all tastes and if you do not like it, none of it, nor, as a whole, while not caring for details, then it is not for you. It would be pleasant of course for those who do like it if those who do not would not feel that they had to go to war against it or give money to try to suppress it, since it offends them or does not please them, but that is too much to expect and anything capable of arousing passion in its favour will surely raise as much passion against it.

The chances are that the first bullfight any spectator attends may not be a good one artistically; for that to happen there must

be good bullfighters and good bulls; artist bullfighters and poor
bulls do not make interesting fights, for the bullfighter who has
ability to do extraordinary things with the bull which are capable of producing the intensest degree of emotion in the
spectator will not attempt them with a bull which he cannot
depend on to charge; so, if the bulls are bad, that is only vicious
rather than brave, undependable in their charges, reserved and
unpredictable in their attacks, it is best that they can be fought
by bullfighters with knowledge of their profession, integrity,
and years of experience rather than artistic ability. Such bullfighters will give a competent performance with a difficult
animal, and because of the extra danger from the bull, and the
skill and courage they must use to overcome this danger, to
prepare for the killing and kill with any degree of dignity, the
bullfight is interesting, even to a person who has never seen
one before. However, if such a bullfighter, skilful, knowing,
brave and competent but without either genius or great inspiration happens to receive in the ring a truly brave bull, one
which charges in a straight line, which responds to all the cites
of the bullfighter, which grows braver under punishment,
and has that technical quality that the Spanish call 'nobility',
and the bullfighter has only bravery and honest ability in the
preparation for killing and killing of bulls and nothing of
the wrist magic and aesthetic vision that, given a bull that will
charge in a straight line, has produced the sculptural art of
modern bullfighting; then he fails completely, he gives an undistinguished, honest performance and he goes on lower down
in the commercial ranking of bullfighting while men in the
crowd who earn, perhaps, less than a thousand pesetas a year
will say, and mean it truly, 'I would have given a hundred
pesetas to have seen Cagancho with that bull'. Cagancho is a
gipsy, subject to fits of cowardice, altogether without integrity,
who violates all the rules, written and unwritten, for the conduct of a matador but who, when he receives a bull that he has
confidence in, and he has confidence in them very rarely, can

do things which all bullfighters do in a way they have never been done before and sometimes standing absolutely straight with his feet still, planted as though he were a tree, with the arrogance and grace that gipsies have and of which all other arrogance and grace seems an imitation, moves the cape spread full as the pulling jib of a yacht before the bull's muzzle so slowly that the art of bullfighting, which is only kept from being one of the major arts because it is impermanent, in the arrogant slowness of his veronicas becomes, for the seeming minutes that they endure, permanent. That is the worst of flowery writing, but it is necessary to try to give the feeling, and to someone who has never seen it a simple statement of the method does not convey the feeling. Anyone who has seen bull-fights can skip such flowerishness and read the facts which are much more difficult to isolate and state. The fact is that the gipsy, Cagancho, can sometimes, through the marvellous wrists that he has, perform the usual movements of bullfighting so slowly that they become, to old-time bullfighting, as the slow motion picture is to the ordinary motion picture. It is as though a diver could control his speed in the air and prolong the vision of a swan dive, which is a jerk in actual life, although in photographs it seems a long glide, to make it a long glide like the dives and leaps we sometimes take in dreams. Other bullfighters who have or have had this ability with their wrists are Juan Belmonte, and, occasionally with the cape, Enrique Torres and Félix Rodríguez.

The spectator going to a bullfight for the first time cannot expect to see the combination of the ideal bull and the ideal fighter for the bull which may occur not more than twenty times in all Spain in a season, and it would be wrong for him to see that the first time. He would be so confused, visually, by the many things he was seeing that he could not take it all in with his eyes, and something which he might never see again in his life would mean no more to him than a regular perform-ance. If there is any chance of his liking the bullfights, the best bullfight for him to see first is an average one, two brave bulls out of six, the four undistinguished ones to give relief to the performance of the two excellent ones, three bullfighters, not too highly paid, so that whatever extraordinary things they do will look difficult rather than easy, a seat not too near the ring so that he will see the entire spectacle rather than, if he is too close, have it constantly broken up into bull and horse, man and bull, bull and man – and a hot sunny day. The sun is very important. The theory, practice and spectacle of bullfighting have all been built on the assumption of the presence of the sun, and when it does not shine over a third of the bullfight is missing. The Spanish say, 'El sol es el mejor torero'. The sun is the best bullfighter, and without the sun the best bullfighter is not there. He is like a man without a shadow.

Chapter 2

The bullfight is not a sport in the Anglo-Saxon sense of the word, that is, it is not an equal contest or an attempt at an equal contest between a bull and a man. Rather it is a tragedy; the death of the bull, which is played, more or less well, by the bull and the man involved and in which there is danger for the man but certain death for the animal. This danger to the man can be increased by the bullfighter at will in the measure in which he works close to the bull's horns. Keeping within the rules for bullfighting on foot in a closed ring formulated by years of experience, which, if known and followed, permit a man to perform certain actions with a bull without being caught by the bull's horns, the bullfighter may, by decreasing his distance from the bull's horns, depend more and more on his own reflexes and judgement of that distance to protect him from the points. This danger of goring, which the man creates voluntarily, can be changed to certainty of being caught and tossed by the bull if the man, through ignorance, slowness, torpidness, blind folly or momentary grogginess, breaks any of these fundamental rules for the execution of the different suertes. Everything that is done by the man in the ring is called a 'suerte'. It is the easiest term to use, as it is short. It means act, but the word act has, in English, a connotation of the theatre that makes its use confusing.

People seeing their first bullfight say, 'But the bulls are so stupid. They always go for the cape and not for the man.'

The bull only goes for the percale of the cape or for the scarlet serge of the muleta if the man makes him and so handles the cloth that the bull sees it rather than the man. Therefore to really start to see bullfights a spectator should go to the novilladas or apprentice fights. There the bulls do not always go for the cloth because the bullfighters are learning before your eyes the rules of bullfighting and they do not always remember or know the proper terrain to take and how to keep the bull after the lure and away from the man. It is one thing to know the rules in principle and another to remember them as they are needed when facing an animal that is seeking to kill you, and the spectator who wants to see men tossed and gored rather than judge the manner in which the bulls are dominated should go to a novillada before he sees a corrida de toros or complete bullfight. It should be a good thing for him to see a novillada first anyway if he wants to learn about technique, since the employment of knowledge that we call by that bastard name is always most visible in its imperfection. At a novillada the spectator may see the mistakes of the bullfighters, and the penalties that these mistakes carry. He will learn something too about the state of training or lack of training of the men and the effect this has on their courage.

One time in Madrid I remember we went to a novillada in the middle of the summer on a very hot Sunday when everyone who could afford it had left the city for the beaches of the north or the mountains and the bullfight was not advertised to start until six o'clock in the evening, to see six Tovar bulls killed by three aspirant matadors who have all since failed in their profession. We sat in the first row behind the wooden barrier and when the first bull came out it was clear that Domingo Hernandorena, a short, thick-ankled, graceless Basque with a pale face who looked nervous and incompletely fed, in a cheap rented suit, if he was to kill this bull would either make a fool of himself or be gored. Hernandorena could not control the nervousness of his feet. He wanted to stand quietly and play the bull with the cape with a slow movement of his arms, but when he tried to stand still as the bull charged his feet jumped away in short, nervous jerks. His feet were obviously not under his personal control and his effort to be statuesque while his feet jittered him away out of danger was very funny to the crowd. It was funny to them, because many of them knew that was how their own feet would behave if they saw the horns coming toward them, and as always, they resented anyone else being in there in the ring, making money, who had the same physical defects which barred them, the spectators, from that supposedly highly paid way of making a living. In their turn the other two matadors were very fancy with the cape and Hernandorena's nervous jerking was even worse after their performance. He had not been in the ring with a bull for over a year and he was altogether unable to control his nervousness. When the banderillas were in and it was time for him to go out with the red cloth and the sword to prepare the bull for killing and to kill, the crowd which had applauded ironically at every nervous move he had made knew something very funny would happen. Below us, as he took the muleta and the sword and rinsed his mouth out with water I could see the muscles of his cheeks twitching. The bull stood against the barrier watching him. Hernandorena could not trust his legs to carry him slowly toward the bull. He knew there was only one way he could stay in one place in the ring. He ran out toward the bull, and ten yards in front of him dropped to both knees on the sand. In that position he was safe from ridicule. He spread the red cloth with his sword and jerked himself forward on his knees toward the bull. The bull was watching the man and the triangle of red cloth, his ears pointed, his eyes fixed, and Hernandorena kneeed himself a yard closer and shook the cloth. The bull's tail rose, his head lowered and he charged and, as he reached the man, Hernandorena rose solidly from his knees into the air, swung over like a bundle, his legs in all directions now, and then dropped to the ground. The bull looked for him, found a widespread moving cape held by another bullfighter instead, charged it, and Hernandorena stood up with sand on his white

DEATH IN THE AFTERNOON

face and looked for his sword and the cloth. As he stood up I saw the heavy, solid grey silk of his rented trousers open cleanly and deeply to show the thigh bones from the hip almost to the knee. He saw it too and looked very surprised and put his hand on it while people jumped over the barrier and ran toward him to carry him to the infirmary. The technical error that he had committed was in not keeping the red cloth of the muleta between himself and the bull until the charge; then at the moment of jurisdiction as it is called, when the bull's lowered head reaches the cloth, swaying back while he held the cloth, spread by the stick and the sword, far enough forward so that the bull following it would be clear of his body. It was a simple technical error.

That night at the café I heard no word of sympathy for him. He was ignorant, he was torpid, and he was out of training. Why did he insist on being a bullfighter? Why did he go down on both knees? Because he was a coward, they said. The knees are for cowards. If he was a coward why did he insist on being a bullfighter? There was no natural sympathy for uncontrollable nervousness, because he was a paid public performer. It was preferable that he be gored rather than run from the bull. To be gored was honourable; they would have sympathized with him had he been caught in one of his nervous uncontrollable jerky retreats, which, although they mocked, they knew were from lack of training, rather than for him to have gone down on his knees. Because the hardest thing when frightened by the bull is to control the feet and let the bull come, and any attempt to control the feet was honourable even though they jeered at it because it looked ridiculous. But when he went on both knees, without the technique to fight from that position; the technique that Marcial Lalanda, the most scientific of living bullfighters, has, and which alone makes that position honourable; then Hernandorena admitted his nervousness. To show his nervousness was not shameful; only to admit it. When, lacking the technique and thereby admitting his inability to control his feet, the matador went down on both knees before the bull, the crowd had no more sympathy with him than with a suicide.

For myself, not being a bullfighter, and being much interested in suicides, the problem was one of depiction and waking in the night I tried to remember what it was that seemed just out of my remembering, and what was the thing that I had really seen and, finally, remembering all around it, I got it. When he stood up, his face white and dirty and the silk of his breeches opened from waist to knee, it was the dirtiness of the rented breeches, the dirtiness of his slit underwear and the clean, clean, unbearably clean whiteness of the thigh bone that I had seen, and it was that which was important.

At the novilladas, too, besides the study of technique, and the consequences of its lack you have a chance to learn about the manner of dealing with defective bulls since bulls which cannot be used in a formal bullfight because of some obvious defect are killed in the apprentice fights. Nearly all bulls develop defects in the course of any fight which must be corrected by the bullfighter, but in the novillada these defects, those of vision for instance, are many times obvious at the start and so the manner of their correcting, or the result of their not being corrected, is apparent.

The formal bullfight is a tragedy, not a sport, and the bull is certain to be killed. If the matador cannot kill him and, at the end of the allotted fifteen minutes for the preparation and killing, the bull is led and herded out of the ring alive by steers to dishonour the killer, he must, by law, be killed in the corrals. It is one hundred to one against the matador de toros or formally invested bullfighter being killed unless he is inexperienced, ignorant, out of training or too old and heavy on his feet. But the matador, if he knows his profession, can increase the amount of the danger of death that he runs exactly as much as he wishes. He should, however, increase this danger, *within the rules provided for his protection*. In other words it is to his credit if

he does something that he knows how to do in a highly dangerous but still geometrically possible manner. It is to his discredit
if he runs danger through ignorance, through disregard of the
fundamental rules, through physical or mental slowness, or
through blind folly.

The matador must dominate the bulls by knowledge and
science. In the measure in which this domination is accomplished with grace will it be beautiful to watch. Strength is of
little use to him except at the actual moment of killing. Once
some one asked Rafael Gomez, 'El Gallo', nearing fifty years
old, a gipsy, brother of José Gomez, 'Gallito', and the last living
member of the great family of gipsy bullfighters of that name,
what physical exercise he, Gallo, took to keep his strength up
for bullfighting.

'Strength,' Gallo said.'What do I want with strength, man?
The bull weighs half a ton. Should I take exercises for strength
to match him? Let the bull have the strength.'

If the bulls were allowed to increase their knowledge as the
bullfighter does, and if those bulls which are not killed in the
allotted fifteen minutes in the ring were not afterwards killed
in the corrals but were allowed to be fought again, they would
kill all the bullfighters, if the bullfighters fought them according
to the rules. Bullfighting is based on the fact that it is the first
meeting between the wild animal and a dismounted man. This
is the fundamental premise of modern bullfighting – that the
bull has never been in the ring before. In the early days of bullfighting bulls were allowed to be fought which had been in the
ring before and so many men were killed in the bull ring that on
20th November 1567, Pope Pius the Fifth issued a Papal edict
excommunicating all Christian princes who should permit bullfights in their countries and denying Christian burial to any
person killed in the bull ring. The Church only agreed to tolerate bullfighting, which continued steadily in Spain in spite of
the edict, when it was agreed that the bulls should only appear
once in the ring.

You would think then that it would make of bullfighting a true sport, rather than merely a tragic spectacle, if bulls that had been in the ring were allowed to reappear. I have seen such bulls fought, in violation of the law, in provincial towns in improvised arenas made by blocking the entrances to the public square with piled-up carts in the illegal capeas, or town-square bullfights with used bulls. The aspirant bullfighters who have no financial backing get their first experience in capeas. It is a sport, a very savage and primitive sport, and for the most part a truly amateur one. I am afraid, however, due to the danger of death it involves, it would never have much success among the amateur sportsmen of America and England who play games. We, in games, are not fascinated by death, its nearness and its avoidance. We are fascinated by victory, and we replace the avoidance of death by the avoidance of defeat. It is a very nice symbolism, but it takes more cojones to be a sportsman when death is a closer party to the game. The bull in the capeas is rarely killed. This should appeal to sportsmen who are lovers of animals. The town is usually too poor to afford to pay for the killing of the bull and none of the aspirant bullfighters has enough money to buy a sword or he would not have chosen to serve his apprenticeship in the capeas. This would afford an opportunity for the man who is a wealthy sportsman, for he could afford to pay for the bull and buy himself a sword as well.

However due to the mechanics of a bull's mental development, the used bull does not make a brilliant spectacle. After his first charge or so he will stand quite still and will only charge if he is certain of getting the man or boy who is tempting him with a cape. When there is a crowd and the bull charges into it he will pick one man out and follow him, no matter how he may dodge, run and twist until he gets him and tosses him. If the tips of the bull's horns have been blunted this chasing and tossing is good fun to see for a little while. No one has to go in with the bull who does not want to, although of course many who want to very little go in to show their courage. It is very exciting for those who are down in the square, that is one test of a true amateur sport, whether it is more enjoyable to player than to spectator (as soon as it becomes enjoyable enough to the spectator for the charging of admission to be profitable the sport contains the germ of professionalism), and the smallest evidence of coolness or composure brings immediate applause. But when the bull's horns are sharp-pointed it is a disturbing spectacle. The men and boys try cape work with sacks, blouses and old capes on the bull just as they do when his horns have been blunted; the only difference is that when the bull catches them and tosses them they are liable to come off the horn with wounds no local surgeon can cope with. One bull which was a great favourite in the capeas of the province of Valencia killed sixteen men and boys and badly wounded over sixty in a career of five years. The people who go into these capeas do so sometimes as aspirant professionals to get free experience with bulls but most often as amateurs, purely for sport, for the immediate excitement, and it is very great excitement; and for the retrospective pleasure, of having shown their contempt for death on a hot day in their own town square. Many go in from pride, hoping that they will be brave. Many find they are not brave at all; but at least they went in. There is absolutely nothing for them to gain except the inner satisfaction of having been in the ring with a bull; itself a thing that anyone who has done it will always remember. It is a strange feeling to have an animal come toward you consciously seeking to kill you, his eyes open looking at you, and see the oncoming of the lowered horn that he intends to kill you with. It gives enough of a sensation so that there are always men willing to go into the capeas for the pride of having experienced it and the pleasure of having tried some bullfighting manoeuvre with a real bull although the actual pleasure at the time may not be great. Sometimes the bull is killed if the town has the money to afford it, or if the populace gets out of control; everyone swarming on him at once with knives, daggers, butcher knives and rocks; a man perhaps between his horns, being swung up and down, another flying through the air, surely several holding its tail, a swarm of choppers, thrusters and stabbers pushing into him, laying on to him or cutting up at him until he sways and goes down. All amateur or group killing is a very barbarous, messy, though exciting business and is a long way from the ritual of the formal bullfight.

The bull which killed the sixteen and wounded the sixty was killed in a very odd way. One of those he had killed was a gipsy boy of about fourteen. Afterwards the boy's brother and sister followed the bull around hoping perhaps to have a chance to assassinate him when he was loaded in his cage after a capea. That was difficult since, being a very highly valued performer, the bull was carefully taken care of. They followed him around for two years, not attempting anything, simply turning up wherever the bull was used. When the capeas were again abolished, they are always being abolished and re-abolished, by government order, the bull's owner decided to send him to the slaughterhouse in Valencia, for the bull was getting on in years anyway. The two gipsies were at the slaughter-house and the young man asked permission, since the bull had killed his brother, to kill the bull. This was granted and he started in by digging out both the bull's eyes while the bull was in his cage, and spitting carefully into the sockets, then after killing him by severing the spinal marrow between the neck vertebrae with a dagger, he experienced some difficulty in this, he asked permission to cut off the bull's testicles, which being granted, he and his sister built a small fire at the edge of the dusty street outside the slaughter-house and roasted the two glands on sticks and when they were done, ate them. They then turned their backs on the slaughter-house and went away along the road and out of town.

Chapter 3

In the modern formal bullfight or corrida de toros there are usually six bulls that are killed by three different men. Each man kills two bulls. The bulls by law are required to be from four to five years old, free from physical defects, and well armed with sharp-pointed horns. They are inspected by a municipal veterinary surgeon before the fight. The veterinary is supposed to reject bulls that are under age, insufficiently armed or with anything wrong with their eyes, their horns or any apparent disease or visible bodily defect such as lameness.

The men who are to kill them are called matadors and which of the six bulls they are to kill is determined by lot. Each matador or killer, has a cuadrilla, or team, of from five to six men who are paid by him and work under his orders. Three of these men who aid him on foot with capes, and at his orders place the banderillas, three-foot wooden shafts with harpoon points, are called peones or banderilleros. The other two, who are mounted on horses when they appear in the ring, are called picadors.

No one is called a toreador in Spain. That is an obsolete word which was applied to those members of the nobility who, in the days before professional bullfighting, killed bulls from horseback for sport. Anyone who fights bulls for money, whether as a matador, banderillero or a picador is called a torero. A man who kills them on horseback with a javelin, using trained thoroughbred horses, is called a rejoneador or a caballero en plaza. A bullfight in Spanish is called a corrida de toros or a running of bulls. A bull ring is called a plaza de toros.

In the morning before the bullfight the representatives of

each matador, usually their oldest or most trusted banderilleros, meet at the corrals of the plaza de toros where the bulls that are to be fought that afternoon are quartered. They look over the bulls, compare their size, weight, height, the length of their horns, width of horns, sharpness of horns, and the condition of their coats. This last is as good an indication as any of their physical condition and probable bravery. There is no sure sign by which bravery may be determined although there are many indications of probable cowardice. The confidential banderilleros question the herder or vaquero who has travelled from the ranch with the bulls and who, while he is in charge of them, is called the mayoral, about the qualities and probable disposition of each bull. The bulls must be divided into three lots of two bulls each by common consent of the representatives assembled and the effort is to have one good bull and one bad bull, good and bad from the bullfighter's standpoint, in each lot. A good bull for the bullfighter is not too big, not too strong, not too much horns, not too much height at shoulder, but above all with good vision, good reaction to colour and movement, brave and frank to charge. A bad bull, for the bullfighter, is too big a bull, too old a bull, too powerful a bull, with too wide horns; but above all a bad bull is one with no reaction to colour or movement or with defective courage and lack of sustained viciousness, so that the bullfighter cannot tell when, whether or how he will charge. The representatives, usually short men in caps, not yet shaven for the day, with a great variety of accents, but all with the same hard eyes, argue and discuss. They say the number 20 has more horns than the 42, but the 42 weighs two arrobas (fifty pounds) more than the 16. The 46 is as big as a cathedral, one calls to him and he raises his head from where he has been feeding, and the 18 is roan-coloured and may be as cowardly as a steer. The lots are made up after much arguing and the numbers of two bulls, those branded on their flanks, are written on three different cigarette papers and the papers rolled up into balls and dropped into a cap. The roan-coloured probable coward has been paired with a medium-weight, black bull with not too long horns and a glossy coat. The cathedral-sized 46 is coupled with the 16 which, being just barely big enough to be passed by the veterinaries and without salient characteristics, is the ideal of the half-bull that looks like a bull but lacks the full development of muscle and knowledge of how to use his horns, that all the representatives have hoped to get for their bullfighter. The number 20 with the wide horns with the needle points is balanced by the 42 which is the next smallest to the 16. The man who holds the cap shakes it and each representative puts in a brown hand and draws out a tight-rolled cigarette paper. They unroll them, read them, perhaps take a final look at the two bulls they have drawn and go off to the hotel to find the matador and tell him what he has to kill.

The matador decides in which order he prefers to take his bulls. He may take the worst one first and hope to rehabilitate himself with the second in case his work with the first turns out badly. Or if he is third in the order to kill he may take the best one first knowing that he will be killing the sixth bull and if it should be getting dark and the crowd wanting to leave he will be pardoned an attempt to finish quickly and in the easiest way possible should this bull turn out to be difficult.

The matadors kill their bulls in turn in the order of their seniority; this dating from their presentation as a matador de toros in the Plaza of Madrid. If any matador is gored so that he is unable to return from the infirmary his bulls were formerly all killed by the senior-ranking matador of those remaining in the ring. Now they are divided between the remaining matadors.

The bullfight usually takes place at five o'clock or five-thirty in the afternoon. At a half-hour past noon of the day of the fight the apartado takes place. This is the sorting out of bulls in the corrals with the aid of steers and, by the use of swinging doors, runways and trap doors, separating them and trapping them into the individual pens or chiqueros where they are to stay and rest until they come out into the ring in the order in which it has been determined they are to be fought. Bulls are not deprived of food and water before fighting as one may read in various guides to Spain nor are they kept in a dark pen for several days. They are in the chiqueros in a dim light for not more than four hours before the bullfight commences. They are not fed there after they leave the corral any more than a boxer would be fed immediately before a fight, but the reason for placing them in the small dimly lighted pens is to have some way of getting them promptly into the ring, and to rest them and keep them quiet before the fight.

Usually only the matadors, their friends and representatives, the bull ring management, the authorities, and a very few spectators attend the apartado. It is usually the first time the matador sees the bulls he is to kill that afternoon. The number of spectators is kept down in most places by putting the price of tickets at five pesetas. The bull ring management wants few people at the sorting in order that the bulls may not have their attention attracted by the spectators who want to see action and so call to the bulls to excite them that they may charge the doors or the walls or each other. If they charge in the corrals they run a risk of injuring their horns or of goring each other and the management would have to replace them in the ring at the expense of a couple of hundred dollars apiece. Many bullfight spectators and hangers-on have a belief that they can talk to the bulls as well or better than the bullfighters. Protected by the high fence or the wall of the corral they try to catch the bull's eye and they utter the guttural 'huh!-huh!-huhs!' that the herders and toreros use to call the bull's attention. If the bull in the pen below raises his great head with the wide horns, solid-looking as wood and smoothly pointed, and the hump of muscle in his neck and shoulders, heavy and wide in repose, rises in a great swelling crest under the black, hairy sheen of his hide and his nostrils widen and he lifts and jerks his horns as he

31

looks towards the spectator then the amateur speaker of bull talk has had a success. If the bull should really charge, driving his horns into the wood, or tossing his head at the talker it would be a triumph. To hold the number of successes and avoid triumphs the management puts the tickets at five pesetas on the theory that anyone able to pay five pesetas to see bulls sorted will be too dignified to try to talk to bulls before bullfights.

There is no way they can be sure of this, and at some places in the country where they have bulls only once a year you see men at the apartado who pay five pesetas only in order to have a better opportunity to exercise their powers as talkers to bulls. But in general the five pesetas reduce the amount of sober talking. The bulls pay little attention to a drunk. I have many times seen drunken men shout at bulls and never seen the bulls pay any attention. The five-peseta atmosphere of dignity in a town like Pamplona, where a man can be drunk twice and eat a meal at the horse fair on five pesetas, gives an almost religious hush to the apartado. No one spends five pesetas there to see the bulls sorted unless he is very rich and dignified. But the atmosphere of the sorting can be very different in other places. I have never seen it quite the same in any two towns. After the sorting everybody goes to the café.

The bullfight itself takes place in a sand-covered ring enclosed by a red wooden fence a little over four feet high. This red wooden fence is called a barrera. Behind it is a narrow circular passageway that separates it from the first row of seats in the amphitheatre. This narrow runway is called the callejon. In it stand the sword-handlers with their jugs of water, sponges, piles of folded muletas and heavy leather sword cases, the bull ring servants, the vendors of cold beer and gaseosas, of iced fruits in nets that float in galvanized buckets full of ice and water, of pastries in flat baskets, of salted almonds, and of peanuts. In it also are the police, the bullfighters who are not in the ring at the moment, several plainclothes policemen ready to arrest amateurs who may jump into the ring, the photographers, and on seats built in it and protected by shields of boards, are the doctors, the carpenters who repair the barrera if it is broken, and the delegates of the government. In some rings the photographers are allowed to circulate in the callejon; in others they must work from their seats.

The seats of the bull ring are uncovered except for the boxes or palcos and the first gallery or grada. From the gallery the seats descend in circular rows to the edge of the rings. These rows of numbered places are called tendidos. The two rows nearest the ring, the front rows of all the seats, are called barreras and contra-barreras. The third row are known as delanteras de tendidos or the front row of the tendidos. The bull ring for numbering purposes is cut into sections as you would cut a pie, and these sections numbered tendidos 1, 2, 3, and so on up to 11 and 12 depending on the size of the ring.

If you are going to a bullfight for the first time the best place for you to sit depends on your temperament. From a box or from the first row in the gallery details of sound and smell and those details of sight that make for the perception of danger are lost or minimized, but you see the fight better as a spectacle and the chances are that, if it is a good bullfight, you will enjoy it more. If it is a bad bullfight, that is, not an artistic spectacle, you will be better off the closer you are, since you can then, for lack of a whole to appreciate, learn and see all the details, the whys and the wherefores. The boxes and the gallery are for people who do not want to see things too closely for fear they may upset them, for people who want to see the bullfight as a spectacle or a pageant, and for experts who can see details even though a long way from them and want to be high enough up so they can see everything that happens in any part of the ring in order to be able to judge it as a whole.

The barrera is the best seat if you want to see and hear what happens and to be so close to the bull that you will have the bullfighter's point of view. From the barrera the action is so near and so detailed that a bullfight that would be soporific from the boxes or the balcony is always interesting. It is from the barrera that you see danger and learn to appreciate it. There too you have an uninterrupted view of the ring. The only other seats, besides the first row in the gallery and the first row in the boxes, where you do not see people between you and the ring, are the sobrepuertas. These are the seats that are built over the doorways through which you enter the various sections of the ring. They are about half-way up to the sides of the bowl and from them you get a good view of the ring and a good perspective, yet you are not as distant as in the boxes or gallery. They cost about half as much as the barreras or the first row of gallery or boxes and they are very good seats.

The west walls of the bull ring building cast a shadow and those seats that are in the shade when the fight commences are called seats of the sombra or shade. Seats that are in the sun when the fight commences but that will be in the shadow as the afternoon advances are called of sol y sombra. Seats are priced according to their desirability and whether they are shaded or not. The cheapest seats are those which are nearest the roof on the far sunny side and have no shade at all at any time. They are the andanadas del sol and on a hot day, close under the roof, they must reach temperatures that are unbelievable in a city like Valencia where it can be 104° Fahrenheit in the shade, but the better seats of the sol are good ones to buy on a cloudy day or in cold weather.

At your first bullfight if you are alone, with no one to instruct you, sit in a delantera de grada or a sobrepuerta. If you cannot get these seats you can always get a seat in a box. They are the most expensive seats and the farthest from the ring, but they give a good panoramic view of the fight. If you are going with someone who really knows bullfighting and want to learn to understand it and have no qualms about details a barrera is the best seat, contrabarrera the next best and sobrepuerta the next.

If you are a woman and think you would like to see a bullfight and are afraid you might be badly affected by it do not sit any closer than the gallery the first time. You might enjoy the fight from there where you will see it as a spectacle and not care for it at all if you sat closer so that the details destroyed the effect of the whole. If you have plenty of money, want not to see but to have seen a bullfight and plan no matter whether you like it or not to leave after the first bull, buy a barrera seat so that someone who has never had enough money to sit in a barrera can make a quick rush from above and occupy your expensive seat as you go out taking your preconceived opinions with you.

That is the way it used to happen at San Sebastian. Due to various grafts of ticket resale and the reliance of the management on the wealthy curiosity trade from Biarritz and the Basque Coast, the barreras, by the time you buy them, cost a hundred pesetas apiece or over. A man could live a week on that in a bullfighters' boarding-house in Madrid, go to the Prado four times a week, buy good seats in the sun for two bullfights, buy the papers afterwards and drink beer and eat shrimps in the Pasaje Alvarez off the Calle de Vitoria, and still have something left to get his shoes shined with. Yet by buying any sort of seat within diving range of the barrera at San Sebastian you could be sure of having a hundred-peseta seat to occupy when the citizens who knew they were morally bound to leave the bull ring after the first bull stand up to make their well-fed, skull and bones-ed, porcelain-ed, beach-tanned, flannelled, Panama-hatted, sport-shod exits. I've seen them go many times when the women with them wanted to stay. They could go to the bullfight, but they had to meet at the Casino after they had seen the first bull killed. If they didn't leave and liked it there was something wrong with them. Maybe they were queer. There was never anything wrong with them. They always left. That was until bullfights became respectable. In nineteen-thirty-one I did not see one leave within range and now it looks as though the good days of the free barreras at San Sebastian are over.

Chapter 4

The best bullfight to see first would be a novillada and the best
place to see a novillada is Madrid. The novilladas usually start
about the middle of March and there is one every Sunday and
usually every Thursday until Easter when the major fights or
corridas de toros start. After Easter, in Madrid, starts the first
subscription season of seven bullfights. Books of tickets for all
seven fights are sold and the best seats are always subscribed
year in and year out. The best of all seats are the barreras in the
middle of the shade where the bullfighters put their capes over
the red wooden barrier. There is where they stand when they
are not in the ring; it is there that they have the bull brought
when they are going out with the muleta; it is to there they
come to sponge off after the killing. A seat there is equivalent in
what you see and hear to being in the corner of a boxer during a
fight or to sitting in the dugout or on the bench in a baseball
or football game.

You will not be able to buy any of those seats during the first
or the second abono or subscription season at Madrid, but you
can get them for the novilladas that come before, between and
after the regular bullfight season, on Sundays and, usually,
Thursdays. When you buy a barrera seat ask where the capes
are put. '¿Adonde se ponen los capotes?' and then ask that you
be given a seat as close as possible to them. The ticket seller may
lie to you in the provinces and give you the worst seat he has
but he may, because you are a foreigner and seem to want to
have a really good seat and know what one is, give you the best
that he has. I have been lied to most in Galicia where the truth in

any business transaction is hard to come at, and treated best in Madrid, and, of all places, Valencia. In most parts of Spain you will find the institution of the subscription or abono and the re-venta. The re-venta are ticket brokers who take over all or most of the unsubscribed tickets from the bull-ring management and sell them at a twenty per cent increase over their face value. The bull rings favour them sometimes because while they buy the tickets at a discount yet they insure the paper being disposed of. If the tickets for the fight are not all sold it is the re-venta that has the big loss, not the bull ring – although the bull ring usually manages to have big losses in some manner or other. Since you will seldom, unless you are living in a town, be there at the time the subscription or abono for a fight or series of fights is opened, and since, in all cases, old seat holders have a right to renew their subscriptions before new ones are taken, and since these sub-scriptions are taken two or three weeks before the fights at some place perhaps difficult to find and open only from, say, four to five in the afternoon, the chances are you must buy your seats from the re-venta.

If you are in a town and you know you are going to the bull-fight buy your seats as soon as you are decided. The chances are there will be nothing in the Madrid papers about any bullfight before it is to take place except a small classified advertisement under Plaza de Toros de Madrid in the column of espectáculos. Bullfights are not written up in the papers in advance in Spain except in the provinces. But in all parts of Spain they are advertised by large coloured posters which give the number of bulls to be killed with the names of the men who are to kill them, the breeder who is furnishing them, the cuadrillas and the place and hour of the fight. There is usually also a list of prices of the various seats. To these prices you must expect to add the twenty-per-cent commission if you buy the tickets from the re-venta.

If you want to see a bullfight in Spain there will be one of some sort in Madrid every Sunday from the middle of March until the middle of November, weather permitting. During the winter there are rarely any fights in Spain except very occasionally in Barcelona and sometimes in Malaga or Valencia. The first formal bullfight of each year is at Castellón de la Plana late in February or early in March for the fiesta of the Magdalena and the last one of the year is usually in Valencia, Gerona, or Ondara in the first part of November, but if the weather is bad these November fights will not take place. There will be fights every Sunday in Mexico City from October until, and probably through, April. There will be novilladas in the spring and summer. Dates of bullfights in other places in Mexico vary. The days on which there will be fights in other towns in Spain than Madrid vary, but, in general, except for Barcelona, where they are held almost as regularly as in Madrid, the dates coincide with the national religious festivals and the times of the local fairs or ferias, which usually commence on the Saint's day of the town. In an appendix to this book I have given a list of the dates of the main ferias, so far as these are fixed, on which bullfights will be held in Spain, Mexico and South and Central America. It is easy, easier than you can believe, in a two or three weeks' trip to Spain to miss a chance to see bullfights, but using this appendix anyone can see a bullfight if they want to be at any of the places on any of the fixed dates, rain permitting. After the first one you will know if you want to see any more.

Aside from the novilladas and the two subscription seasons at Madrid the best place to see a series of bullfights in the early spring is at the feria in Sevilla where there are at least four fights on successive days. This feria starts after Easter. If you are in Sevilla for Easter ask anyone when the feria starts or you can find the dates from the big posters advertising the fights. If you are in Madrid before Easter go to any of the cafés around the Puerta del Sol, or the first café on your right on the Plaza de Canalejas going down the Calle de San Jeronimo from the Puerta del Sol toward the Prado and you will find a poster on the wall advertising the feria of Sevilla. In this same café you will always find in the summer the posters or cartels advertising the ferias of Pamplona, Valencia, Bilbao, Salamanca, Valladolid, Cuenca, Malaga, Murcia and many others.

On Easter Sunday there are always bullfights in Madrid, Sevilla, Barcelona, Murcia, Zaragoza, and novilladas in Granada, Bilbao, Valladolid and many other places. There is also a bullfight in Madrid on the Monday after Easter. On the 29th of April of each year there is a bullfight and fair at Jerez de la Frontera. This is an excellent place to visit with or without bulls, and is the home of sherry and everything distilled from it. They will take you through the cellars of Jerez and you may taste many different grades of wines and brandies, but it is best to do this on another day than the one you plan to go to the corrida. There will be two fights in Bilbao on either the 1st, 2nd or 3rd of May, depending on whether one of those dates falls on a Sunday. Those would be good fights to go to if you were, say, at Biarritz or St Jean de Luz for Easter. There is a fine road to Bilbao from anywhere along the Basque coast. Bilbao is a rich, ugly, mining city where it gets as hot as St Louis, either St Louis, Missouri, or St Louis, Senegal, and where they love bulls and dislike bullfighters. When they like a bullfighter in Bilbao they buy bigger and bigger bulls for him to fight until he finally has a disaster with them, either moral or physical. Then the Bilbao enthusiast says, 'See – they are all alike – all cowards, all fakes. Give them big enough bulls and they will prove it.' If you want to see how big bulls can be produced, how much horn they can carry on their heads, how they can look up over the barrera so that you think you are going to have them in your lap, how tough a crowd can be and how thoroughly bullfighters can be terrorized, go to Bilbao. They do not have as big bulls in May as they do during their big-bull seven-corrida fair which starts the middle of August, but in May it will not be as hot in Bilbao as it will be in August. If you do not mind heat, really heavy, damp, lead and zinc mining heat, and want to see big, wonderfully presented bulls, the August feria in

39

Bilbao is the place. Cordoba has the only other feria in May
where more than two bullfights are given and its dates vary,
but on the 16th there is always a bullfight at Talavera de la
Reina; on the 20th one at Ronda, and on the 30th one at
Aranjuez.

There are two ways to go to Sevilla by road from Madrid.
One goes by Aranjuez, Valdepenas, and Cordoba and is called
the highroad of Andalucia, and the other is by Talavera de la
Reina, Trujillo and Merida and is called the road of Extremadura. If you are in Madrid in May and driving to the south you
can see the fight at Talavera de la Reina on the 16th if you go by
the Extremadura road. It is a fine road, smooth and rolling,
Talavera is a good place in fair time and the bulls, nearly always
furnished by a local breeder, the widow Ortega, are modere-
ately big, vicious, difficult, and dangerous. It was there that José
Gomez y Ortega, called Gallito or Joselito, who was probably
the greatest bullfighter that ever lived, was killed on the 16th of
May 1920. The bulls of the widow Ortega are famous because
of that accident and as they do not make a brilliant fight and are
big and dangerous they will usually be killed, now, by the
disinherited of the profession.

Aranjuez is only forty-seven kilometres from Madrid on a
billiard-smooth road. It is an oasis of tall trees, rich gardens and
a swift river set in brown plain and hills. There are avenues of
trees like the background of Velasquez canvases, and on 30th
May you can drive out there, if you have money, or get a
special-rate third-class round-trip railway ticket, or go on a bus
if you haven't (there will be a special bus leaving from the Calle
Victoria opposite the Passaje Alvarez), and, coming from the
hot sun of the bare, desert country, suddenly, under the shade of
the trees, see brown-armed girls with baskets of fresh strawberries piled on the smooth, bare, cool ground, strawberries you
cannot reach around with thumb and forefinger, damp and
cool, packed on green leaves in wicker baskets. The girls and
the old women sell them and bunches of wonderful asparagus,

each stalk as thick as your thumb, to the crowd that comes off
the special train from Madrid and Toledo and the people who
drive into the town in motor-cars and ride in on buses. You
can eat at booths where they grill steaks and roast chickens over
a charcoal fire and drink all the Valdepenas wine you can hold
for five pesetas. You can lie in the shade or walk and see the
sights until time for the bullfights. You can find the sights in
Baedeker. The bull ring is at the end of a hot, wide, dusty
street that runs into the heat from the cool forest shade of the
town, and the professional cripples and horror and pity inspirers
that follow the fairs of Spain line this road, wagging stumps,
exposing sores, waving monstrosities and holding out their caps
in their mouths when they have nothing left to hold them with,
so that you walk a dusty gauntlet between two rows of horrors
to the ring. The town is Velasquez to the edge and then straight
Goya to the bull ring. The ring itself dates from before Goya. It
is a lovely building in the style of the old ring at Ronda and you
can sit in a barrera seat and drink wine and eat strawberries in
the shade with your back to the sand and watch the boxes fill
and see the girls from Toledo and all the surrounding country
of Castille come in and drape their shawls over the front of the
boxes, sitting, with much fan waving, to smile and talk with the
pleasant, conscious confusion of amateur beauties under inspection. This girl inspection is a big part of bullfighting for the
spectator. If you are near-sighted you can carry a pair of opera
or field-glasses. They are taken as an additional compliment. It
is best not to neglect a single box. The use of a good pair of
glasses is an advantage. They will destroy for you some of the
greatest and most startling beauties who will come in with
cloudy white lace mantillas, high combs and complexions and
wonderful shawls and who through the glasses will show the
gold teeth and flour-covered swartness of someone you saw
last night perhaps somewhere else and who is attending the fight
to advertise the house; but in some box you might not have
noticed without the glasses you may see a beautiful girl. It is

very easy for the traveller in Spain, seeing the flour-faced fatness of the flamenca dancers and the hardy ladies of the brothels, to write that all talk of beautiful Spanish women is nonsense. Whoring is not a highly paid profession in Spain and the Spanish whore works too hard to keep her looks. Do not look for beautiful women on the stage, in the brothels or the canta honda places. You look for them in the evening at the time of the paseo when you can sit in a chair at a café or on the street and have all the girls of the town walk by you for an hour, passing not once but many times as they walk up the block, make the turn and come back, walking three or four abreast; or you look for them carefully with glasses in the boxes at the bull ring. It is not polite to focus the glasses on anyone not in a box, nor is it polite to use them from the ring itself in those rings where the admirers of girls are allowed to stay in the ring to circle about before the fight and congregate before any special beauties. To use glasses when standing on the sand of the ring is the mark of a voyeur, a looker in the worst sense; that is a looker rather than a do-er. But to use the glasses on the boxes from a barrera seat is legitimate, and a compliment, and means of communication and almost an introduction. There is no better preliminary introduction than acceptable sincere admiration and there is no way admiration at a certain distance can be conveyed or any response noted better than with a good-looking pair of racing glasses. Even if you never look at girls the glasses are good to watch the killing of the last bull if it is getting dusk and the bull is being killed on the far side of the ring.

Aranjuez would be a fine place to see your first bullfight. It would be a good place if you were only going to see one bull-fight, much better than Madrid, since it has all the colour and picturesqueness that you want when you are still in the spectacle stage of appreciation. Later on what you will want at a bullfight, good bulls and good matadors being given, is a good public, and a good public is not the public of a one bullfight fiesta where everyone drinks and has a fine time, and the women come in costume, nor is it the drunken, dancing, bull-running public of Pamplona, nor the local, patriotic, bullfighter worshippers of Valencia. A good public is Madrid, not the days of the benefit fights with elaborate decorations, much spectacle and high prices, but the serious public of the abonos who know bull-fighting, bulls, and bullfighters, who know the good from the bad, the faked from the sincere and for whom the bullfighter must give his absolute maximum. The picturesque is for when you are young, or if you are a little drunk so that it will all seem real, or if you never grow up, or if you have a girl with you who has never seen it, or for once in a season, or for those who like it. But if you really want to learn about bullfighting, or if you ever get to feel strongly about it, sooner or later you will have to go to Madrid.

There is one town that would be better than Aranjuez to see your first bullfight in if you were only going to see one and that is Ronda. That is where you should go if you ever go to Spain on a honeymoon or if you ever bolt with anyone. The entire town and as far as you can see in any direction is romantic background, and there is an hotel there that is so comfortable, so well run and where you eat so well and usually have a cool breeze at night that, with the romantic background and the modern comfort, if a honeymoon or an elopement is not a success in Ronda it would be as well to start for Paris and both commence making your own friends. Ronda has everything you wish for a stay of that sort, romantic scenery, you can see it if necessary without leaving the hotel, beautiful short walks, good wine, sea-food, a fine hotel, practically nothing else to do, two resident painters who will sell you water colours that will frame as attractive souvenirs of the occasion; and really, in spite of all this, it is a fine place. It is built on a plateau in a circle of mountains and the plateau is cut by a gorge that divides the two towns and ends in a cliff that drops sheer to the river and the plain below where you see the dust rising from the mule trains along the road. The people who settled it when the Moors were driven away, came from Cordoba and the north of Andalucia, and the bullfight and the fair that starts the 20th of May celebrate the conquest of the town by Ferdinand and Isabella. Ronda was one of the cradles of modern bullfighting. It was the birthplace of Pedro Romero, one of the first and greatest of professional fighters and, in our times, of Niño de la Palma, who started to be great but after his first severe goring developed a cowardice which was only equalled by his ability to avoid taking risks in the ring. The bull ring at Ronda was built toward the end of the eighteenth century and is of wood. It stands at the edge of the cliff and after the bullfight when the bulls have been skinned and dressed and their meat sent out for sale on carts, they drag the dead horses over the edge of the cliff and the buzzards that have circled over the town and high in the air over the ring all day, drop down to feed on the rocks below the town.

There is one other feria with a series of bullfights that sometimes comes in May although the date is movable, and it may not come until June, and that is Cordoba. Cordoba has a good country feria and May is the best time to visit that city because of the heat that comes in the summer. The three hottest towns in Spain when the heat really comes are Bilbao, Cordoba and Sevilla. By hottest more is meant than mere degrees of temperature; I mean the heavy, airless heat of nights when you cannot sleep, nights when it is hotter than in the day, and no coolness to get to, Senegal heat, when it is too hot to sit in the café except early in the morning, too hot to do anything after lunch but lie on the bed in the room, dark from the strip of curtain pulled down over the balcony, and wait for the time for the bullfight.

Valencia is hotter in temperature sometimes and hotter in fact when the wind blows from Africa, but there you can always go out on a bus or the tramway to the port of Grau at night and swim at the public beach or, when it is too hot to swim, float out with as little effort as you need and lie in the barely cool water and watch the lights and the dark of the boats and the rows of eating shacks and swimming cabins. At Valencia, too, when it is hottest, you can eat down at the beach for a peseta or two pesetas at one of the eating pavilions where they will serve you beer and shrimps and a paella of rice, tomato, sweet peppers, saffron and good sea-food, snails, crawfish, small fish, little eels, all cooked together in a saffron-coloured mound. You can get this with a bottle of local wine for two pesetas and the children will go by barelegged on the beach and there is a thatched roof over the pavilion, the sand cool under your feet, the sea with the fishermen sitting in the cool of the evening in the black felucca-rigged boats that you can see, if you come to swim the next morning, being dragged up the beach by six yoke of oxen. Three of these eating shacks on the beach are named Granero, after the greatest bullfighter Valencia ever produced, who was killed in the ring in Madrid in 1922. Manuel Granero, after having ninety-four fights the year before, died leaving nothing but debts, the half-million pesetas he made all spent on publicity, propaganda, subsidies to news-paper men and taken by parasites. He was twenty years old when he was killed by a Veragua bull that lifted him once, then tossed him against the wood of the foot of the barrera and never left him until the horn had broken up the skull as you might break a flowerpot. He was a fine-looking boy who had studied the violin until he was fourteen, studied bullfighting until he was seventeen and fought bulls until he was twenty. They really worshipped him in Valencia and he was killed before they ever had time to turn on him. Now there is a pastry that is named for him and three rival eating pavilions Granero on different parts of the beach. The next bullfighter they got to worship in Valencia was called Chaves and he had well-vaselined hair, a big face, a double chin, and a big stomach that he puffed out toward the bull as soon as the horns were past to give a sensation of great danger. The Valencians, who are a people who worship bullfighters, Valencian bullfighters, rather than enjoy the bull-fights, were mad about Chaves for a time. As well as his stomach and his great air of arrogance he had a pair of gigantic buttocks which he threw out when he drew his stomach in and everything he did he did with great style. We had to watch him all through one feria. We saw him in five fights, if I remember correctly, and once of Chaves is enough for anyone who is not his neighbour. But on the last fight while he was attempting to stab a big Miura bull somewhere, anywhere, in the neck, the Miura elongated that neck just enough to catch Chaves under the armpit and he hung a little and then made a big-stomached pinwheel around the horn. It took a long time to cure the tears and the destruction in the arm muscle, and he is now so prudent that he does not even advance his stomach toward the bull after the horn is past. They have turned on him in Valencia now too, where they have two new bullfighters as idols, and the one time I saw him a year ago he was not so well fed looking as formerly and standing in the shade he began sweating the minute he saw the bull come out. But he has one consolation. In his home town of Grau, the port of Valencia, where they have turned on him too, they have named a public monument after him. It is an iron monument on the corner of the street where the tramcar turns that runs to the beach. In America it would be called a comfort station, and on the circular iron wall is written in white paint, *El Urinario Chaves*.

Chapter 5

The bad thing about going to Spain in the spring to see bull-fights is the rain. It may rain everywhere you go, especially in May and June, and that is why I prefer the summer months. It rains then, too, sometimes, but never yet have I seen it snow in Spain in July and August although it snowed in August of 1929 in some of the mountain summer resorts of Aragon and in Madrid it snowed one year on May 15th and was so cold they called off the bullfights. I remember having gone down that year to Spain thinking spring would be well along, and all day on the train we rode through country as bare and cold as the badlands in November. I could hardly recognize the country as the same I knew in the summer and when I got off the train at night in Madrid snow was blowing outside the station. I had no overcoat and stayed in my room writing in bed or in the nearest café drinking coffee and Domecq brandy. It was too cold to go out for three days and then came lovely spring weather. Madrid is a mountain city with a mountain climate. It has the high cloudless Spanish sky that makes the Italian sky seem senti-mental and it has air that is actively pleasurable to breathe. The heat and the cold come and go quickly there. I have watched, on a July night when I could not sleep, the beggars burning news-papers in the street and crouching around the fire to keep warm. Two nights later it was too hot to sleep until the coolness that comes just before morning.

Madrileños love the climate and are proud of these changes. Where can you get such a variation in any other large city? When they ask you at the café how you slept, and you say it was too bloody hot to sleep until just before morning, they tell you that is the time to sleep. There is always that coolness just before daylight at the hour a man should go to sleep. No matter how hot the night you always get that. It really is a very good climate if you do not mind changes. On hot nights you can go to the Bombilla to sit and drink cider and dance and it is always cool when you stop dancing there in the leafiness of the long plantings of trees where the mist rises from the small river. On cold nights you can drink sherry brandy and go to bed. To go to bed at night in Madrid marks you as a little queer. For a long time your friends will be a little uncomfortable about it. Nobody goes to bed in Madrid until they have killed the night. Appointments with a friend are habitually made for after midnight at the café. In no other town that I have ever lived in, except Constantinople during the period of the Allied occupation, is there less going to bed for sleeping purposes. It may be based on the theory that you stay up until that cool time that comes just before daylight but that cannot have been the reason at Constantinople, because we always used that cool time to take a ride out along the Bosphorus to see the sun rise. Seeing the sun rise is a fine thing. As a boy, fishing or shooting, or during the war you used to see it rather regularly; then, after the war, I do not remember seeing it until Constantinople. There seeing it rise was the traditional thing to do. In some way it seemed to prove something if, after whatever you had been doing, you went out along the Bosphorus and saw the sun rise. It finished off everything with a healthy outdoor touch. But being away from such things one forgets them. At Kansas City during the Republican Convention of 1928, I was driving out to my cousins' house in the country at an hour that I felt was much too late in the evening when I noted the glow of a tremendous fire. It looked exactly as it did the night the stockyards burned and, while I felt there was little I could do about it, still I felt that I should go. I turned the motor-car toward the fire. When the car came to the top of the next hill I saw what it was. It was the sunrise.

The ideal weather to visit Spain and to see bullfights and the time when there are most bullfights to see is in the month of September. The only drawback to that month is that the bullfights are not so good. The bulls are at their best in May and June, still good in July and early in August, but by September the pastures are pretty well burned up by the heat and the bulls lean and out of condition, unless they have been fed up on grain which makes them fat, sleek and glossy, and very violent for a few minutes, but as unfit for fighting as a boxer that has trained exclusively on potatoes and ale. Then, too, in September, the bullfighters are fighting nearly every day and have so many contracts and the prospect of making so much money in a short time, if they are not injured, that they take the minimum of chances. This does not always hold true and if there is a rivalry existing between two fighters they may each put out everything they have, but many times the fights are spoiled by poor bulls in bad condition and by bullfighters who have either been wounded and come back too quickly while still in bad physical condition in order not to lose their contracts or by bullfighters who are worn out after a heavy season. September may be a splendid month if there are new fighters who have only just taken the alternativa, and in their first season are giving all they have to try to make names for themselves and get contracts for the next year. If you wanted to, and had a fast enough motorcar, you could see a bullfight some place in Spain on every single day in September. I guarantee you would be worn out getting to them without having to fight in them and then you would have some idea of the physical strain a bullfighter goes through toward the end of the season in moving about the country from one place to another.

Of course there is no law that compels them to fight so often. They fight for money, and if they get tired, worn out and unable to do their best through trying to fill so many contracts it does not help the spectator any who has paid money to see them. But when you yourself are travelling the same way, stopping at the same hotel, seeing the bullfight through the eyes of the bullfighter rather than the spectator who is paying a good price to see the bullfighter only once in a year perhaps, it is hard not to get the bullfighter's point of view about his engagements. Truly enough, from any point of view, the bullfighter has no right to sign a contract which means that he must leave immediately after the fight is over in a motor-car, the capes and muletas folded into baskets that are roped on over the baggage trunks, the sword cases and suitcases piled in the front and the whole cuadrilla packed tightly into the big motor-car, a huge headlight on the front, to leave for a run of perhaps five hundred miles, driving all night, and through all the dust and heat of the next day, to arrive in the town where they are to fight in the afternoon with barely time to wash off the dust, bathe, and shave before dressing for the corrida. In the ring the bullfighter may be tired and stale, and you understand because you know the trip he has just made, having made such a trip yourself, and know that, with a good night's rest, he will be different the next day, but the spectator who has paid his money to see him on that one day does not forgive, whether he understands or not. He calls it hoggishness for money and if the bullfighter cannot take advantage of a fine bull and get all there is out of him he feels he has been defrauded – and he has been.

There is another reason for seeing your first and last bullfight in Madrid, for the spring fights there are not during the feria season and the bullfighters are at their best; they are trying for triumphs which will bring them contracts for the various ferias, and, unless they have been in Mexico for the winter with the resultant fatigue, and often staleness, of a double season and the faults they acquire from working with the smaller and less difficult Mexican bulls, they should be in the very best of condition. Madrid is a strange place anyway. I do not believe anyone likes it much when he first goes there. It has none of the look that you expect of Spain. It is modern rather than picturesque, no costumes, practically no Cordoban hats, except on the heads of phonies, no castanets, and no disgusting fakes like the gipsy caves at Granada. There is not one local-coloured place for tourists in the town. Yet when you get to know it, it is the most Spanish of all cities, the best to live in, the finest people, month in and month out the finest climate and while the other big cities are all very representative of the province they are in, they are either Andalucian, Catalan, Basque, Aragonese, or otherwise provincial. It is in Madrid only that you get the essence. The essence, when it is the essence, can be in a plain glass bottle and you need no fancy labels, nor in Madrid do you need any national costumes; no matter what sort of building they put up, though the building itself may look like Buenos Aires, when you see it against that sky you know it is Madrid. If it had nothing else than the Prado it would be worth spending a month in every spring, if you have the money to spend a month in any European capital. But when you can have the Prado and the bullfight season at the same time with El Escorial not two hours to the north and Toledo to the south, a fine road to Avila and a fine road to Segovia, which is no distance from La Granja, it makes you feel very badly, all question of immortality aside, to know that you will have to die and never see it again.

The Prado is altogether characteristic of Madrid. From the outside it looks as unpicturesque as an American High School building. The pictures are so simply arranged, so easy to see, so well-lighted and with no attempt, with one exception, the Velasquez of the small maids of honour, to theatricalize or set off masterpieces that the tourist looking in the red or blue guide book to see which are the famous ones feels vaguely disappointed. The colours have kept so wonderfully in the dry mountain air and the pictures are so simply hung and easy to see that the tourist feels cheated. I have watched them being puzzled. These cannot be great pictures, the colours are too fresh and they are too simple to see. These pictures are hung as though in a modern dealer's gallery where they are being shown off to their best and clearest advantage in order to be sold. It cannot be right, the tourist thinks. There must be a catch somewhere. They get their money's worth in Italian galleries where they cannot find any given picture nor see it any too well if they do find it. That way they feel they are seeing great art. Great art should have great frames and needs either red plush or bad lighting to back it up. It is as though after having known of certain things only through reading pornographic literature the tourist should be introduced to an attractive woman quite unclothed, with no draperies, no concealments and no conversation and only the plainest of beds. He would probably want a book to aid him or at least a few properties or suggestions. That may be one reason there are so many books on Spain. For one person who likes Spain there are a dozen who prefer books on her. France sells better than books on France.

The longest books on Spain are usually written by Germans who make one intensive visit and then never return. I should say that it is probably a good system, if one has to write books on Spain, to write them as rapidly as possible after a first visit as several visits could only confuse the first impressions and make conclusions much less easy to draw. Also the one-visit books are much surer of everything and are bound to be more popular. Books like Richard Ford's have never had the popularity of the bedside mysticism of such a book as *Virgin Spain*. The author of this book once published a piece in a now dead little magazine called *S4N* explaining how he did his writing. Any historian of letters wanting to explain certain phenomena of our writing can look it up in the files of that magazine. My copy is in Paris or I could quote it in full, but the gist of it was how this writer lay naked in his bed in the night and God sent him things to write, how he 'was in touch ecstatically with the plunging and immobile all'. How he was, through the courtesy of God, '*everywhere* and *everywhen*'. The italics are his or maybe they are God's. It didn't say in the article. After God sent it he wrote it. The result was that unavoidable mysticism of a man who writes a language so badly he cannot make a clear statement uncomplicated by whatever pseudo-scientific jargon is in style at the moment. God sent him some wonderful stuff about Spain, during his short stay there preparatory to writing of the soul of the country, but it is often nonsense. The whole thing is what, to make a belated entry into the pseudo-scientific field, I call erectile writing. It is well known, or not known, whichever you prefer, that due to a certain congestion or other, trees for example look different to a man in that portentous state and a man who is not. All objects look different. They are slightly larger, more mysterious, and vaguely blurred. Try it yourself. Now there has or had arisen in America a school of writers who (this is old Dr Hemingstein, the great psychiatrist deducing) had, it would seem, by conserving these congestions, sought to make all objects mystic through the slight distortion of vision that unrelieved turgidness presents. The school seems to be passing now, or to have passed, and it was an interesting mechanical experiment while it lasted, and full of pretty phallic images drawn in the manner of sentimental valentines, but it would have amounted to more if only the vision of these writers had been a little more interesting and developed, when, say, not so congested.

I wonder what such a book as *Virgin Spain* would have been like if written after a few good pieces of that sovereign specific for making a man see clearly. Perhaps it was. We pseudo-scientific coves may be all wrong. But to those inner-searching Viennese eyes peering out from under the shaggy brows of old Dr Hemingstein, that masterful deducer, it seems as though, had the brain been cleared sufficiently, by a few good pieces, there might have been no book at all.

This too to remember. If a man writes clearly enough anyone can see if he fakes. If he mystifies to avoid a straight statement, which is very different from breaking so-called rules of syntax or grammar to make an effect which can be obtained in no other way, the writer takes a longer time to be known as a fake and other writers who are afflicted by the same necessity will praise him in their own defence. True mysticism should not be confused with incompetence in writing which seeks to mystify where there is no mystery but is really only the necessity to fake to cover lack of knowledge or the inability to state clearly. Mysticism implies a mystery and there are many mysteries; but incompetence is not one of them; nor is over-written journalism made literature by the injection of a false epic quality. Remember this too: all bad writers are in love with the epic.

Chapter 6

If you go first to a corrida in Madrid you can go down into the ring and walk about before the fight.* The gates into the corrals and the patio de caballos are open and there in the courtyard you will see the line of horses against the wall, and the picadors arriving on the horses they have ridden in from town, these horses having been ridden from the bull ring by the red-bloused monos or bull-ring servants to the lodging in the town where the picadors live, so the picador, dressed in his white shirt, narrow black four-in-hand tie, brocaded jacket, wide sash, bowl-topped hat with the pompom on the side and the thick buckskin trousers that cover the steel leaf armour over the right leg, may mount and ride through the streets and in the traffic along the carretera de Aragon out to the ring; the mono sometimes riding behind his saddle, sometimes on another horse he has led out; these few horsemen in the stream of carriages, carts, taxis and motor-cars serving to advertise the bullfights, to tire the horses ridden, and to spare the matador from having to provide room for the picador in his coach or motor. As you ride toward the ring the best way to go is on one of the horse-drawn buses that leave the Puerta del Sol. You can sit on the top and see all the other people who are going and if you watch the crowd of vehicles you will see a motor-car pass packed full of bullfighters in their costumes. All you will see will be their heads with the flat black-topped hats, their gold or silver brocade-covered shoulders and their faces.

* You can no longer walk about in the ring, by government order. You may visit the patio de caballos and other dependencies.

If, in one car, there are several men in silver or dark jackets and only one in gold and while the others may be laughing, smoking and joking, his face is still, he is the matador and the others are his cuadrilla. The ride to the ring is the worst part of the day for the matador. In the morning the fight is still a long way off. After lunch it is still a long way off, then, before the car is ready or the carriage comes, there is the preoccupation of dressing. But once in the car or the carriage the fight is very near and there is nothing he can do about it during all that closely packed ride to the ring. It is closely packed because the upper part of a bull-fighter's jacket is heavy and thick at the shoulders and the mata-dor and his banderilleros, now that they ride in the motor-car, crowd each other tightly when they are dressed in their fighting clothes. There are some that smile and recognize friends on the ride, but nearly all are still-faced and detached. The matador, from living every day with death, becomes very detached, the measure of his detachment of course is the measure of his imagination and always on the day of the fight and finally during the whole end of the season, there is a detached something in their minds that you can almost see. What is there is death and you cannot deal in it each day and know each day there is a chance of receiving it without having it make a very plain mark. It makes this mark on everyone. The banderilleros and the picadors are different. Their danger is relative. They are under orders; their responsibility is limited; and they do not kill. They are under no great strain before a fight. Ordin-arily though, if you wish to see a study in apprehension, see an ordinarily cheerful and careless picador after he has been to the corrals, or the sorting of the bulls, and seen that these are really very big and powerful. If I could draw I would make a picture of a table at the café during a feria with the banderilleros sitting before lunch reading the papers, a boot-black at work, a waiter hurrying somewhere and two returning picadors, one a big brown-faced, dark-browed man usually very cheerful and a great joker, the other a grey-haired, neat, hawk-nosed, trim-waisted little man, both of them looking the absolute embodiment of gloom and depression.

'¿Qué tal?' asks one of the banderilleros.

'Son grandes,' says the picador.

'¿Grandes?'

'¡Muy grandes!'

There is nothing more to be said. The banderilleros know everything that is in the picador's mind. The matador may be able to assassinate the big bull, if he swallows his pride and puts away his honour, as easily as any small bull. The veins of the neck are in the same place and as easily reached with the point of the sword. There is no greater chance of a banderillero's being caught if the bull is big. But there is nothing the picador can do to help himself. After the bulls are above a certain age and weight, when they hit the horse it means the horse goes up into the air and perhaps he comes down with the picador under him, perhaps the picador is thrown against the barrier and pinned under the horse, or if they lean forward gallantly, put their weight on the vara and try to punish the bull during the encounter it means they fall between the bull and the horse when the horse goes and must lie there, with the bull looking for them with the horn, until the matador can take the bull away. If the bulls are really big, each time they hit the horse the picador will fall and he knows this and his apprehension when 'they are big' is greater than any the matador, unless he is a coward, can feel. There is always something the matador can do if he keeps his nerve. He may sweat ink, but there is a way to fight each bull no matter how difficult. The picador has no recourse. All he can do is turn down the customary bribe from the horse contractor for accepting an undersized mount and insist on a good strong horse, tall enough to keep him above the bull at the start, try to peg him well once and hope for not the worst.

By the time you see the matadors standing in the opening of the patio de caballos their worst time of apprehension is over.

The crowd around them has removed that loneliness of the ride with people who know them all too well, and the crowd restores their characters. Nearly all bullfighters are brave. Some are not. This seems impossible since no man who was not brave would get into the ring with a bull, but in certain special cases natural ability and early training, commencing the training with calves where there is no danger, have made bullfighters of men with no natural courage. There are only about three of these, I will go into their cases later, and they are among the most interesting phenomena of the ring, but the usual bullfighter is a very brave man, the most common degree of bravery being the ability temporarily to ignore possible consequences. A more pronounced degree of bravery, which comes with exhilaration, is the ability not to give a damn for possible consequences; not only to ignore them but to despise them. Nearly all bullfighters are brave and yet nearly all bullfighters are frightened at some moment *before* the fight begins.

The crowd starts to thin in the patio de caballos, the bullfighters line up, the three matadors abreast, their banderilleros and picadors behind them. The crowd goes from the ring, leaving it empty. You go to your seat, and, if you are in a barrera, you buy a cushion from the vendor below, sit on it, and with your knees pressing the wood, look out across the ring to the doorway of the patio you have just left with the three matadors, the sun shining on the gold of their suits, standing in the doorway, the other bullfighters, on foot and mounted, making a mass behind them. Then you see the people around you looking up above them toward a box. It is the president coming in. He takes his seat and waves a handkerchief. If he is on time there is a burst of clapping; if he is late there is a storm of whistling and booing. A trumpet blows and from the patio two mounted men in the costume of the time of Philip II ride out across the sand.

They are the alguacils or mounted bailiffs and it is through them that all orders by the president, who represents the constituted authority, are transmitted. They gallop across the ring, doff their hats, bow low before the president and presumably having received his authorization gallop back to place. The music starts, and from the opening in the courtyard of the horses comes the procession of the bullfighters; the paseo or parade. The three, if there are six bulls, four, if there are eight, matadors walk abreast, their dress capes are furled and wrapped around their left arms, their right arms balance, they walk with a loose-hipped stride, their arms swinging, their chins up, their eyes on the president's box. In single file behind each matador comes his cuadrilla of banderilleros and his picadors in the order of their seniority. So they come across the sand in a column of three or four. As the matadors come in front of the president's box they bow low and remove their black hats or monteras – the bow is serious or perfunctory, depending on their length of service or degree of cynicism. At the start of their careers all are as devoutly ritual as altar boys serving a high mass and some always remain so. Others are as cynical as night club proprietors. The devout ones are killed more frequently. The cynical ones are the best companions. But the best of all are the cynical ones when they are still devout; or after; when having been devout, then cynical, they become devout again by cynicism. Juan Belmonte is an example of the last stage.

After they have bowed to the president they replace their hats, settling them carefully, and go to the barrera. The procession breaks up as, all having saluted, the matadors remove their heavy gold brocaded and jewelled parade capes and send them or pass them to friends or admirers to spread along the front of the wall protecting the first rows of seats, or sometimes send them by a sword handler to someone, usually a singer, a dancer, a quack doctor, an aviator, a cinema actor, a politician or someone notorious in the news of the day who happens to be in a box. Very young matadors or very cynical ones send their capes to bullfight impresarios from other towns who may be in Madrid, or to the bullfight critics. The best ones send them to friends. It is better not to have one sent to you. It is a pleasant compliment if the bullfighter has a good day and does well, but if he does badly it is too much responsibility. To have an obvious allegiance to a bullfighter who through bad luck, a bad bull, some accident that makes him lose confidence, or bad nerves from coming back to the ring in poor physical shape after a goring, disgraces himself and finally makes the public so indignant that he may have to be protected by the police as he goes out of the ring, head down, under a bombardment of thrown leather cushions, makes one conspicuous when the sword handler comes dodging around the falling cushions to reclaim the cape. Or perhaps, anticipating the disaster, the sword handler has come for the cape before the last bull so that you can see the cape, so proudly received, drawn tightly around the disgraced shoulders, being carried sprinting across the ring, the cushions sailing, a few of the more violent spectators being charged by the police as they pursue your matador. The bander-illeros give their capes to friends to display too, but as these capes are regal looking only at a distance, are often thin, well-sweated and lined with that same striped material that seems to form the lining for vests all over the world and as the banderil-leros do not take the conferring of this favour seriously, the honour is only nominal. While the capes are being thrown and spread and the fighting capes taken from the barrera, the bull-ring servants smooth the sand of the ring that has been disturbed by the procession of the mounted picadors, the harnessed mules for handling of dead bulls and horses and the hooves of the horses of the alguacils. Meantime the two matadors (it is infer-red that this is a six-bull fight) who are not killing retire with their cuadrillas into the callejon or narrow passageway between the red fences of the barrera and the first seats. The matador whose bull is to come out selects one of the heavy percale fighting capes. These are usually rose-coloured on the outside and yellow inside with a wide stiffened collar, and big and full enough so that if the matador should put it over his shoulders the bottom of it would fall to his knees or just below and he would be able to wrap himself completely in it. The matador who is to kill places himself behind one of the little flat plank shelters which are built out from the barrera, wide enough for two men to stand in and just narrow enough to dodge behind, the alguacils ride up to under the president's box to ask for the key to the red door of the toril where the bull is waiting. The president throws it and the alguacil tries to catch it in his plumed hat. If he does the crowd claps. If he misses it whistles. But it does not take any of this seriously. If it is not caught a bull-ring servant picks it up and hands it to the alguacil who gallops across the ring and hands it to the man who stands ready to open the door of the toril, gallops back, salutes the president and gallops out while the servants smooth away the traces of the horse marks on the sand. This smoothing completed there is no one in the ring but the matador behind his little shelter or burladero and two banderilleros, one on each side of the ring, tight against the fence. It is very quiet and everyone is looking at the red plank door. The president gives a signal with his handkerchief, the trumpet sounds and the very serious, white-haired wide old man, his name is Gabriel, in a sort of burlesque bullfighter's suit (it was bought for him by popular subscription) unlocks the door of the toril and pulling heavily on it runs backward to expose the low passageway that shows as the door swings open.

Chapter 7

At this point is is necessary that you see a bullfight. If I were to describe one it would not be the one that you would see, since the bullfighters and the bulls are all different, and if I were to explain the possible variations as I went along the chapter would be interminable. There are two sorts of guide books; those that are read before and those that are to be read after, and the ones that are to be read after the fact are bound to be incomprehensible to a certain extent before; if the fact is of enough importance in itself. So with any book on mountain ski-ing, sexual intercourse, wing shooting, or any other thing which it is impossible to make come true on paper, or at least impossible to attempt to make more than one version of at a time on paper, it being always an individual experience, there comes a place in the guide book where you must say do not come back until you have ski-ed, had sexual intercourse, shot quail or grouse, or been to the bullfight, so that you will know what we are talking about. So from now on it is inferred that you have been to the bullfight.

You went to the bullfight? How was it?

It was disgusting. I couldn't stand it.

All right, we will give you an honourable discharge but no refund.

How did you like it? It was terrible. How do you mean terrible? Just terrible. It was terrible, awful, horrible. Good. You get an honourable discharge, too.

How did it seem to you? I was simply bored to death. All right. You get the hell out of here.

Didn't anybody like the bullfight? Didn't anybody like the bullfight at all? No answer. Did you like it, sir? I did not. Did you like it, madame? Decidedly not.

An old lady in the back of the room: What is he saying? What is that young man asking?

Someone near her: He's asking if anyone liked the bullfight.

Old lady: Oh, I thought he was asking if any of us wanted to be bullfighters.

Did you like the bullfight, madame?

Old lady: I liked it very much.

What did you like about it?

Old lady: I liked to see the bulls hit the horses.

Why did you like that?

Old lady: It seemed so sort of homey.

Madame, you are a mystic. You are not among friends here. Let us go to the Café Fornos where we can discuss these matters at leisure.

Old lady: Wherever you wish, sir, provided it is clean and wholesome.

Madame, there is no wholesomer place in the Peninsula.

Old lady: Will we see the bullfighters there?

Madame, the place is packed with them.

Old lady: Then let us be off.

Fornos is a café frequented only by people connected with the bullfights and by whores. There is smoke, hurrying of waiters, noise of glasses, and you have the noisy privacy of a big café. We can discuss the fight, if you wish, and the old lady can sit and look at the bullfighters. There are bullfighters at every table and for all tastes, and all the other people in the café live off bullfighters in some way or another. A shark rarely has more than four remoras or sucking fish that fasten to him or swim along with him, but a bullfighter, when he is making money, has dozens. The old lady does not care to discuss the bullfight. She liked it; she is now looking at the bullfighters and never discusses things she has enjoyed even with her most intimate friends. We talk about it because there were a number of things you say you did not understand.

When the bull came out did you notice that one of the banderilleros ran across his course trailing a cape and that the bull followed the cape driving at it with one horn? They run him that way always, at the start, to see which horn he favours. The matador, standing behind his shelter, watches the bull run by the trailing cape and notices whether he follows the zig-zagging cape on both his right and his left sides, this showing whether he sees with both eyes and which horn he prefers to hook with. He also notices whether he runs straight or if he has a tendency to cut ground toward the man as he charges. The man who went out with the cape in both hands after the bull had been run, and cited him from in front, standing still as the bull charged, and with his arms moving the cape slowly just ahead of the bull's horns, passing the bull's horns close by his body with slow movement of the cape, seeming to keep him controlled, in the folds of the cape, bringing him past his body each time as he turned and recharged; doing this five times and then finishing off with a swirl of the cape that turned the man's back on the bull and, by cutting the bull's charge brusquely, fixed him to the spot; that man was the matador and the slow passes that he made were called veronicas and the half pass at the end a media-veronica. Those passes were designed to show the matador's skill and art with the cape, his domination of the bull and also to fix the bull in a certain spot before the entry of the horses. They are called veronicas after St Veronica who wiped the face of Our Lord with a cloth and are so called because the saint is always represented holding the cloth by the two corners in the position the bullfighter holds the cape for the start of the veronica. The media-veronica that stops the bull at the end of the passes is a recorte. A recorte is any pass with the cape that, by causing the bull to try to turn in less than his own length, stops him brusquely or checks his rush by cutting his course and doubling him on himself.

The banderilleros are never supposed to use both hands on the cape when the bull first comes out. If they use only one hand the cape will be trailed and when they turn it at the end of a run the bull will turn easily and not sharply and brusquely. He will do this because the turn of the long cape gives him an indication of the turn to make and gives him something to follow. With the cape held in both hands the banderillero can snap it away from the bull, flop it brusquely out of his sight and stop him dead, and turn him sharply so that he twists his spinal column, lames himself, has his speed cut, not by being worn down, but by laming, and make him unfit for the rest of the fight. Only the matador is supposed to use two hands on the cape during the early part of the fight. Strictly speaking the banderilleros, who are also called peones, are never supposed to use two hands on the cape except when bringing the bull out from a position he has taken and refused to leave. But in the way bullfighting has developed, or decayed, with emphasis increasingly placed on the manner of execution of the various passes rather than their effect, the banderilleros now do much of the work of preparing the bull for killing that was formerly done by the matador; and matadors without resources or science, whose only ability is their plastic or artistic talent, have their bulls, if these offer the slightest difficulty, prepared, worn down, dominated and everything but killed by the skilled and destructive cape of an experienced banderillero.

It may seem foolish to speak of almost killing such an animal as a fighting bull with a cape. Of course you could not kill, but you can so damage the spinal column, twist the legs and lame the animal and, by abusing its bravery, force it to charge uselessly again and again, each time recorting it ferociously, that you may tire it, lame it, and deprive it of all speed and a great part of its natural forces. We speak of killing a trout with a rod. It is the effort made by the trout that kills it. A catfish arrives at the side of the boat in full possession of all its force and strength.

A tarpon, a trout or a salmon will often kill himself fighting the rod and line if you hold him long enough.

It was for this reason that banderilleros were prohibited from caping the bull with both hands. The matador was supposed to do all of the preparation for killing and the killing himself. The picadors were to slow the bull, to change his tempo, and to bring down the carriage of his head. The banderilleros were supposed to run him at the start, to place the banderillas quickly and in such a position as to correct any faults of hooking if they existed, and never to do anything to destroy the strength of the bull, in order that he might come intact into the hands of the matador who was supposed, with the muleta, to correct any tendencies toward hooking to one side or the other, to place him in position for killing and to kill him from in front, making him lower his head with the red serge of the muleta and killing him with the sword, driving it in high up at the top of the angle between the two shoulder blades.

As the corrida has developed and decayed there has been less emphasis on the form of killing, which was once the whole thing, and more on the cape work, the placing of the banderillas and the work with the muleta. The cape, the banderillas and the muleta have all become ends in themselves rather than means to an end and the bullfight has both lost and gained thereby.

In the old days the bulls were usually bigger than they are now; they were fiercer, more uncertain, heavier, and older. They had not been bred down to a smaller size to please the bull-fighters, and they were fought at the age of four and a half to five years instead of three and a half to four and a half years. Matadors often had from six to twelve years of apprenticeship as banderilleros and as novilleros before becoming formal matadors. They were mature men, knew bulls thoroughly, and faced bulls which were brought to the highest point of physical force, strength, knowledge of how to use their horns and general difficulty and danger. The whole end of the bullfight was the final sword thrust, the actual encounter between the man

and the animal, what the Spanish call the moment of truth, and
every move in the fight was to prepare the bull for that killing.
With such bulls it was not necessary to give emotion for the
man to pass the animal as deliberately close to him with the cape
as was possible. The cape was used to run the bulls, to protect
the picadors, and the passes that were made with it, by our
modern standards, were exciting because of the size, strength,
weight and fierceness of the animal and the danger the matador
ran in making them rather than by the form or the slowness of
their execution. It was exciting that the man should pass such
a bull at all, that a man should be in the ring with and dominate
such an animal furnished the emotion rather than that he should
deliberately, as now, try to pass the points of the horn as mathe-
matically close to his body as possible without moving his feet.
It is the decadence of the modern bull that has made modern
bullfighting possible. It is a decadent art in every way and like
most decadent things it reaches its fullest flower at its rottenest
point, which is the present.

It is impossible, day in and day out, to fight bulls that are
really bulls, huge, strong, fierce and fast, knowing how to use
their horns and old enough so that they have their full growth,
with the technique that has been developed, starting with Juan
Belmonte, in modern bullfighting. It is too dangerous. Belmonte invented the technique. He was a genius, who could
break the rules of bullfighting and could torear, that is the only
word for all the actions performed by a man with the bull, as it
was known to be impossible to torear. Once he had done it all
bullfighters had to do it, or attempt to do it since there is no
going back in the matter of sensations. Joselito who was strong
(Belmonte was weak), healthy (Belmonte was sickly), who had
an athlete's body, gipsy grace and an intuitive and acquired
knowledge of bulls that was never surpassed by any bullfighter;
Joselito for whom everything in bullfighting was easy, who
lived for bullfighting, and seemed to have been made and bred
almost to the measurement of what a great bullfighter should

be, had to learn Belmonte's way of working. Joselito, the heritor of all great bullfighters, probably the greatest bullfighter that ever lived, learned to torear as Belmonte did. Belmonte worked that way because of his lack of stature, his lack of strength, because of his feeble legs. He did not accept any rules made without testing whether they might be broken, and he was a genius and a great artist. The way Belmonte worked was not a heritage, nor a development; it was a revolution. Joselito learned it, and during the years of their competition, when they each had around a hundred corridas a year, he used to say, 'They say that he, Belmonte, works closer to the bull. It looks as though he does. But that isn't true. I really work closer. But it is more natural so it doesn't look so close.'

Anyway, the decadent, the impossible, the almost depraved, style of Belmonte was grafted and grown into the great healthy, intuitive genius of Joselito and in his competition with Juan Belmonte, bullfighting for seven years had a golden age in spite of the fact that it was in the process of being destroyed.

They bred the bulls down in size; they bred down the length of horn; they bred them for suavity in their charges as well as fierceness because Joselito and Belmonte could do finer things with these smaller, easier bulls. They could do fine enough things with any bulls that came out of the torils; they were not helpless with any of them but, with the smaller, easier bulls they were certain to do the wonderful things that the public wanted to see. The big bulls were easy for Joselito although they were difficult for Belmonte. All bulls were easy for Joselito and he had to make his own difficulties. The competition ended when Joselito was killed in the ring on 16th May 1920. Belmonte went on one more year, then retired, and bullfighting was left with the new decadent method, the almost impossible technique, the bred-down bulls and, as bullfighters, only the bad ones, the hardy, tough ones who had not been able to learn the new method and so no longer pleased, and a crop of new ones, decadent, sad and sickly enough, who had the method but no knowledge of bulls, no apprenticeship, none of the male courage, faculties or genius of Joselito, and none of the beautiful unhealthy mystery of Belmonte.

Old lady: I saw nothing decadent or rotten about the spectacle we observed today.

Nor did I, today, madame, for the matadors were Nicanor Villalta, the courageous telephone pole of Aragon; Luis Fuentes Bejarano, the valorous and worthy workman, the pride of Union Labour, and Diego Mazquiaran, Fortuna, the brave butcher boy of Bilbao.

Old lady: They all seemed to me to be most valorous and manly chaps. In what way, sir, do you speak of decadence?

Madame, they are most manly chaps although Villalta's voice is a shade high sometimes, and the decadence I speak of does not apply to them but to the decay of a complete art through a magnification of certain of its aspects.

Old lady: Sir, you are hard to understand.

I will explain later, madame, but indeed decadence is a difficult word to use since it has become little more than a term of abuse applied by critics to anything they do not yet understand or which seems to differ from their moral concepts.

Old lady: I always understood it to mean that there was something rotten as there is at courts.

Madame, all our words from loose using have lost their edge, but your inherent concepts are most sound.

Old lady: If you please, sir, I do not care for all this discussion of words. Are we not here to be instructed about the bulls and those who fight them?

If you so wish, but start your writer to talking of words and he will go on until you are wearied and wish he could show more skill in using them and preach less of their significance.

Old lady: Can you not stop then, sir?

Have you ever heard of the late Raymond Radiguet?

Old lady: I cannot say I have.

He was a young French writer who knew how to make his

career not only with his pen but with his pencil if you follow me, madame.

Old lady: You mean?

Not exactly, but something of the sort.

Old lady: You mean he – ?

Precisely. When the late Radiguet was alive he often wearied of the tenuous, rapturous and querulous society of his literary protector, Jean Cocteau, and spent the nights at an hotel near the Luxembourg Gardens with one of two sisters who were then working as models in the quarter. His protector was greatly upset and denounced this as decadence, saying, bitterly, yet proudly of the late Radiguet, 'Bébé est vicieuse – il aime les femmes'. So you see, madame, we must be careful chucking the term decadence about since it cannot mean the same to all who read it.

Old lady: It repelled me from the first.

Then let us return to the bulls.

Old lady: Gladly, sir. But what finally happened to the late Radiguet?

He caught typhoid fever from swimming in the Seine and died of it.

Old lady: Poor chap.

Poor chap, indeed.

Chapter 8

Those years after Joselito's death and the retirement of Belmonte were the worst bullfighting has gone through. The bull ring had been dominated by the two figures that, in their own art, remembering of course that it is an impermanent and so minor art, were comparable to Velasquez and Goya, or, in writing, to Cervantes and Lope de Vega, though I have never cared for Lope, but he has the needed reputation for the comparison, and when they were gone it was as though in English writing Shakespeare had suddenly died, and Marlowe retired and the field left to Ronald Firbank who wrote very well about what he wrote about but was, let us say, a specialist. Manuel Granero of Valencia was the one bullfighter the afición had great faith in. He was one of three boys who had, with protection and money furnished, been made into bullfighters by the best mechanical means and instruction; practising with calves on the bull ranches around Salamanca. Granero had no bullfighting blood in his veins and his immediate family had wanted him to be a violinist, but he had an ambitious uncle and natural talent for bullfighting, aided by much courage, and he was the best of the three. The other two were Manuel Jiminez, Chicuelo, and Juan Luis de la Rosa. As children they were all perfectly trained miniature bullfighters and the three of them all had pure Belmontistic styles, beautiful execution in everything they did, and they were all three called phenomenons. Granero was the soundest, the healthiest, and the bravest and he was killed in Madrid in the May following the death of Joselito.

Chicuelo was the son of a matador of that same name who

had been dead some years from tuberculosis. He was reared, trained and launched and managed as a matador by his uncle, Zocato, who had been a banderillero of the old school and was a good business man and a heavy drinker. Chicuelo was short, unhealthily plump, without a chin, with a bad complexion, tiny hands and with the long eyelashes of a girl. Trained in Sevilla and then on the ranches around Salamanca, he was as perfect a miniature bullfighter as could be manufactured, and he was about as authentic a bullfighter, really, as a little porcelain statuette. After the death of Joselito and Granero and the retirement of Belmonte bullfighting had him. It had Juan Luis de la Rosa who was Chicuelo in everything but the uncle and the way he was built in the altogether. Someone, not a relative, had put up the money for his education and he was another perfectly manufactured product. It had Marcial Lalanda, who knew bulls from being brought up among them – he was the son of the overseer of the breeding ranch of the Duke of Veragua, and he was advertised as the successor of Joselito. All he had as successor at that time was his knowledge of bulls, and a certain way of walking as he cited the bulls for the banderillas. I saw him often in those days and he was always a scientific bullfighter, but he was not strong and he was listless. He seemed to take no pleasure in bullfighting, to derive no emotion or elation from it and to have much controlled, but depressing, fear. He was a sad and unemotional bullfighter, although he was technically skilful and completely intelligent, and for once that he was good in the ring, he was mediocre and uninteresting a dozen times. He, Chicuelo and La Rosa all fought as though they were condemned to it rather than if as they had chosen it. I believe that no one of them could ever completely forget the death of Joselito and of Granero. Marcial had been in the ring when Granero was killed and had been unjustly accused of not having made an effort to take the bull away from him in time. He was very bitter about this.

Bullfighting, then, too, had two brothers, the Anllos, from

Aragon. One, the older, Ricardo, they were both called Nacional, was of medium height and thick set, a monument of probity, courage, undistinguished but classic style and bad luck. The second, Juan, called Nacional II, was tall, with a thin mouth and slanting eyes. He was ungraceful, angular, very brave and with a style of fighting as ugly as you could see.

There was Victoriano Roger, Valencia II, the son of a banderillero. Born in Madrid, he was trained by his father and he too had an older brother who was a failure as a matador. A boy of the same vintage as Chicuelo and company, he managed a cape beautifully, was arrogant, quarrelsome and brave as the bull itself in Madrid, but anywhere else let his nerves master him and felt his honour was secure in provincial disasters, if he could only triumph in Madrid. This confining of their personal honour to Madrid is the mark of those bullfighters who make a living from the profession but never dominate it.

With Julian Saiz, Saleri II, a very complete bullfighter and a splendid banderillero who had competed at one time with Joselito for a season, but who had become the embodiment of caution and safety before all things; Diego Mazquiaran, Fortuna, brave, stupid, a great killer, but of the old school, and Luis Freg, a Mexican, short, brown, with Indian hair, in his late thirties, heavy on his feet, the muscles of his legs gnarled like an old oak with the scars where the bulls had punished him for his slowness, his awkwardness and his never-varying courage with the sword; with a few more veterans and a good many more failures, those were about all the lot in those first years after the two great ones were gone.

Freg, Fortuna and the elder of the Nacionals did not please because the new way of fighting had made their styles old-fashioned and there were no longer the big bulls that, with a brave, competent man in the ring, made all that was needed for a bullfight. Chicuelo was wonderful until he was first touched by a bull. Then, utterly cowardly if the bull offered any difficulties, he was good about twice a year thereafter, only giving all

73

his repertoire when he found a bull without any bad ideas that would move past him without deviation as though it were mounted on rails. In between the beauty of his performances with the mechanically perfect bull that he awaited all season, and his occasional, nerved up, good, scientific work with a difficult bull, came some of the saddest exhibitions of cowardice and shamelessness it would be possible to see. La Rosa was gored once, frightened for ever, and quickly disappeared from circulation. He was very talented as a bullfighter, but he was even more talented in another respect and he is still fighting in South America and, by combining his two talents, living very well.

Valencia II started every season as brave as a fighting cock, worked closer to the bulls each time he appeared in Madrid, until the bull had only to reach a little with its horn to catch him, toss him, gore him and send him to hospital; and when he recovered his courage was gone until the next season.

There were a few others, too. One called Gitanillo, in spite of the name he was no gipsy but had only worked as horsetender for a gipsy family in his youth, was short, arrogant and really brave; in Madrid, at least. In the provinces, like all cheap bullfighters, he relied on his Madrid reputation. He was one of the sort that does everything but eat the bulls raw. He was unskilful at everything and relied on such business as, when the bull was tired or fixed for a moment, turning his back on the animal a foot or so in front of the horns and then kneeling, smiling at the crowd. He was gored badly nearly every season, and finally recovered from a terrible horn wound that transfixed his chest, destroyed a good part of the lung and pleura and left him a cripple for life.

A doctor in Soria hit Juan Anllo, Nacional II, over the head with a bottle in an argument during a bullfight at which Nacional II, a spectator, was defending the conduct of the fighter in the ring who was dealing with a difficult animal. The police arrested the bullfighter but not the assailant and Nacional II lay in jail all night with the red dust of Soria on his clothes and in his hair, dying with his skull fractured and a blood clot on his brain while the people of the jail treated him as a drunk, trying various expedients to rouse him from his unconsciousness. He never roused. That rid bullfighting of one of the really brave men who were matadors during this decadence.

A year before another had died, one who looked as though he were going to be one of the greatest of all. He was Manuel Garcia, Maera. He was a boy with Juan Belmonte in the barrio of Triana in Sevilla and when Belmonte, who worked as a day labourer, had no one to protect him, to send him to a bullfight school and furnish him with money to learn to fight by practising with the calves, wanted to practise with the cape, he and Maera and sometimes Varelito, another local boy, would swim across the river, their capes and a lantern on a log, and, dripping and naked, climb the fence into the corral to where the fighting bulls were kept at Tablada to rouse one of the great full-grown fighting bulls from his sleep. While Maera held the lantern Belmonte passed the bull with the cape. When Belmonte became a matador, Maera, tall, dark, thin-hipped, gaunt-eyed, his face blue black even after a close shave, arrogant, slouching, and sombre, went with him as a banderillero. He was a great banderillero and in the years with Belmonte, fighting ninety to a hundred times in a season, working with all sorts of bulls, he came to know bulls as well as anyone, even Joselito. Belmonte never placed the banderilleras since he could not run. Joselito nearly always placed banderillas in the bulls he killed and in their competition Belmonte used Maera as an antidote to Joselito. Maera could banderillear as well as Joselito, and Belmonte kept him dressed in the worst-fitting, most awkward suits a bullfighter could wear so that he would seem more of a peon; to hold down his personality, and make it seem that he, Belmonte, had a banderillero, a mere peon, who could compete as a banderillero with the great matador, Joselito. In the last year Belmonte fought Maera asked him for an increase of wages. He was getting two hundred and fifty pesetas a fight and he asked

75

for three hundred. Belmonte, although he was then making ten thousand a fight, refused the increase. 'All right, I'll be a matador and I'll show you up,' Maera said. 'You'll be ridiculous,' Belmonte told him. 'No,' said Maera, 'you'll be ridiculous when I'm through.'

At first as a matador, Maera had many of the faults and manners of a peon to overcome, such faults as too much movement (a matador should never run), and he was also styleless with the cape. He was capable and scientific but unfinished with the muleta, and he killed trickily but well. But he had a complete knowledge of bulls and a valour that was so absolute and such a solid part of him that it made everything easy that he understood; and he understood it all. Also he was very proud. He was the proudest man I have ever seen.

In two years he corrected all his faults with the cape, he got to manage the muleta beautifully; he was always one of the finest, most emotional and finished banderilleros that ever nailed a pair; and he became one of the best and most satisfying matadors I have ever watched. He was so brave that he shamed those stylists who were not, and bullfighting was so important and so wonderful to him that, in his last year, his presence in the ring raised the whole thing from the least effort, get-rich-quick, wait-for-the-mechanical bull basis it had fallen to and, while he was in the ring, it again had dignity and passion. If Maera was in the plaza it was a good bullfight for at least two bulls, and as often as he intervened in the fighting of the other four. When the bulls did not come to him he did not point out the fact to the crowd asking for their indulgence and sympathy; he went to the bulls, arrogant, domineering, and disregarding danger. He gave emotion always and, finally, as he steadily improved his style, he was an artist. But all the last year he fought you could see he was going to die. He had galloping consumption and he expected to die before the year was out. In the meantime he was very occupied. He was gored badly twice but he paid no attention to it. I saw him fight on a Sunday with a five-inch wound in his armpit that he received on a Thursday. I saw the wound, saw it dressed before and after the fight, and he paid no attention to it. It hurt as a torn wound made by a splintered horn hurts after two days but he paid no attention to the pain. He acted as though it were not there. He did not favour it or avoid lifting the arm; he ignored it. He was a long way beyond pain. I never saw a man to whom time seemed so short as it did to him that season.

The next time I saw him he had been gored in the neck in Barcelona. The wound was closed with eight stitches and he was fighting, his neck bandaged, the day after. His neck was stiff and he was furious. He was furious at the stiffness he could do nothing about and the fact that he had to wear a bandage that showed above his collar.

A young matador who must watch the observance of all etiquette, to command a respect he may not always inspire, never eats with his cuadrilla. He eats apart, thus keeping the gulf between master and servant that he cannot maintain if he mixes with those who work for him. Maera always ate with the cuadrilla; they all ate at one table; they all travelled together, and lived, sometimes in crowded ferias, all in the same room, and they all respected him as I have seen no matador respected by his cuadrilla.

He had trouble with his wrists. They are the part of the body that are of most vital use to a good bullfighter. As the trigger finger of a rifleman is sensitive and educated to the tiniest degrees of squeezing to approach and release the discharge of his piece, so it is with his wrists that a bullfighter controls and makes the delicacy of art with the cape and muleta. All the sculpturing that he does with the muleta is done with the wrist and it is with the wrist that he sinks the banderillas, and with the wrist, stiff this time, the chamois-wrapped, lead-weighted pommel of the sword held in the palm of his hand, that he kills. Maera, killing one time, driving in as the bull charged and leaning hard, shoulder forward, after the sword, struck the point of

77

the sword on one of the vertebrae, inside the opening between the shoulder blades. He was driving and the bull was driving and the sword buckled nearly double and then shot up into the air. As it buckled it dislocated his wrist. He picked the sword up in his left hand and carried it over to the barrera and with his left hand pulled out a new sword from the leather sheath his sword handler offered him.

'And the wrist?' the sword handler asked.

'Damn the wrist,' Maera said.

He went toward the bull, squared him with two passes with the muleta, putting it in front of his damp muzzle and quickly withdrawing it as the bull's forefeet rose to follow it and then fell into the right position for killing, holding both the sword and muleta in his left hand, he lifted the sword to his right hand, profiled, and went in. Again he hit bone, insisted, and the sword buckled, shot into the air, and fell. This time he didn't go for a new sword. He picked up the sword with his right hand, and as he lifted it I could see the sweat on his face from the pain. He chopped the bull into position with the red cloth, profiled, sighted along the blade and went in. He went in as though he would drive through a stone wall, his weight, his height and all on to the sword and it hit bone, doubled, not so far this time because his wrist gave quicker, buckled, and fell. He lifted the sword with his right hand and the wrist would not hold it and it dropped. He lifted the wrist and banged it against his doubled left fist, then picked up the sword in his left hand, placed it in his right and as he held it you could see the sweat come down his face. The second matador tried to get him to go to the infirmary and he shook himself away and cursed them all.

'Let me alone,' he said, 'and go and hang yourselves.'

He went in twice more and hit the bone both times. Now at any time he could have, without danger or pain, slipped the sword into the neck of the bull, let it go into the lung or cut the jugular and killed him with no trouble. But his honour demanded that he kill him high up between the shoulders, going in as a man should, over the horn, following the sword with his body. And on the sixth time he went in this way and the sword went in too. He came out from the encounter, the horn just clearing his belly as he shrugged over it as he passed and then stood tall and sunken-eyed, his face wet with sweat, his hair down on his forehead, watching the bull as he swung, lost his feet and rolled over. He pulled the sword out with his *right* hand, as punishment for it I suppose, but shifted it to his left, and carrying it point down, walked over to the barrera. His rage was all over. His right wrist was swollen to double its size. He was thinking about something else. He would not go to the infirmary to get it bandaged.

Somebody asked about his wrist. He held it up and sneered at it.

'Go to the infirmary, man,' one of the banderilleros said. 'Put yourself inside.' Maera looked at him. He wasn't thinking about his wrist at all. He was thinking about the bull.

'He was made out of cement,' he said. 'Bloody bull made out of cement.'

Anyway he died that winter in Seville with a tube in each lung, drowned with pneumonia that came to finish off the tuberculosis. When he was delirious he rolled under the bed and fought with death under the bed, dying as hard as a man can die. I thought that year he hoped for death in the ring but he would not cheat by looking for it. You would have liked him, madame. Era muy hombre.

Old lady: Why wouldn't Belmonte pay him more money when he asked for it?

That is a strange thing about Spain, madame. Of all things financial that I have any acquaintance with, the dirtiest in regard to money is bullfighting. A man's ranking is made by the amount he receives for fighting. But in Spain a man feels that the less he pays his subordinates the more man he is, and in the same way the nearer he can bring his subordinates to slaves the more man he feels he is. This is especially true of matadors who have come from the lowest ranks of the people. They are affable, generous, courteous, and well liked by all who are superior to them in station, and miserly with those who work for them.

Old lady: Is this true of all?

No, and certainly being surrounded by fawning parasites a matador could be excused any bitterness or desire to protect his earnings. But in general I say there is no man meaner about money with his inferiors than your matador.

Old lady: Was your friend Maera, then, mean about money?

He was not. He was generous, humorous, proud, bitter, foul-mouthed and a great drinker. He neither sucked after intellectuals nor married money. He loved to kill bulls and lived with much passion and enjoyment, although the last six months of his life he was very bitter. He knew he had tuberculosis and took absolutely no care of himself; having no fear of death he preferred to burn out, not as an act of bravado, but from choice. He was training his younger brother and believed he would be a great matador. The younger brother, also afflicted in the lungs, turned out to be a coward. It was a great disappointment to us all.

Chapter 9

Of course if you should happen to go to a bullfight and not see any of the decadent matadors there would be no need for all this explanation of the decadence of bullfighting. But if at your first bullfight you should see, instead of whatever your idea of how a matador should look, a fat, weak-faced, long-eyelashed little man with great delicacy of wrist and skill with, and horror of, bulls, this requires some explanation. That is how Chicuelo looks today, ten years after his first appearance as a phenomenon. He still has contracts, because people are always in the hope that his bull, the perfect bull that he waits for, will come out of the toril and he will unroll his beautiful, pure, improved over Belmonte even, repertoire of linked passes. You may see him twenty times in a season and never see him give a complete performance once, but when he is good he is wonderful.

Of the others who dominated with their names and with the hopes they roused, but never with consistent triumphs, the period immediately after Joselito and Belmonte, Marcial Lalanda has become a masterly, dependable, skilful, able and sincere bullfighter. He can deal with any and all bulls and can do skilful and sincere work with them all. He is confident and secure. His nine years of service have ripened him and given him confidence and pleasure in his work rather than frightened him. As a complete, scientific torero he is the best there is in Spain.

Valencia II is the same as he was at the start, in ability and limitations, except that he has grown fat and prudent and a badly-sewn wound at the corner of one eye has distorted his face so that he has lost his cockiness. He does beautiful work with the cape, has a few tricks with the muleta, but they are only tricks, and in the main he only defends himself with it. He gives everything he has in Madrid when he is capable of nerving himself to it and in the provinces he is as cynical as ever. He is nearly through as a matador.

There are two matadors I have said nothing about because they were no part of the decadence of the fighting bull but rather individual cases. They would have been the same at any epoch. These two are Nicanor Villalta and Niño de la Palma. But first I must explain why there should be so much discussion of individuals. Individuals are interesting, madame, but they are not all. In this case it is because, with the decadence of bullfighting, it has become altogether a matter of the individual. Someone has seen a bullfight. You ask who were the matadors. If they remember the names you know exactly what sort of bullfight they may have seen. For, now, certain matadors are only capable of certain things. They have become as much specialists as doctors. In the old days you went to a doctor and he fixed up, or tried to fix up, whatever was wrong with you. So in the old days you went to a bullfight and the matadors were matadors; they had served a real apprenticeship, knew bullfighting, performed as skilfully as their ability and courage permitted with cape, muleta, banderillas, and they killed the bulls. It is of no use to describe the state of specialization doctors have reached, nor to speak of the aspects of this which are most repellent and ridiculous because everyone has some contact with them sooner or later, but a person who is going to the bullfights does not know that this malady of specialization has spread to bullfighting so that there are matadors who are only good with the cape and useless at anything else. The spectators may not watch the cape work closely, it all being new and strange to their eyes, and they will then think that the rest of the performance of that particular matador is representative of bullfighting and judge it, bullfighting, accordingly, when, in reality, it is the sorriest parody of the way bulls should be fought.

What is needed in bullfighting today is a complete bullfighter who is at the same time an artist to save it from the specialists; the bullfighters who can do only one thing, and who do it superlatively, but who require a special, almost made-to-order bull to bring their art to its highest point or, sometimes, to be able to have any art at all. What it needs is a god to drive the half-gods out. But waiting for a messiah is a long business and you get many fake ones. There is no record in the Bible of the number of fake messiahs that came before Our Lord, but the history of the last ten years of bullfighting would record little else.

It is because you may see some of these fake messiahs in action that it is important to know about them. You do not know whether you have seen a bullfight or not until you know whether the bulls were really bulls and the matadors really bullfighters.

For instance, you might see Nicanor Villalta. If you saw him in Madrid you could think he was splendid and see something very fine because, in Madrid, he keeps his feet together when he uses the cape and muleta and thus keeps from being grotesque, and he always, in Madrid, kills very valiantly. Villalta is a strange case. He has a neck three times as long as that of the average man. He is six feet tall to start with and those six feet are mostly legs and neck.

You cannot compare it with the neck of a giraffe because the giraffe's neck looks natural. Villalta's neck looks as though it were being stretched out right before your eyes. It seems to stretch like rubber but it never snaps back. It would be wonderful if it did. Now a man with such a neck, if he keeps his feet together, looks fairly normal; if he keeps his feet together, bends backward at the waist and inclines that neck toward the bull, a certain effect is produced which while not aesthetic is not completely grotesque, but once he spreads his legs and his long arms apart no valour can save him from being utterly ridiculous. One night in San Sebastian, as we walked along the concha, Villalta talked about his neck, in his Aragonese sort of baby-talk dialect, cursed it, and told us how he had to concentrate always, remember always, in order not to be grotesque. He invented a sort of gyroscopic way of using the muleta, of making his unnatural *natural* passes, his feet tight together, his gigantic muleta (spread out it would be large enough for a respectable hotel bed sheet) in the right hand, spread by the sword, he spins slowly with the bull. No one passes the bull closer, no one works closer to the bull, and no one spins as he, the master, spins. With the cape he is not good, he is much too fast with it and too snatchy, and killing he goes in straight and follows the sword well with his body, but he often, instead of dropping the left hand low so that the bull follows it and uncovers the vital spot between his shoulders, blinds the bull with the red volume of his muleta and relies on his height to carry him over the horns and let him get the sword well in. Sometimes, however, he kills absolutely correctly and according to the rules. Lately his killing has been almost classical and very consistent. Everything he does he does bravely, and everything he does in his own way, so that if you see Nicanor Villalta that is not bullfighting either. But you should see him once in Madrid where he puts out everything he has and if he has a bull that permits him to keep his feet together, and only one of six will, you will see something very strange, very emotional and very, thank God, except for the great courage employed, unique.

If you see Niño de la Palma the chances are you will see cowardice in its least attractive form; its fat-rumped, prematurely bald from using hair fixatives, prematurely senile form. He, of all the young bullfighters who came up in the ten years after Belmonte's first retirement, raised the most false hopes and proved the greatest disappointment. He started bullfighting in Malaga, and he only fought twenty-one times in the ring, in contrast to the eight to ten years of apprenticeship of the run of old-time bullfighters, before he was made a full-fledged matador. There were two great bullfighters who became full matadors when they were only sixteen years of age, Costillares and Joselito, and because they seemed to skip all apprenticeship and found a royal road to learning, many boys have been given premature and disastrous elevation. Niño de la Palma was a great sample of this. The only cases where these early alternatives were justified were where the boys had served years as child bullfighters and came from bullfighting families, so they could make up in early paternal or fraternal training and counsel what they lacked in experience. Even then it was only successful if they were super-geniuses. I say super-geniuses because every matador is a genius. You cannot learn to be a full matador any more than you can learn to be a major-league ballplayer, an opera singer, or a good professional boxer. You can learn to play baseball, to box, or to sing, but unless you have a certain degree of genius you cannot make your living at baseball or boxing or singing in opera. In bullfighting this genius, which must be there to start with, is further complicated by the necessity of physical courage to face wounding and possible death after the wounding has become reality through its first experience. Cayetano Ordonez, Niño de la Palma, in his first season as a matador, promoted in the spring after some beautiful performances as a novillero in Sevilla, Malaga and some incomplete ones in Madrid, looked like the messiah who had come to save bullfighting if ever anyone did.

I tried to describe how he looked, and a couple of his fights in a book one time. I was present the day of his first presentation as a matador in Madrid and I saw him in Valencia that year in competition with Juan Belmonte, returned from retirement, do two faenas that were so beautiful and wonderful that I can remember them pass by pass today. He was sincerity and purity of style itself with the cape, he did not kill badly, although, except when he had luck, he was not a great killer. He did kill several times recibiendo, receiving the bull on the sword in the old manner, and he was beautiful with the muleta. Gregorio Corrochano, the bullfighter critic of the influential newspaper

A.B.C., in Madrid, said of him, 'Es de Ronda y se llama Cayetano'. He is from Ronda, the cradle of bullfighting, and they call him Cayetano, a great bullfighter's name; the first name of Cayetano Sanz, the greatest old-time stylist. The phrase went all over Spain. Translated freely it might be, in its implications, as though a great young golfer many years from now should come from Atlanta again and his name be Bobby Jones. Cayetano Ordonez looked like a bullfighter, he acted like a bullfighter and for one season he was a bullfighter. I saw him in most of his fights and in all his best ones. At the end of the season he was gored severely and painfully in the thigh, very near the femoral artery.

That was the end of him. The next year he had the most contracts of any matador in the profession, signed because of his first splendid year, and his actions in the ring were a series of disasters. He could hardly look at a bull. His fright as he had to go in to kill was painful to see and he spent the whole season assassinating bulls in the way that offered him least danger, running across their line of charge and shoving the sword at their necks, sticking them in the lungs, anywhere he could reach without bringing his body within range of the horns. It was the most shameful season any matador had ever had up until that year in bullfighting. What had happened was that the horn wound, the first real goring, had taken all his valour. He never got it back. He had too much imagination. Several times, in succeeding years, he nerved himself to give good performances in Madrid so that by the publicity they would give him in the press he would still obtain contracts. The Madrid papers are distributed and read all over Spain and a triumph by a bullfighter in the capital is read about all over the peninsula while a triumph in the provinces goes no farther than the immediate neighbourhood and is always discounted in Madrid because the fighters' managers always announce triumphs by telephone and telegram from wherever their fighters appear in the provinces even though the fighter may have nearly been lynched by the disgusted spectators. But these nerved-up performances were the brave actions of a coward.

Now the brave actions of a coward are very valuable in psychological novels and are always extremely valuable to the man who performs them, but they are not valuable to the public who, season in and season out, pay to see a bullfighter. All they do is give that bullfighter a seeming value which he does not have. Going sometimes to church in his bullfighting clothes to pray before the fight, sweating under the armpits, praying that the bull will embiste, that is charge frankly and follow the cloth well; oh, blessed Virgin, that thou wilt give me a bull that will embiste well; blessed Virgin, give me this bull; blessed Virgin, that I should touch this bull in Madrid today on a day without wind; promising something of value or a pilgrimage, praying for luck, frightened sick, and then that afternoon perhaps such a bull comes out and the fighter's face drawn with the strain of maintaining a bravery that is not there; sometimes simulating almost successfully the light-heartedness of a great faena; the cowardly bullfighter by a taut unnatural nerve-strained effort, abrogating his imagination, does a splendid and brilliant performance. One of these a year in Madrid in the springtime gives him enough contracts to keep him in circulation, but they are really of no importance. If you see one you are fortunate, but you will go to see that matador twenty times in the year and never see another.

Thinking about all this you must have either the bullfighter's standpoint or the spectator's. It is the matter of death that makes all the confusion. Bullfighting is the only art in which the artist is in danger of death and in which the degree of brilliance in the performance is left to the fighter's honour. In Spain honour is a very real thing. Called pundonor, it means honour, probity, courage, self-respect, and pride in one word. Pride is the strongest characteristic of the race and it is a matter of pundonor not to show cowardice. Once it has been shown, truly and unmistakably shown, honour is gone and then a bullfighter may give purely cynical performances, dosing his effort, only creating danger for himself if there is financial need for improving his standing and obtaining contracts. A bullfighter is not always expected to be good, only to do his best. He is excused for bad work if the bull is very difficult, he is expected to have off-days, but he is expected to do the best he can with the given bull. But once his honour is gone you cannot be sure that he will do his best or that he will do anything at all except technically fulfil his obligation by killing his bull as safely, dully, and dishonestly as he can. Having lost his honour he goes along living through his contracts, hating the public he fights before, telling himself that they have no right to hoot and jeer at him who faces death when they sit comfortable and safe in the seats, telling himself he can always do great work if he wants to and they can wait until he wants. Then in one year he finds that he no longer can do good work even when he has a good bull and makes the great effort to nerve himself, and the next year is usually the one in which he retires. Because a Spaniard must have some honour, and when he no longer has the honour-among-thieves sort of belief that he can be good if he only wants to as sustenance, then he retires and he gains honour with himself for that decision. This honour thing is not some fantasy that I am trying to inflict on you in the way writers on the peninsula give out their theories on its people. I swear it is true. Honour to a Spaniard, no matter how dishonest, is as real a thing as water, wine, or olive oil. There is honour among pickpockets and honour among whores. It is simply that the standards differ.

Honour in the bullfighter is as necessary to a bullfight as good bulls and it is because there are a half-dozen bullfighters, some of them with the greatest talent, who possess the very minimum of it; this condition being caused by early exploitation of the bullfighter with consequent cynicism or sometimes permanent cowardice caused by wounds, to be differentiated from the temporary loss of nerve that may always follow a goring, that you may see bad bullfights altogether aside from the shortcomings and incompletely trained fighters.

Now, what puzzles you, madame? What would you like explained?

Old lady: I notice that when one of the horses was hit by the bull some sawdust came out. What explanations have you for that, young man?

Madame, that sawdust was placed in the horse by a kindly veterinarian to fill a void created by the loss of other organs.

Old lady: Thank you, sir. You made me understand it all. But surely the horse could not permanently replace those organs with sawdust?

Madame, it is only a temporary measure, and one that no one can well approve of.

Old lady: And yet I find it very cleanly, that is if the sawdust be pure and sweet.

Madame, no sweeter, purer sawdust ever stuffed a horse than that used in the Madrid ring.

Old lady: I am very glad to hear it. Tell me who is the gentleman smoking the cigar and what are those things he is eating?

Madame, that is Dominguin, the successful promoter, ex-matador and manager of Domingo Ortega, and he is eating shrimps.

Old lady: Let us order some, if it be not too difficult, and eat them ourselves. He has a kindly face.

He has indeed, but do not loan him money. The shrimps here are of the best, although they are larger across the street and are there known as langostinos. Waiter, three orders of gambas.

Old lady: What did you call them, sir?

Gambas.

Old lady: The word means limb in the Italian tongue if I am not mistaken.

Author: There is an Italian restaurant not far from here if you should wish to dine there.

Old lady: Is it frequented by the bullfighters?

Author: Never, madame. It is full of politicians who are becoming statesmen while one watches them.

Old lady: Then let us dine elsewhere. Where do the matadors eat?

Author: They eat in modest pensions.

Old lady: Do you know such a one?

Author: I do indeed.

Old lady: I would like to know them better.

Author: The modest pensions?

Old lady: No, sir, the bullfighters.

Author: Madame, many of them are racked with disease.

Old lady: Tell me of their diseases that I may judge for myself. Are they affected with mumps?

Author: Nay, madame, mumps claims but few victims amongst them.

Old lady: I have had the mumps and so I do not fear them. As for these other diseases, are they rare and strange like their costumes?

Author: No, they are most common. We will discuss them later.

Old lady: But tell me first before you go; was this Maera the bravest bullfighter you have known?

Author: He was, madame, because, of the naturally brave ones, he was most intelligent. It is easier to be stupid and naturally brave than to be exceedingly intelligent and still completely brave. No one would deny that Marcial Lalanda is brave, but his bravery is all of intelligence and was acquired. Ignacio Sanchez Mejias, who married the sister of Joselito and was an excellent banderillero, but with a heavy style, was very brave, but he laid his bravery on as with a trowel. It was as though he were constantly showing you the quantity of hair on his chest or the way in which he was built in his more private parts. That is not the function of bravery in bullfighting. It should be a quality whose presence permits the fighter to perform all acts he chooses to attempt, unhampered by apprehension. It is not something to club the public with.

Old lady: I have never been clubbed with it yet.

Author: Madame, you will be clubbed silly with it if you ever see Sanchez Mejias.

Old lady: When can I see him?

Author: He is now retired, but if he should lose his money you would see him fight again.

Old lady: You do not seem to care for him.

Author: Although I respect his bravery, his skill with the sticks and his insolence, I do not care for him as a matador, nor as a banderillero, nor as a person. Therefore I devote little space to him in this book.

Old lady: Are you not prejudiced?

Author: Madame, rarely will you meet a more prejudiced man nor one who tells himself he keeps his mind more open. But cannot that be because one part of our mind, that which we act with, becomes prejudiced through experience and still we keep another part completely open to observe and judge with?

Old lady: Sir, I do not know.

Author: Madame, neither do I and it may well be that we are talking nonsense.

Old lady: That is an odd term and one I did not encounter in my youth.

Author: Madame, we apply the term now to describe un-soundness in an abstract conversation, or, indeed, any overmetaphysical tendency in speech.

Old lady: I must learn to use these terms correctly.

Chapter 10

There are three acts to the fighting of each bull and they are called in Spanish los tres tercios de la lidia, or the three thirds of the combat. The first act, where the bull charges the picadors, is the suerte de varas, or the trial of the lances. Suerte is an important word in Spanish. It means, according to the dictionary: Suerte, f., chance, hazard, lots, fortune, luck, good luck, haphazard; state, condition, fate, doom, destiny, kind, sort; species, manner, mode, way, skilful manoeuvre; trick, feat, juggle, and piece of ground separated by landmark. So the translation of trial or manoeuvre is quite arbitrary, as any translation must be from the Spanish.

The action of the picadors in the ring and the work of the matadors who are charged with protecting them with their capes when they are dismounted make up the first act of the bullfight. When the president signals for the end of this act and the bugle blows the picadors leave the ring and the second act begins. There are no horses in the ring after the first act except the dead horses which are covered with canvas. Act one is the act of the capes, the pics and the horses. In it the bull has the greatest opportunity to display his bravery or cowardice.

Act two is that of the banderillas. These are pairs of sticks about a yard long, seventy centimetres to be exact, with a harpoon-shaped steel point four centimetres long at one end. They are supposed to be placed, two at a time, in the humped muscle at the top of the bull's neck as he charges the man who holds them. They are designed to complete the work of slowing up the bull and regulating the carriage of his head which has

92

been begun by the picadors; so that his attack will be slower, but surer and better directed. Four pairs of banderillas are usually put in. If they are placed by the banderilleros or peones they must be placed, above all other considerations, quickly and in the proper position. If the matador himself places them he may indulge in a preparation which is usually accompanied by music. This is the most picturesque part of the bullfight and the part most spectators care for the most when first seeing fights. The mission of the banderilleros is not only to force the bull by hooking to tire his neck muscles and carry his head lower, but also, by placing them at one side or another, to correct a tendency to hook to that side. The entire act of the banderillas should not take more than five minutes. If it is prolonged the bull becomes discomposed and the fight loses the tempo it must keep, and if the bull is an uncertain and dangerous one he has too many opportunities to see and charge men unarmed with any lure, and so develops a tendency to search for the man, the bundle, as the Spanish call him, behind the cloth when the matador comes out for the last act with the sword and muleta.

The president changes the act after three or at most four pairs of banderillas have been placed and the third and final division is the death. It is made up of three parts. First the brindis or salutation of the president and dedication or toasting of the death of the bull, either to him or to some other person by the matador, followed by the work of the matador with the muleta. This is a scarlet serge cloth which is folded over a stick which has a sharp spike at one end and a handle at the other. The spike goes through the cloth which is fastened to the other end of the handle with a thumb screw so that it hangs in folds along the length of the stick. Muleta means literally crutch, but in bullfighting it refers to the scarlet-serge-draped stick with which the matador is supposed to master the bull, prepare him for killing and finally hold in his left hand to lower the bull's head and keep it lowered while he kills the animal by a sword thrust high up between his shoulder blades.

These are the three acts in the tragedy of the bullfight, and it is the first one, the horse part, which indicates what the others will be, and in fact, makes the rest possible. It is in the first act that the bull comes out in full possession of all of his faculties, confident, fast, vicious and conquering. All his victories are in the first act. At the end of the first act he has apparently won. He has cleared the ring of mounted men and is alone. In the second act he is baffled completely by an unarmed man and very cruelly punished by the banderillas so that his confidence and his blind general rage go and he concentrates his hatred on an individual object. In the third act he is faced by only one man who must, alone, dominate him by a piece of cloth placed over a stick, and kill him from in front, going in over the bull's right horn to kill him with a sword thrust between the arch of his shoulder blades.

When I first saw bullfights the only part that I did not like was the banderillas. They seemed to make such a great and cruel change in the bull. He became an altogether different animal when the banderillas were in and I resented the loss of the free, wild quality he brought with him into the ring; that quality that reaches its greatest expression when he faces the picadors. When the banderillas are in he is done for. They are the sentencing. The first act is the trial, the second act is the sentencing and the third the execution. But afterwards when I learned how much more dangerous the bull becomes as he goes on the defensive, how, after the banderillas have sobered him and his speed of foot has been cut he aims every horn stroke, as a hunter aims at an individual bird in a covey rather than shooting at them all and missing, and finally, when I learned the things that can be done with him as an artistic property when he is properly slowed and still has kept his bravery and his strength, I kept my admiration for him always, but felt no more sympathy for him than for a canvas or the marble a sculptor cuts or the dry powder snow your skis cut through.

I know no modern sculpture, except Brancusi's, that is in any way the equal of the sculpture of modern bullfighting. But it is an impermanent art as singing and the dance are, one of those that Leonardo advised men to avoid, and when the performer is gone the art exists only in the memory of those who have seen it and dies with them. Looking at photographs, reading descriptions or trying to recall it too often can only kill it in the memory of an individual. If it were permanent it could be one of the major arts, but it is not and so it finishes with whoever makes it, while a major art cannot even be judged until the unimportant physical rottenness of whoever made it is well buried. It is an art that deals with death, and death wipes it out. But it is never truly lost, you say, because in all arts all improvements and discoveries that are logical are carried on by someone else; so nothing is lost, really, except the man himself. Yes, and it would be very comforting to know that if at his death all the painter's canvases disappeared with him, that Cézanne's discoveries, for example, were not lost but would be used by all his imitators. Like hell it would.

Suppose a painter's canvases disappeared with him and a writer's books were automatically destroyed at his death and only existed in the memory of those that had read them. That is what happens in bullfighting. The art, the method, the improvements of doing, the discoveries remain; but the individual, whose doing of them made them, who was the touchstone, the original, disappears and until another individual, as great, comes, the things, by being imitated, with the original gone, soon distort, lengthen, shorten, weaken and lose all reference to the original. All art is only done by the individual. The individual is all you ever have and all schools only serve to classify their members as failures. The individual, the great artist when he comes, uses everything that has been discovered or known about his art up to that point, being able to accept or reject in a time so short it seems that the knowledge was born with him, rather than that he takes instantly what it takes the ordinary man a lifetime to know, and then the great artist goes beyond what has been done or known and makes something of his own. But there is sometimes a long time between great ones and those that have known the former great ones rarely recognize the new ones when they come. They want the old, the way it was that they remember it. But the others, the contemporaries, recognize the new great ones because of their ability to know so quickly, and finally even the ones who remember the old do. They are excused from not recognizing at once because they, in the period of waiting, see so many false ones that they become so cautious that they cannot trust their feelings; only their memory. Memory, of course, is never true.

After you get a great bullfighter, you may lose him most easily from disease; much more easily than by death. Of the only two really great ones since Belmonte retired neither ever made a full career. Tuberculosis took one and syphilis ruined the other. They are the two occupational diseases of the matador. He starts the corrida in the hot sun, in a sun that is often so hot that people with little money will gladly pay three times as much for their ticket to be able to sit in the shade. He wears a heavy, gold-brocaded jacket that makes him sweat in the sun as a boxer sweats skipping rope in training. From this heat, in this perspiration, with no chance for a shower or an alcohol rub to close the pores, the matador, as the sun goes down, and the shadow of the amphitheatre falls on the sand, stands, comparatively inactive but in readiness to aid, while his companions kill their last bulls. Often at the end of summer and in the early fall in the high plateaus of Spain it is cold enough for you to need an overcoat at the end of a bullfight in a town where it is so hot in the sun at the beginning of the fight that you were liable to sunstroke if you were bareheaded. Spain is a mountain country and a good part of it is African, and in the fall and end of summer when the sun is gone the cold comes quickly and deadly for anyone who must stand in it, wet with sweat, unable even to wipe himself dry. A boxer takes every precaution to avoid catching cold when he is in a sweat, and a bullfighter can take none. That would be enough to account for the number who get tuberculosis even without the fatigue of the nightly journeying, and dust and daily fighting during the feria season of August and September.

Syphilis is another thing. Boxers, bullfighters, and soldiers contract syphilis for the same reasons that make them choose those professions. In boxing most sudden reversals of form, the majority of cases of what is called punch drunkenness, of 'walking on the heels' are products of syphilis. You cannot name the individuals in a book because it is libellous, but anyone of the profession will tell you of a dozen recent cases. There are always recent cases. Syphilis was the disease of the crusaders in the Middle Ages. It was supposed to be brought to Europe by them, and it is a disease of all people who lead lives in which a disregard of consequences dominates. It is an industrial accident, to be expected by all those who lead irregular sexual lives and from their habits of mind would rather take chances than use prophylactics, and it is a to-be-expected end, or rather phase, of the life of all fornicators who continue their careers far enough. A few years ago I had the opportunity of observing the rakes' progress of some citizens who, in college, were great moral influences, but after coming out into the world discovered the joys of immorality, which, as believers in Yale in China, they had never indulged in as young men, and, delivering themselves to these joys, seemed to believe that they had discovered, if not indeed invented, sexual intercourse. They believed this was this great new thing that they had just discovered and were most joyously promiscuous until their first experience with disease which they then believed they too had discovered and invented. Surely one could never have known of this dreadful thing, nor could have experienced it or it would not have been allowed to exist, and they became again, for a time, preachers and practisers of the greatest purity of life or, at least, limited their activities to a narrower social circle. There has been much change in fashion in morals and many who were formerly destined for teachers in fashionable Sunday-school classes are now our most prominent rounders. Like the bullfighters who are ruined by their first goring they have really no vocation as rounders, but it is a trial to watch or to hear them during their discovery of what Guy de Maupassant classed among the diseases of adolescence, and of what, incidentally, to justify his right so to speak, he died of. They say, 'He jests at scars who never felt a wound'. But he jests very well at scars who is covered with them, or at least men once did, although now our jesters will be most humorous about anything which happens to anyone else, and the moment they are touched by anything themselves cry out, 'But you don't understand. This is really serious!' and become great moralists or abandon the whole thing through something as banal as suicide. Probably venereal diseases must exist as bulls must have horns in order to keep all things in their proper relation, or the numbers of Casanovas and of matadors would be so great there would be practically no one else. But I would give much to have it eliminated in Spain, because of what it can do to a great matador. Though even if we did without it in Spain it could be acquired in other places or men would go upon a crusade and bring it back from somewhere.

You cannot expect a matador who has triumphed in the afternoon by taking chances not to take them in the night and 'mas cornadas dan las mujeres'. Three things keep boys from promiscuous intercourse, religious belief, timidity, and fear of venereal diseases. The last is most commonly the basis of appeal made by the Y.M.C.A. and other institutions for clean living. Against these influences in a bullfighter is the tradition which demands that a torero have many affairs, his inclinations, the fact that there will always be women after him, some for himself, some for his money and plenty for both, and his contempt for venereal diseases as danger. But, says the old lady, do many bullfighters contract these diseases?

Madame, they contract them as all men do who go with

women thinking only of the women and not of their future health.

Old lady: But why do they not take thought for their health?

Madame, it is difficult. Truly it is not a thought that comes into the head of a man if he is well pleased. Even though a woman be a whore, yet if she be a good whore a man thinks well of her at the time and sometimes after.

Old lady: And are these illnesses then all from commercial women?

No, madame, they come often from friends or the friends of friends, or from anyone you may bed with here, there, or indeed, anywhere.

Old lady: It must be most dangerous then to be a man.

It is indeed, madame, and but few survive it. 'Tis a hard trade and the grave is at the end of it.

Old lady: Would it not be better if these men all married and bedded only with their wives?

For their souls' good, yes, and for their bodies', too. But as bullfighters many are ruined if they marry if they love their wives truly.

Old lady: And their wives? What of them?

Of their wives who can speak who has not been one? If the husband has no contracts he does not make a living. But at each contract he risks death and no man can go into the ring and say that he will come out alive. It is not like being wife to a soldier, for your soldier earns his living when there is no war; nor your sailor, for he is long gone, but his ship is his protection; nor your boxer, for he does not face death. It is like being wife to no other man and I would not wish it for her if I had a daughter.

Old lady: Have you a daughter, sir?

No, madame.

Then at least, we need not worry for her. But I that daughters did not get these illnesses.

will find no man who is a man who will

not bear some marks of past misfortune. Either he has been hit here, or broken this or contracted that, but a man throws off many things and I know a champion at golf who never putted so well as with the gonorrhoea.

Old lady: Have you no remedy then?

Madame, there is no remedy for anything in life. Death is a sovereign remedy for all misfortunes and we'd do best to leave off all discoursing now and get to table. Within our time the scientists may well abolish these old diseases and we'll live to see the end of all morality. But meantime I would rather dine on suckling pig at Botin's than sit and think of casualties my friends have suffered.

Old lady: Then let us dine. Tomorrow you can tell us more about the bullfights.

Chapter 11

The fighting bull is to the domestic bull as the wolf is to the dog. A domestic bull may be evil tempered and vicious as a dog may be mean and dangerous, but he will never have the speed, the quality of muscle and sinew and the peculiar build of the fighting bull, any more than the dog will have the sinews of the wolf, his cunning and his width of jaw. Bulls for the ring are wild animals. They are bred from a strain that comes down in direct descent from the wild bulls that ranged over the Peninsula and they are bred on ranches with thousands of acres of range where they live as free ranging animals. The contacts with men of the bulls that are to appear in the ring are held to the absolute minimum.

The physical characteristics of the fighting bull are its thick and very strong hide with glossy pelt, small head, but wide forehead; strength and shape of horns, which curve forward; short, thick neck with the great hump of muscle which erects when the bull is angry; wide shoulders, very small hooves and length and slenderness of tail. The female of the fighting bull is not as heavily built as the male; has a smaller head; shorter and thinner horns; a longer neck, a less pronounced dewlap under the jaw; is not as wide through the chest, and has no visible udder. I have frequently seen these cows in the ring in the amateur fights in Pamplona charging like bulls, tossing the amateurs about, and they were invariably spoken of by the visiting foreigners as steers, since they showed no visible signs of their cowhood and gave no evidence of femininity. It is in the female of the fighting bull that you see most plainly the difference between the savage and domestic animal.

One of the things one hears oftenest about bullfighting is the statement that a cow is much more dangerous when charging than a bull as the bull shuts his eyes while a cow keeps hers open. I do not know who started this, but there is no truth in it. The females that are used in amateur fights almost invariably make for the man rather than the cape, cut in on him rather than charge straight, and will often single out one particular man or boy and pursue him through a crowd of half a hundred, but they do this not because of any innate superior intelligence in the female, as Virginia Woolf might suppose, but because female calves, since they are never to appear in the ring in normal fights and since there is no objection to their becoming completely educated in all the phases of bullfighting, are used exclusively for the bullfighters to train on with cape and muleta. Either a bull calf or a cow calf, if passed a few times with cape or muleta, learns all about it, remembers, and, if it is a bull, becomes consequently useless for a formal bullfight where everything is built on the basis of this being the bull's first encounter with a dismounted man. If the bull is unfamiliar with cape or muleta and charges straight, the man can create the danger himself by working as close to the bull's charge as possible and will be able to attempt a variety of passes, selecting them himself and arranging them in an emotional sequence rather than being forced into them as defensive measures. If the bull has been fought before, he will cut in constantly on the man, will chop with his horns into the cloth looking for the man, and will create all the danger himself, putting the man constantly in retreat and on the defensive and making any clarity of passes or brilliance of fight impossible.

The bullfight has been so developed and organized that the bull has just time enough, coming into the ring completely unfamiliar with dismounted men, to learn to distrust all their artifices and reach the summit of his danger at the moment of killing. The bull learns so rapidly in the ring that if the bullfight drags, is badly done, or is prolonged an extra ten minutes he becomes almost unkillable by the means prescribed in the rules of the spectacle. It is for this reason that bullfighters always practise and train with female calves which, after a few sessions, become so educated, the fighters say, that they can talk Greek and Latin. After this education, they are released in the ring for the amateurs; sometimes with naked horns, sometimes with the points covered with a leather ball, they come in as fast and lithe as deer to practise on the amateur capemen and aspirant bull-fighters of all sorts in the capeas; to toss, rip, gore, pursue and inspire with terror these amateurs until, when the vacas tire, steers are let into the ring to take them out to rest in the corrals until their next appearance. The fighting cows, or vaquillas, seem to enjoy these appearances. They are not goaded, no divisa is placed in their shoulders, they are not irritated to make them charge and they seem to enjoy charging and tossing as much as a fighting cock does fighting. Of course they receive no punishment while the bull's bravery is judged by the manner in which he behaves under punishment.

The manoeuvring of fighting bulls is made possible by the operation of the herd instinct which makes it possible to drive bulls in groups of six or more where one bull, if detached from the herd, will charge instantly and repeatedly anything, man, horse, or any moving object, vehicle or otherwise, until he is killed; and by the use of trained steers or cabestros to herd and decoy the fighting bulls as wild elephants are caught and herded by elephants which have been tamed. It is one of the most interesting of all phases of bullfighting to see the steers work in the operations of loading, separating, putting the bulls into the runways that lead to the shipping cages and in all the many operations connected with the raising, transporting, and unloading of fighting bulls.

In the old days before they were shipped in their cages by railroad, or now, since the building of good roads in Spain, sometimes in motor trucks, an excellent and much less fatiguing way, bulls were driven along the roads in Spain, the fighting bulls surrounded by steers and the whole herd guarded by the mounted herders carrying their protective lances, much like those the picadors use, raising a cloud of dust as they moved and sending the inhabitants of villages running into their houses to slam and lock doors and look through the windows at the wide, dusty backs, the great horns, the quick eyes and damp muzzles, the belled necks of the cabestros and the short jackets, brown faces and wide high-crowned grey hats of the herdsmen moving along through the streets. When they are together, moving in the herd, they are quiet because the feeling of numbers gives them confidence and the herd instinct makes them follow the leader. Bulls are still driven in that way in the provinces away from the railways and occasionally one will desmandar or unherd. One year when we were in Spain this happened before the last house of a little village outside of Valencia. The bull stumbled and went to his knees and the others were past when he got to his feet. The first thing he saw was an open door with a man standing in it. He charged at once, lifted the man clear out of the door, and swung him back over his head. Inside the house he saw no one and went straight through. In the bedroom a woman sat in a rocking chair. She was old and had not heard the commotion. The bull demolished the chair and killed the old woman. The man who had been tossed in the doorway came in with a shotgun to protect his wife who was already lying where the bull had tossed her into a corner of the room. He fired point blank at the bull but only tore up his shoulder. The bull caught the man, killed him, saw a mirror, charged that, charged and smashed a tall, old-fashioned armoire and then went out into the street. He went a little way down the road, met a horse and cart, charged and killed the horse and overturned the cart. The driver stayed inside it. The herders by this time were coming back down the road, their galloping horses raising a great dust. They drove out two steers that picked the bull up and, as soon as there was a steer on each side of him, his crest lowered, he dropped his head and trotted, between the two steers, back to the herd.

Bulls in Spain have been known to charge a motor-car and even, getting on to the tracks, to stop a train, refusing to back up or leave the track when the train stopped and when, with much blowing of the whistle the train finally advanced, charging the engine blindly. A really brave fighting bull is afraid of nothing on earth and in various towns in Spain, in special and barbarous exhibitions, a bull has charged an elephant repeatedly; bulls have killed both lions and tigers, charging these animals as blithely as they go for the picadors. A true fighting bull fears nothing and, to me, is the finest of all animals to watch in action and repose. From a standing start a fighting bull will outrun a horse for twenty-five yards although a horse will beat him in fifty yards. The bull can turn on his feet almost as a cat does, he can turn much quicker than a polo pony, and at four years he has the strength in his neck and shoulder muscles to lift a horse and rider and throw them over his back. Many times I have seen a bull attack the inch-thick wooden planks of the barrera with his horns, or horn rather, for he uses either the one or the other, and splinter the planks into bits, and there is, in the bull ring museum at Valencia, a heavy iron stirrup that a bull from the ranch of Don Esteban Hernandez perforated with a horn stroke to the depth of four inches. This stirrup is preserved not because it is unique for having the horn driven through it but because of the fact that on this occasion the picador was miraculously not wounded by the horn stroke.

There is a book, now out of print in Spain, called *Toros Célebres*, which chronicles, alphabetically, by the names the breeders gave them, the manner of dying and feats of some three hundred and twenty-two pages of celebrated bulls. At random you can take Hechicero, or the Wizard, from the ranch of Concha and Sierra, a grey bull fought in Cadiz in 1844 who sent to the hospital all the picadors of all the matadors of the fight, a minimum of seven men, in addition to killing seven horses. Vibora, or the Viper, from the ranch of Don José Bueno, a black bull, fought at Vista Alegra, the 9th of August 1908, as he came into the ring, jumped the barrera and gored the bull-ring carpenter, Luis Gonzales, giving him an enormous wound in the right thigh. The matador charged to kill Vibora was unable to do so and he was returned to the corrals. That is not the sort of case which would be long remembered, except, perhaps, by the carpenter, and Vibora was probably included in the book more because of the timeliness of his action and the recent impression he had made on possible buyers of the book than for any permanent motive. There is no record of what the matador named Jaqueta, whose only appearance in history is this one action, went through before he was declared unable to kill Vibora, and the bull may have been more memorable for more than the not exceptional goring of the carpenter. I have seen two carpenters gored myself and have never written a line about it.

The bull Zaragoza, raised by the Lesireas ranch, while being taken to the ring at Moetia, Portugal, on the 2nd of October, 1898, broke out of his cage and pursued and wounded many people. He pursued a boy who ran into the town hall, and the bull, pursuing the boy, climbed the stairs to the first floor, where, according to the book, he caused great destruction. He probably did.

Comisario, of the ranch of Don Victoriano Ripamilan, a red bull with the eye of a partridge and wide horns, was the third bull fought in Barcelona on the 14th of April 1895. He jumped the barrera and got into the grandstand, and, driving through the spectators, the book says, produced the imagined disorder and damage. The civil-guard, Isidro Silva, drove his sabre into him and the corporal of the civil-guards, Ubaldo Vigueres, shot at him with his carbine, the bullet passing through the neck muscles of the bull and lodging in the left breast of the bull-ring servant, Juan Recaseus, who died on the spot. Comisario was finally lassoed and killed with dagger strokes.

None of these occurrences belong to the realm of pure bull-fighting except the first, nor does the case of Huron, a bull of the ranch of Don Antonio Lopez Plata, which fought a Bengal tiger on the 24th of July 1904 in the Plaza of San Sebastian. They fought in a steel cage and the bull whipped the tiger, but in one of his charges broke the cage apart and the two animals came out into the ring in the midst of the spectators. The police, attempting to finish the dying tiger and the very live bull, fired several volleys which 'caused grave wounds to many spectators'. From the history of these various encounters between bulls and other animals I should say they were spectacles to stay away from, or at least to view from one of the higher boxes.

The bull Oficial, from the ranch of the Arribas brothers, fought in Cadiz the 5th of October 1884, caught and gored a banderillero, jumped the barrera and gored the picador Chato three times, gored a civil-guard, broke the leg and three ribs of a municipal guard, and the arm of a night watchman. He would have been an ideal animal to turn loose when the police are clubbing manifestants in front of the city hall. Had he not been killed a strain of police-hating bulls might have been bred which would give the populace the advantage they lost in street fighting with the disappearance of the paving stone. A paving stone at short range is more effective than a club or sabre. The disappearance of cobble and paving stones has been more of a deterrent to the overthrowing of governments than machine guns, tear bombs and automatic pistols. For it is in the clashes when the government does not want to kill its citizens but to club, ride down and beat them into submission with the flat of a sabre that a government is overthrown. Any government that uses machine guns once too often on its citizens will fall automatically. Régimes are kept in with the club and the blackjack, not the machine gun or bayonet, and while there were paving stones there was never an unarmed mob to club.

The type of bull the aficionados of bullfighting rather than police-fighting would remember is Hechicero, whose feats were performed in the ring against trained bullfighters and in the face of punishment. It is the difference between street fights which are usually more exciting, portentous and useful, but out of place here, and the winning of a championship in boxing. Any bull might, on escaping, kill a number of people and smash up much property without taking punishment, but in the confusion and excitement of a bull getting into the grandstand the people who are in his way are in much less danger than a bullfighter is at the moment of killing, for the bull, when confused and in a mob of people, charges blindly and does not aim his horn strokes. A bull that jumps the barrera, unless he makes the leap while pursuing the man, is not a brave bull. He is a cowardly bull who is simply trying to escape the ring. The really brave bull welcomes the fight, accepts every invitation to fight, does not fight because he is cornered, but because he wants to, and this bravery is measured, and can only be measured, by the number of times he freely and willingly, without pawing, threatening, or bluffing, accepts combat with the picador and whether, when the steel point of the pic is sunk in his muscles of neck or shoulder, he insists under the iron and continues his charge after he begins to really receive punishment, until man and horse are thrown. A brave bull is one that, without any hesitation and in approximately the same part of the ring, will charge the picadors four times, paying no attention to the punishment he receives and each time charging with the steel in him until he has reversed the rider and horse.

It is only by his conduct against the pic that the bravery of a bull can be judged and appreciated, and the bravery of the bull is the primal root of the whole Spanish bullfight. The bravery of a truly brave bull is something unearthly and unbelievable. This bravery is not merely viciousness, ill-temper, and the panic-bred courage of a cornered animal. The bull is a fighting animal and where the fighting strain has been kept pure and all cowardice bred out he becomes often, when not fighting, the quietest and most peaceful acting in repose, of any animal. It is not the bulls that are most difficult to handle that make the best fights. The best of all fighting bulls have a quality, called nobility by the Spanish, which is the most extraordinary part of the whole business. The bull is a wild animal whose greatest pleasure is combat and which will accept combat offered to it in any form, or will take up anything it believes to be an offer of combat; yet the very best fighting bulls of all often recognize and know the mayoral or herder who is in charge of them on the ranch and on their trip to the ring, and will even allow him to stroke and pat them. I have seen a bull which in the corrals allowed the herder to stroke its nose, curry it like a horse, and even mount on its back, go into the ring without any preliminary excitement or goading, charge the picadors again and again, kill five horses, do its best to kill banderilleros and matador, and be, in the ring, vicious as a cobra and brave as a charging lioness.

Of course not all bulls are noble, for one that the mayoral can make friends with, there are fifty that will charge even when he is bringing them food if they see any movement which makes them think he is challenging them. Neither are all bulls brave. When they are two years old they are tested for bravery by the breeder, being confronted with a picador on horseback either in a closed corral or on the open range. The year before they were branded, being thrown by men on horseback who tumble them over with a long blunt pole, and when, at two years, they are tested against the steel-tipped lances of the picadors they already have their numbers and names, and the breeder makes a note of the manifestations of bravery given by each one. Those that are not brave, if the bull breeder is scrupulous, are marked for veal. The others are marked in the book according to their bravery shown, so that when he makes up a corrida of six bulls to ship away to some ring the breeder may dose the quality as he desires.

Branding is done as it is on ranches in the cattle-raising country of the American west except for the precautions necessary for separating the calves from their mothers, the necessity not to injure their horns or eyes and the complications of the marking. The branding irons are heated in a big fire and consist of the brand of the bull raiser, which is usually a combination of letters or a crest, and ten irons bearing the numbers 0, 1, 2, 3, 4, 5, 6, 7, 8, 9. The branding irons have a wooden handle and the points that are in the fire are heated red hot. The calves are in one corral, the fire and the irons in another; the two connected by a swinging door, and when the door is open the vaqueros drive them, one at a time, into the branding corral where they are thrown and held. It takes from four to five men to hold a fighting-bull calf still and they must be careful not to injure the budding horns, for a calf whose horns are injured will never be accepted for a formal bullfight, and the breeder then must sell him for a novillada or defective bullfight and lose at least two-thirds of his probable value. Also they must be very careful of their eyes since a straw in the eye may make a defect of vision that will unfit the bull for the ring. When they are branded one man holds the head, and the others the legs, body and tail. The calf's head is usually placed on a sack of straw to protect it as much as possible, the legs are tied together and the tail pulled forward between the legs. The main brand is placed on the right hindquarters and the numbers along the flank. Both male and female calves are numbered. After the brands are on, the ears are slit or clipped with the sign of the ranch and the hairs at the end of the tails of the male calves are snipped with scissors so that they will grow out long and silky. Then the calf is released, gets up furious, charges everything and anything it sees and finally goes out of the opened door of the branding corral. The herradero of branding day is the noisiest, dustiest, and most confused of all operations in bullfighting. When a Spaniard wishes to describe the utter confusion of a bad bullfight he compares it to a herradero.

The actual testing for bravery, the part of it which takes place in a closed corral, is the quietest of operations. Bulls are tested when they are two years old. At a year they are too young and not powerful enough to stand it, and at three years they are too powerful, too dangerous and would remember it too well. If they are tested in a closed corral this will be either square or round, fitted with burladeros or plank shelters for a few men with capes to stand behind. These are professional fighters, or amateurs who have been invited to the testing, being promised the chance of practising with the female calves, and they take the calves in turn for their workouts.

The whole corral is usually about thirty yards across, or half the size of a major bull ring, the two-year-old bulls are in an adjacent corral and are let into the testing corral one at a time. When they come in, a picador, who wears the leather chaps and short jacket of a bull herder, is waiting for them, holding a long pic about twelve feet long and with a triangular steel point slightly shorter than that used in the actual fight. He places his horse with his back turned toward the gate the young bull has entered by and waits quietly. No one in the corral says a word and the picador does nothing to excite the bull, for the most important part of the testing is the willingness with which the bull charges without being harassed or annoyed in any way.

When the young bull charges everyone notes his style; whether he charges from a distance, without pawing the ground first or without any preliminary bellowing; when he comes at the horse whether he keeps his feet well back and thrusts with full power, keeping on pushing to reach the man and animal when the steel goes into his muscle, using the full force of his hind legs and the small of his back; or whether he gets his feet forward and only chops with his neck to try and get rid of the pic, turning quickly and quitting the charge when he is punishèd. If he does not charge at all, he is, if the owner is scrupulous, certified for castration and the meat market. If he is sentenced to this the owner calls out 'buey' or ox instead of saying 'toro', which means the bull has been approved for the ring.

If the bull knocks over horse and man, and sometimes even at two years they are able to, the bullfighters must take him away with their capes, but ordinarily the bulls are not allowed to see the capes at all. When they have charged the picador once, or at most twice, if their style and probable bravery could not be judged in the first charge, the gate to the open range is opened and they are allowed to go free. How they accept this freedom, whether they are eager or reluctant for it; hurrying off or turning at the gate to look back, wanting to charge again, are all valuable indications of how they will act in the ring.

Most breeders are reluctant to have the bulls charge more than once. They feel that a bull has only so many pics in him to accept. That if he takes two or three in the testing that is three less he will take in the ring, and so they put their faith in the lineage of the bulls and do the real testing on those bulls that are to be used at stud and on the cows. They believe that the get of an exceptional bull and really brave females are all proper bulls, and they call every two-year-old 'toro' that is perfect of horn and body without making any practical test of their bravery.

Cows which are to be used for breeding are sometimes allowed to charge the testing picador as many as twelve or fifteen times and are passed with both cape and muleta by the bullfighters to test their charging quality and their aptitude for following the cloth. It is most important that the cows be of great bravery and that they take the cloth well, as these are qualities which they transmit to their offspring. They should be strong, well built, and sturdy. On the other hand if they have defects of horn this is not important as these are not generally transmissible. A tendency to shorter horns can be transmitted and breeders who are trying to make their product highly acceptable to bullfighters so that these will select this breeder's bulls when they have an opportunity in their contracts to specify the bulls to be fought, often try to breed down the length of horn by careful selection, trying to keep the length of horn to the minimum that the government delegates will allow and breed for a low-slanting horn which will pass below the knee when the bull's head is lowered in charging rather than a high horn that will pass higher and more dangerously as the man goes in to kill.

Bulls that are to be used in breeding are tested with the greatest rigour. After they have been used for breeding for some years if they are then sent to the ring you may always recognize them. They seem to know all about the picadors. They will charge bravely often, but will be able to knock the pic out of the man's hands with their horns, and I have seen one ignoring pic and horse, reach up and hook the man out of the saddle. If they have, too, been tested with cape and muleta they become, often, absolutely unkillable, and a bullfighter who has signed a contract to kill two 'new bulls' is perfectly within his rights to refuse these bulls or to kill these learnéd animals in any way that he can. By law every bull that has appeared in the ring must be killed immediately thereafter to prevent bulls being used more than once. But this law is often broken in the provinces, and is always broken in capeas or amateur fights which have long been forbidden by law. A stud-bull that has been thoroughly tested has not the skill of these criminals, but he has been obviously fought before and any intelligent spectator can see the difference at once. In the testing of bulls it is important not to confuse the power of the young bull with his bravery. A bull may be strong enough in a single charge, if the pic should slip, to overthrow the rider and mount and make a fine showing while, if the pic should have held firm, he might have been quiet under the punishment, refused to insist and finally turned his head. Bulls are tested in corrals in Castilla, the country around Salamanca, Navarra, and Extremadura, but in Andalucia they are usually tested in the open range.

Those who advocate testing in the open say that the true bravery of a bull can only be shown that way since in the corral he feels himself cornered, and any cornered animal will fight.

In open-range testing though, the bulls are ridden after until they turn; are toppled by the long poles carried by the horsemen or are roused in some way before they charge the picador, while in the corral they are let absolutely alone and harassed in no way; so the two ways are about equal in advantage; the testing on the open range, with a crowd of mounted guests, is more picturesque, and the corral method is nearer to approximating the actual conditions of the bull ring.

All of the operations of bull raising to one who loves bull-fighting are of great fascination and in the testings one has much eating, drinking, companionship, practical joking, bad amateur cape-work by the aristocracy, often excellent amateur cape-work by the visiting bootblacks who aspire to be matadors, and long days with the smell of cold, fall air, of dust and leather and lathered horses, and the big bulls not so far away looking very big in the fields, calm and heavy, and dominating the landscape with their confidence.

Fighting bulls are raised in the provinces of Navarra, Burgos, Palensia, Logroño, Zaragoza, Valladolid, Zamora, Segovia, Salamanca, Madrid, Toledo, Albacete, Extremadura, and Andalucia, but the principal regions are Andalucia, Castilla, and Salamanca. The biggest bulls and the best bred come from Andalucia and Castilla, and those which are made nearest to order for the bullfighters from Salamanca. Navarra still raises many bulls, but their cast, type, and bravery have deteriorated greatly in the last twenty years.

All brave bulls may be roughly divided into two classes: those that are made, bred and created for bullfighters, and those that are bred to please their breeders. Salamanca stands at one extreme and Andalucia at the other.

But, you say, there is very little conversation in this book. Why isn't there more dialogue? What we want in a book by this citizen is people talking; that is all he knows how to do and now he doesn't do it. The fellow is no philosopher, no savant, an incompetent zoologist, he drinks too much and cannot punc-

tuate readily and now he has stopped writing dialogue. Someone ought to put a stop to him. He is bull crazy. Citizen, perhaps
you are right. Let us have a little dialogue.

What do you ask, madame? Is there anything you would like
to know about the bulls?

Yes, sir.

What would you like to know? I'll tell you absolutely
anything.

It is a difficult thing to ask, sir.

Do not let that trouble you; talk to me frankly; as you would
to your doctor, or to another woman. Do not be afraid to ask
what you would really like to know.

Sir, I would like to know about their love life.

Madame, you have come to just the man.

Then tell me, sir.

Madame, I will. It is as good a subject as another. It combines
popular appeal, a touch of sex, a world of useful information,
and it lends itself to dialogue. Madame, their love lives are
tremendous.

I had thought as much, sir, but can you not give us some
statistics?

Most readily. The little calves are born in the winter months.

It was not of the little calves that we wished most to hear.

But you must be patient, madame. All these things but lead
to the little calves and so, indeed, they must be taken to start
from them too. The little calves are born in three months of the
winter and, counting backward nine months on your fingers,
as who, being married, has not counted forward nine months
on their fingers many times, you find that if the calves are born
in December, January and February the bulls have been let run
with the cows during April, May, and June, when as a fact, they
most usually are. In a good ranch there are from two hundred
to four hundred cows and for every fifty cows there is one bull.
The usual ranch has two hundred cows and four seed bulls.
These bulls are from three to five years old and older. When a

bull is first turned loose with the cows no one knows how he will act, although were a bookmaker present he would lay you odds that the bull would show enthusiasm for his companions. But sometimes a bull will have nothing to do with them nor they with him and they will fight savagely with their horns, making a clatter of horn on horn you can hear across the field. Sometimes such a bull will change his attitude toward one of the cows, but this is rare. At other times the bulls range quietly with the cows but will leave them to return to the other bulls, who, being destined for the ring, are never let run with the cows at all. But the ordinary result is that which the bookmaker would lay you odds would occur, and a single bull would do for more than fifty cows, but if there were too many he would finally weaken and end in impotence. Are these the facts you care to hear or do I speak too baldly?

No one could say, sir, you place the facts in any but a straight-forward Christian way and we find them most instructive.

This gratifies me and I will tell you of an odd occurrence. The bull is polygamous as an animal, but occasionally an individual is found that is monogamous. Sometimes a bull on the range will come to so care for one of the fifty cows that he is with, that he will make no case of all the others and will only have to do with her and she will refuse to leave his side on the range. When this occurs they take the cow from the herd and if the bull does not then return to polygamy he is sent with the other bulls that are for the ring.

I find that a sad story, sir.

Madame, all stories, if continued far enough, end in death, and he is no true-story teller who would keep that from you. Especially do all stories of monogamy end in death, and your man who is monogamous while he often lives most happily, dies in the most lonely fashion. There is no lonelier man in death, except the suicide, than that man who has lived many years with a good wife and then outlived her. If two people love each other there can be no happy end to it.

Sir, I do not know what you mean by love. It does not sound well as you say it.

Madame, it is an old word and each one takes it new and wears it out himself. It is a word that fills with meaning as a bladder with air and the meaning goes out of it as quickly. It may be punctured as a bladder is punctured and patched and blown up again and if you have not had it it does not exist for you. All people talk of it, but those who have had it are all marked by it, and I would not wish to speak of it further since of all things it is the most ridiculous to talk of and only fools go through it many times. I would sooner have the pox than to fall in love with another woman, loving the one I have.

What has this to do with the bulls, sir?

Nothing, madame, nothing at all, it is only conversation to give you your money's worth.

I find the subject interesting. What way are people marked who have had this thing, or is that only a way of speaking?

All those who have really experienced it are marked after it is gone, by a quality of deadness. I say this as a naturalist, not to be romantic.

This does not amuse me.

Nor is it designed to, madame, but only to give you your money's worth.

But often you amuse me very much.

Madame, with a little luck I will amuse you again.

Chapter 12

No one can say, on seeing a fighting bull in the corrals, whether that bull will be brave in the ring although, usually, the quieter the bull is, the less nervous he seems, the calmer he is, the more chance that he will turn out brave. The reason for this is that the braver he is, usually, the more confident he is and the less he bluffs. All supposed exterior signs of danger that a bull gives, such as pawing the ground, threatening with his horns, or bellowing are forms of bluffing. They are warnings given in order that combat may be avoided if possible. The truly brave bull gives no warning before he charges except the fixing of his eye on his enemy, the raising of the crest of muscle in his neck, the twitching of an ear, and, as he charges, the lifting of his tail. A completely brave bull, if he is in perfect condition, will never open his mouth, will not even let his tongue out, during the course of the entire fight and, at the finish, with the sword in him, will come toward the man while his legs support him, his mouth tight shut to keep the blood in.

Now what makes a bull brave is first the strain of fighting blood which can only be kept pure by conscientious testing in the tientas, and second his own health and condition. Health and condition will not replace scrupulous breeding, but lack of them will ruin the natural inherited bravery of an animal, will make his body incapable of responding to it, or else cause the bravery to burn up as a fire of straw, burning out in a single flare and the bull being then empty and hollow. Health and condition are determined, granting there has been no disease on the ranch, by pasture and water.

It is the differences of pasture and water in different parts of Spain caused by the different climates, the changes in composition of the soil and the distances the stock must go to water from their pastures that make entirely different types of bulls. Spain is more a continent than a country in regard to climates, for the climate and vegetation of the north, of Navarra for example, has nothing in common with that of Valencia or Andalucia and none of those three, except parts of Navarra, have any resemblance to the high plateau of Castilla. So the bulls raised in Navarra, Andalucia, and Salamanca differ greatly, and this is not due to them coming from differing strains. Navarrese bulls are almost a different race, smaller and usually of a reddish colour, but when bull raisers in Navarra have taken seed bulls and cows from an Andalucian ranch and tried to transplant them to Navarra they have invariably taken on the present vices of the northern bulls, nervousness, uncertainty in attack, and lack of true bravery, and have lost their original character without gaining any of the quickness, courage, and deerlike speed that characterized the old strains of Navarra. Bulls in Navarra are about bred out due to inbreeding of the original Navarrese strain and the selling of their best cows to France a number of years ago for use in the *Course Landaise*, a French form of bull fête, and the inability of the Andalucian and Castillian strains to retain their type and bravery on the northern ranges although many costly experiments have been made to develop a new and brave Navarrese strain. The best fighting bulls come from Andalucia, Colmenar, Salamanca, and, exceptionally, Portugal. The most typical bulls are those of Andalucia. The Andalucian breeds have been taken to Salamanca and perverted by breeding them down in size and in length of horn in order to please the bullfighters. Salamanca is an ideal province for bull breeding. The pastures and water are good, and the bulls from there are sold at under four years and often, to make them appear larger and older, are fed on grain for a time, which gives them a false size, covering the natural muscle with fat, giving them a false well-being, causing them to tire quickly and to be short of wind. Many bulls from Salamanca, if fought at four and a half to five years, hence having their natural size and not needing to be fed up on grain to reach the government-required poundage, with a year more on the range and the consequent added maturity, would be the ideal fighting bulls except for a tendency that they have to lose frankness and bravery when they have passed their fourth year. Occasionally you will see such a corrida in Madrid, but on the publicity they receive from such a splendid lot of bulls and with the aid and connivance of the bullfighters the same breeders that send such an ideal corrida to the capital will sell fifteen or twenty other corridas throughout the provinces in a season which will be composed of bulls under the minimum age, stuffed on grain to make them seem big, giving the minimum of danger because of their lack of experience in using their horns, and helping in every way, by depriving the spectacle of that which makes it, the true fighting bull, to contribute to the decadence of bullfighting.

For the third factor in the making of a bull, after breeding and condition, is age. With any one of these three factors lacking you cannot have a complete fighting bull. A bull is not mature until after his fourth year. It is true that after his third year he looks mature, but he is not. Maturity brings strength, resistance, but above all, knowledge. Now the knowledge of a bull consists principally in his memory of experience, he forgets nothing, and in his knowledge of, and ability to use, his horns. It is the horn that makes bullfighting, and the ideal bull is one whose memory is as clean as possible from any experience of bullfighting, so that he will learn everything that he is to learn in the ring; being dominated if the bullfighter works him properly, and dominating the bullfighter if his work is deficient or cowardly; and for this bull to provide the most real danger and put the bullfighter to the necessary test of knowledge of how to handle a bull properly he must know how to use his horns. At four years a bull has this knowledge, he has acquired it by fighting on the range, the only way he can acquire it. To see two bulls fight is a beautiful sight. They use their horns as a fencer does his weapon. They strike, parry, feint, block, and have an exactitude of aim that is amazing. When they both know how to use the horn the combat usually ends as does a fight between two really skilful boxers, with all dangerous blows stopped, without bloodshed and with mutual respect. They do not have to kill each other for a decision. The bull that loses is the first one that breaks and turns acknowledging the other's superiority. I have seen them fight again and again for small causes that I was not able to make out; coming head on, feinting with their master horn, the horns clattering as they knocked together, the blows being parried and countered, then, suddenly one bull would wheel and turn and gallop off. Once though, in the corrals after a fight in which one bull turned away admitting he was beaten, the other followed him and charged, getting the horn in the defeated bull's flank and throwing him over. Before the bull that was down could get to his feet the other was on him, driving the horn in with chopping thrusts of his neck and head; driving in all the time. The defeated bull got to his feet once, wheeled to face head-on, but in the first horn exchange he was caught in the eye, then went down under another charge. The bull killed him without letting him get to his feet again. Before the fight, two days later, that same bull killed another in the corrals, but when he came into the ring he was one of the best animals, both for bullfighters and public, that I have ever seen. His horn knowledge had been acquired as it should be. He had no vices with the horn, he simply knew how to use it, and the matador, Félix Rodriguez, dominated him, did splendid work with the cape and muleta and killed him perfectly.

A three-year-old bull may know how to use his horns, but it is exceptional. He has not had enough experience. Bulls over five years know too well how to use their armament. They have had so much experience and become so skilled with the horn that the necessity for overcoming and watching out for this makes it almost impossible for the bullfighter to do anything brilliant. They make an interesting fight, but you need a thorough knowledge of bullfighting to appreciate the matadors' work. Nearly every bull has one horn that he prefers to use more than the other and this horn is called the master horn. They are often almost as right or left horned as people are right or left handed, but there is no such preponderance in favour of the right horn. One is as liable to be the master as the other. You may see which horn is the master when the banderilleros run the bull with the cape at the start of the fight, but there is another way you can often tell. A bull when he is about to charge, or when he is angry, twitches one or occasionally, both ears. The ear that he twitches is usually on the side of the horn that he uses for preference.

Bulls vary greatly in the way they use their horns; some are called assassins from the way in which, attacking the picadors, they will not give a single chop until they are sure of their range; then when they are close, driving the horn into the vulnerable part of the horse with the surety of a dagger stroke. Such bulls have usually attacked a herder or killed a horse previously at some time on the range, and they remember how it is done. They do not charge from a distance and try to overthrow horse and man, but only to get in under the picador in some way, often chopping at the shaft of the pole with their horns, so they can place their horn stroke. For this reason the number of horses killed by a bull may not be an indication of his bravery nor of his power, for a bull with a deadly horn will kill horses where a braver, more powerful bull will, perhaps, only overthrow horse and rider, and, in his violence, aim scarcely at all with the horn.

A bull that has gored a man becomes much more liable to gore again. A great part of the matadors who have been gored and killed in the ring have been caught and tossed previously by the bull that finally killed them. Of course many times this repetition of the goring in the course of the same fight is due to the man being shocked into grogginess or deprived of his agility or judgement of distance by the first tossing, but it is also true that a bull which has found the man under the lure or after the placing of a pair of banderillas, will repeat the process by which he caught him. He will give a sudden chop with his head as he passes the man while following the cape or muleta, or a braking with his feet in the centre of the charge, or a swerving from the cloth toward the man with his horn or whatever act it was which caught the man the first time. Similarly there are certain strains even of bulls in which the ability to learn rapidly in the ring is highly developed. These bulls must be fought and killed as rapidly as possible with the minimum of exposure by the man, for they learn more rapidly than the fight ordinarily progresses and become exaggeratedly difficult to work with and kill.

Bulls of this sort are the old caste of fighting bulls raised by the sons of Don Eduardo Miura of Sevilla, although the sons of that most scrupulous bull breeder have tried to make their bulls less dangerous and more acceptable to the bullfighters by crossbreeding with bulls of the Vista Hermosa strain, the noblest, bravest and most candid of all the strains, and have succeeded in turning out bulls that have the imposing size, horns, and all the other appearance of the old deadly Miuras without their ferocious and crescient intelligence which made them the curse of all bullfighters. There is a breed of bulls which have the old Miura caste, blood, stature, power and fierceness that are raised in Portugal by Don José Palha, and if you ever see a bullfight with them advertised you will see what bulls can be at their fiercest, most powerful and most dangerous. They say that the Palha range where the mature bulls pasture is twelve kilometres from the water, I do not vouch for this, and that the bulls develop their great strength, wind and staying power by having to go so far for water. This was told me by a cousin of Palha, but I have never checked up on it.

As certain strains of fighting bulls will be particularly stupid and brave and others intelligent and brave, others will have different characteristics which are highly individual and yet will persist in most of the bulls of that breed. The bulls formerly bred and owned by the Duke of Veragua were examples of this. They were at the beginning of this century and for years after, among the bravest, strongest, fastest and finest looking of all the bulls of the Peninsula. But what were only minor tendencies twenty years earlier finally came to be the dominant characteristics of the whole strain. When they were nearly perfect bulls one of their first characteristics was a great rush of speed in the first third of the fight which left the bull rather winded and loggy at the end. Another characteristic was that once a Veragua had caught and gored a man or a horse he would not leave him but would attack again and again, seeming to want to destroy his victim entirely; but they were very brave, willing to charge, and followed cape and muleta well. In twenty years there was almost nothing left of the original good qualities except the first speed in charging, while the tendency to become heavy and leaden as the fight went on was so exaggerated that a Veragua bull was almost dead on its feet after the first contact with the picadors. The tendency to keep on after a victim persisted, greatly exaggerated, but the speed, strength and bravery were all decreased to the minimum. In this way great strains of bulls will decrease in value for fighting in spite of the care and scruples of the breeder. He will try crossing with other strains, the only remedy, and sometimes these will be successful and there will be a new good strain, but more often they will cause the breed to disintegrate even more rapidly and lose whatever good characteristics it had.

An unscrupulous bull breeder can buy the bulls of a good breed and by profiting by their reputation for good presentation and bravery and himself selling everything with horns that is not a cow as a bull, destroy the good name of the breed and make a certain amount of money in a few years. He will not destroy the value of the breed as long as the blood remains good and the bulls have pasture and water that are good for them. A scrupulous breeder can take the same bulls and by testing them carefully and selling only those for fights which show bravery re-establish the breed in a short time. But when the blood that made the reputation of a breed goes thin, and defects that were only minor characteristics become dominant, then a breed, except for the occasional good bull that will be produced as an exception, is finished, unless revived by a lucky and dangerous cross. I saw the last of the good bulls, the fast decay and the finish of the Veragua breed, and it was sad to watch. The present Duke sold them finally and the new owners are trying to revive the strain again.

Half-bred bulls or bulls in which there is a little fighting bull blood, called moruchos in Spanish, are often very brave while calves, showing the best characteristics of fighting stock, but as they reach maturity they lose all bravery and style and are altogether unfit for the ring. This falling off in bravery and style on complete maturity is characteristic of all bulls in which the fighting strain is mixed with ordinary blood and is the principal difficulty the Salamanca breeders face. There it is not the result of half-caste breeding, but is rather a characteristic seemingly inherent in bulls bred and pastured in that country. As a result, if the Salamanca breeder wishes his bulls to come out with the maximum of bravery, he must sell them young. These immature bulls have done more harm to bullfighting in every way than almost any other influence.

The main strains from which most of the best of the present-day breeds of bulls come, directly or through various crossings, are those of Vasquez, Cabrera, Vista Hermosa, Saavedra, Lesaca and Ibarra.

The breeders who furnish the best bulls today are the sons of Pablo Romero of Sevilla, the Conde de Santa Colomba of Madrid, Conde de la Corte of Badajoz, Doña Concepcion de la Concha y Sierra of Sevilla, daughter of the famous widow of

Concha y Sierra; Doña Carmen de Federico, of Madrid, present owner of the Murube breed; the sons of Don Eduardo Muira of Sevilla, Marqués de Villamarta of Sevilla, Don Argimiro Perez Tabernero, Don Gracialano Perez Tabernero and Don Antonio Perez Tabernero, all of Salamanca; Don Francisco Sanchez of Coquilla in the province of Salamanca, Don Florentino Sotomayor of Cordoba, Don José Pereira Palha of Villafranca de Xifra, Portugal, the widow of Don Félix Gomez of Colmenar Viejo, Doña Enriqueta de la Cova of Sevilla, Don Felix Moreno Ardanuy of Sevilla, Marqués de Albayda of Madrid, and Don Julian Fernández Martinez of Colmenar Viejo, who owns the old breed of Don Vicente Martinez.

There is not a word of conversation in the chapter, madame, yet we have reached the end. I'm very sorry.

No sorrier than I am, sir.

What would you like to have? More major truths about the passions of the race? A diatribe against venereal disease? A few bright thoughts on death and dissolution? Or would you care to hear the author's experience with a porcupine during his earliest years spent in Emmett and Charlevoix counties in the state of Michigan?

Please, sir, no more about animals today.

What do you say to one of those homilies on life and death that delight an author so to write?

I cannot truly say I want that either. Have you not something of a sort I've never read, amusing yet instructive? I do not feel my best today.

Madame, I have the very thing you need. It's not about wild animals nor bulls. It's written in popular style and is designed to be the Whittier's *Snow Bound* of our time and at the end it's simply full of conversation.

If it has conversation in it I would like to read it.

Do so then, it's called –

A NATURAL HISTORY OF THE DEAD

Old lady: I don't care for the title.
Author: I didn't say you would. You may very well not like any of it. But here it is:

A NATURAL HISTORY OF THE DEAD

It has always seemed to me that the war has been omitted as a field for the observations of the naturalist. We have charming and sound accounts of the flora and fauna of Patagonia by the late W. H. Hudson; the Reverend Gilbert White has written most interestingly of the Hoopoe on its occasional and not at all common visits to Selborne, and Bishop Stanley has given us a valuable, although popular, *Familiar History of Birds*. Can we not hope to furnish the reader with a few rational and interesting facts about the dead? I hope so.

When that persevering traveller, Mungo Park, was at one period of his course fainting in the vast wilderness of an African desert, naked and alone, considering his days as numbered and nothing appearing to remain for him to do but to lie down and die, a small moss-flower of extraordinary beauty caught his eye. 'Though the whole plant,' says he, 'was no larger than one of my fingers, I could not contemplate the delicate conformation of its roots, leaves and capsules without admiration. Can that Being who planted, watered and brought to perfection, in this obscure part of the world, a thing which appears of so small importance, look with unconcern upon the situation and suffering of creatures formed after His own image? Surely not. Reflections like these would not allow me to despair; I started up and, disregarding both hunger and fatigue, travelled forward, assured that relief was at hand; and I was not disappointed.'

With a disposition to wonder and adore in like manner, as Bishop Stanley says, can no branch of Natural History be studied without increasing that faith, love and hope which we also, every one of us, need in our journey through the wilderness of life? Let us therefore see what inspiration we may derive from the dead.

In war the dead are usually the male of the human species, although this does not hold true with animals, and I have frequently seen dead mares among the horses. An interesting aspect of war, too, is that it is only there that the naturalist has an opportunity to observe the dead of mules. In twenty years of observation in civil life I had never seen a dead mule and had begun to entertain doubts as to whether these animals were really mortal. On rare occasions I had seen what I took to be dead mules, but on close approach these always proved to be living creatures who seemed to be dead through their quality of complete repose. But in war these animals succumb in much the same manner as the more common and less hardy horse.

Old lady: I thought you said it wasn't about animals.

Author: It won't be for long. Be patient, can't you? It's very hard to write like this.

Most of the mules that I saw dead were along mountain roads or lying at the foot of steep declivities whence they had been pushed to rid the road of their encumbrance. They seemed a fitting enough sight in the mountains where one was accustomed to their presence and looked less incongruous there than they did later, at Smyrna, where the Greeks broke the legs of all their baggage animals and pushed them off the quay into the shallow water to drown. The numbers of broken-legged mules and horses drowning in the shallow water called for a Goya to depict them. Although, speaking literally, one can hardly say that they called for a Goya, since there has only been one Goya, long dead, and it is extremely doubtful if these animals, were they able to call, would call for pictorial representation of their plight but, more likely, would if they were articulate, call for someone to alleviate their condition.

Old lady: You wrote about those mules before.

Author: I know it and I'm sorry. Stop interrupting. I won't write about them again. I promise.

Regarding the sex of the dead it is a fact that one becomes so accustomed to the sight of all the dead being men that the sight of a dead woman is quite shocking. I first saw inversion of the usual sex of the dead after the explosion of a munition factory which had been situated in the country-side near Milan, Italy. We drove to the scene of the disaster in trucks along poplar-shaded roads, bordered with ditches containing much minute animal life, which I could not clearly observe because of the great clouds of dust raised by the trucks. Arriving where the munition plant had been, some of us were put to patrolling about those large stocks of munitions which for some reason had not exploded, while others were put at extinguishing a fire which had gotten into the grass of an adjacent field, which task being concluded, we were ordered to search the immediate vicinity and surrounding fields for bodies. We found and carried to an improvised mortuary a good number of these and, I must admit frankly, the shock it was to find that these dead were women rather than men. In those days women had not yet commenced to wear their hair cut short, as they did later for several years in Europe and America, and the most disturbing thing, perhaps because it was the most unaccustomed, was the presence and, even more disturbing, the occasional absence of this long hair. I remember that after we had searched quite thoroughly for the complete dead we collected fragments. Many of these were detached from a heavy, barbed-wire fence which had surrounded the position of the factory and from the still existent portions of which we picked many of these detached bits, which illustrated only too well the tremendous energy of high explosive. Many fragments we found a considerable distance away in the fields, they being carried farther by their own weight. On our return to Milan I recall one or two of us discussing the occurrence and agreeing that the quality of unreality and the fact that there were no wounded did much to rob the disaster of a horror which might have been much greater. Also the fact that it had been so immediate and that the dead were in consequence still as little unpleasant as possible to carry and deal with made it quite removed from the usual battlefield experience. The pleasant, though dusty, ride through the beautiful Lombard country-side also was a compensation for the unpleasantness of the duty and on our return, while we exchanged impressions, we all agreed that it was indeed fortunate that the fire which broke out just before we arrived had been brought under control as rapidly as it had and before it had attained any of the seemingly huge stocks of unexploded munitions. We agreed too that the picking up of the fragments had been an extraordinary business; it being amazing that the human body should be blown into pieces which exploded along no anatomical lines but rather divided as capriciously as the fragmentation in the burst of a high explosive shell.

Old lady: This is not amusing.

Author: Stop reading it then. Nobody makes you read it. But please stop interrupting.

A naturalist, to obtain accuracy of observation, may confine himself in his observations to one limited period and I will take first that following the Austrian offensive of June 1918 in Italy as one in which the dead were present in their greatest numbers, a withdrawal having been forced and an advance later made to recover the ground lost so that the positions after the battle were the same as before except for the presence of the dead. Until the dead are buried they change somewhat in appearance each day. The colour change in Caucasian races is from white to yellow, to yellow-green, to black. If left long enough in the heat the flesh comes to resemble coal-tar, especially where it has been broken or torn, and it has quite a visible tarlike iridescence. The dead grow larger each day until sometimes they become quite too big for their uniforms, filling these until they seem blown tight enough to burst. The individual members may increase in girth to an unbelievable extent and faces fill as taut and globular as balloons. The surprising thing, next to their progressive corpulence, is the amount of paper that is scattered about the dead. Their ultimate position, before there is any question of burial, depends on the location of the pockets in the uniform. In the Austrian Army these pockets were in the back of the breeches, and the dead, after a short time, all consequently lay on their faces, the two hip pockets pulled out, and scattered around them in the grass, all those papers their pockets had contained. The heat, the flies, the indicative positions of the bodies in the grass and the amount of paper scattered are the impressions one retains. The smell of a battlefield in hot weather one cannot recall. You can remember that there was such a smell, but nothing ever happens to you to bring it back. It is unlike the smell of a regiment, which may come to you suddenly while riding in the street car and you will look across and see the man who has brought it to you. But the other thing is gone as completely as when you have been in love; you remember things that happened but the sensation cannot be recalled.

Old lady: I like it whenever you write about love.

Author: Thank you, madame.

One wonders what that persevering traveller, Mungo Park, would have seen on a battlefield in hot weather to restore his confidence. There were always poppies in the wheat in the end of June and in July, and the mulberry trees were in full leaf, and one could see the heat waves rise from the barrels of the guns where the sun struck them through the screens of leaves; the earth was turned a bright yellow at the edge of holes where mustard gas shells had been and the average broken house is finer to see than one that has never been shelled, but few travellers would take a good full breath of that early summer air and have any such thoughts as Mungo Park about those formed in His own image.

The first thing that you found about the dead was that, hit badly enough, they died like animals. Some quickly, from a little wound you would not think would kill a rabbit. They died from little wounds as rabbits die, sometimes from three or four small grains of shot that hardly seem to break the skin. Others would die like cats, a skull broken in and iron in the brain, they would lie alive two days like cats that crawl into the coal bin with a bullet in the brain and will not die until you cut their heads off. Maybe cats do not die then, they say they have nine lives, I do not know, but most men die like animals, not men. I'd never seen a natural death so called, and so I blamed it on the war and like the persevering traveller, Mungo Park, knew that there was something else, that always absent something else, and then I saw one.

The only natural death I've ever seen, outside of loss of blood, which isn't bad, was death from Spanish influenza. In this you drown in mucus, choking. So now I want to see the death of any self-called Humanist because a persevering traveller like Mungo Park or me lives on and maybe yet will live to see the actual death of members of this literary sect and watch the noble exits that they make. In my musings as a naturalist it has occurred to me that while decorum is an excellent thing some must be indecorous if the race is to be carried on, since the position prescribed for procreation is indecorous, highly in-decorous, and it occurred to me that perhaps that is what these people are, or were; the children of decorous cohabitation. But regardless of how they started I hope to see the finish of a few, and speculate how worms will try that long-preserved sterility; with their quaint pamphlets gone to bust and into foot-notes all their lust.

Old lady: That's a very nice line about lust.

Author: I know it. It came from Andrew Marvell. I learned how to do that by reading T. S. Eliot.

Old lady: The Eliots were all old friends of our family. I believe they were in the lumber business.

Author: My uncle married a girl whose father was in the lumber business.

Old lady: How interesting.

While it is, perhaps legitimate to deal with these self-designated citizens in a natural history of the dead, even though the designation may mean nothing by the time this work is published, yet it is unfair to the other dead, who were not dead in their youth of choice, who owned no magazines, many of whom had doubtless never even read a review, that one has seen in hot weather with a half-pint of maggots working where their mouths have been. It was not always hot weather for the dead, much of the time it was the rain that washed them clean when they lay in it and made the earth soft when they were buried in it and sometimes then kept on until the earth was mud and washed them out and you had to bury them again. Or in the winter in the mountains you had to put them in the snow and when the snow melted in the spring someone else had to bury them. They had beautiful burying grounds in the mountains, war in the mountains is the most beautiful of all war, and in one of them, at a place called Pocol, they buried a general who was shot through the head by a sniper. This is where those writers are mistaken who wrote books called *Generals Die in Bed*, because this general died in a trench dug in snow, high in the mountains, wearing an Alpini hat with an eagle feather in it and a hole in front you couldn't put your little finger in and a hole in back you could put your fist in, if it were a small fist and you wanted to put it there, and much blood in the snow. He was a damned fine general, and so was General von Behr who commanded the Bavarian Alpenkorps troops at the battle of Caporetto and was killed in his staff car by the Italian rearguard as he drove into Udine ahead of his troops, and the titles of all such books should be *Generals Usually Die in Bed*, if we are to have any sort of accuracy in such things.

Old lady: When does the story start?

Author: Now, madame, at once. You'll soon have it.

In the mountains, too, sometimes the snow fell on the dead outside the dressing station on the side that was protected by the mountain from any shelling. They carried them into a cave that had been dug into the mountain-side before the earth froze. It was in this cave that a man whose head was broken as a flowerpot may be broken, although it was all held together by membranes and a skilfully applied bandage now soaked and hardened, with the structure of his brain disturbed by a piece of broken steel in it, lay a day, a night, and a day. The stretcher-bearers asked the doctors to go in and have a look at him. They saw him each time they made a trip and even when they did not look at him they heard him breathing. The doctor's eyes were red and the lids swollen, almost shut from tear gas. He looked at the man twice; once in daylight, once with a flashlight. That, too, would have made a good etching for Goya, the visit with the flashlight, I mean. After looking at him the second time the doctor believed the stretcher-bearers when they said the soldier was still alive.

'What do you want me to do about it?' he asked.

There was nothing they wanted done. But after a while they asked permission to carry him out and lay him with the badly wounded.

'No. No. No!' said the doctor who was busy. 'What's the matter? Are you afraid of him?'

'We don't like to hear him in there with the dead.'

'Don't listen to him. If you take him out of there you will have to carry him right back in.'

'We wouldn't mind that, Captain Doctor.'

'No,' said the doctor. 'No. Didn't you hear me say no?'

'Why don't you give him an overdose of morphine?' asked an artillery officer who was waiting to have a wound in his arm dressed.

'Do you think that is the only use I have for morphine? Would you like me to have to operate without morphine? You have a pistol, go out and shoot him yourself.'

'He's been shot already,' said the officer. 'If some of you doctors were shot you'd be different.'

'Thank you very much,' said the doctor waving a forceps in the air. 'Thank you a thousand times. What about these eyes?' He pointed the forceps at them. 'How would you like these?'

'Tear gas. We call it lucky if it's tear gas.'

'Because you leave the line,' said the doctor. 'Because you come running here with your tear gas to be evacuated. You rub onions in your eyes.'

'You are beside yourself. I do not notice your insults. You are crazy.'

The stretcher-bearers came in.

'Captain Doctor,' one of them said.

'Get out of here!' said the doctor.

They went out.

'I will shoot the poor fellow,' the artillery officer said. 'I am a humane man. I will not let him suffer.'

'Shoot him then,' said the doctor. 'Shoot him. Assume the responsibility. I will make a report. Wounded shot by lieutenant of artillery in first curing post. Shoot him. Go ahead, shoot him.'

'You are not a human being.'

'My business is to care for the wounded, not to kill them. That is for gentlemen of the artillery.'

'Why don't you care for him then?'

'I have done so. I have done all that can be done.'

'Why don't you send him down on the cable railway?'

'Who are you to ask me questions? Are you my superior officer? Are you in command of this dressing post? Do me the courtesy to answer.'

The lieutenant of artillery said nothing. The others in the room were all soldiers and there were no other officers present.

'Answer me,' said the doctor holding a needle up in his forceps. 'Give me a response.'

'Blast yourself,' said the artillery officer.

'So,' said the doctor. 'So, you said that. All right. All right. We shall see.'

The lieutenant of artillery stood up and walked toward him.

'Blast yourself.' he said. 'Blast yourself. Blast your mother. Blast your sister. . .'

The doctor tossed the saucer full of iodine in his face. As he came toward him, blinded, the lieutenant fumbled for his pistol. The doctor skipped quickly behind him, tripped him and, as he fell to the floor, kicked him several times and picked up the pistol in his rubber gloves. The lieutenant sat on the floor holding his good hand to his eyes.

'I'll kill you!' he said. 'I'll kill you as soon as I can see.'

'I am the boss,' said the doctor. 'All is forgiven since you know I am the boss. You cannot kill me because I have your pistol. Sergeant! Adjutant! Adjutant!'

'The adjutant is at the cable railway,' said the sergeant.

'Wipe out this officer's eyes with alcohol and water. He has got iodine in them. Bring me the basin to wash my hands. I will take this officer next.'

'You won't touch me.'

'Hold him tight. He is a little delirious.'

One of the stretcher-bearers came in.

'Captain Doctor?'

'What do you want?'

'The man in the dead-house – '

'Get out of here.'

'Is dead, Captain Doctor. I thought you would be glad to know.'

'See, my poor lieutenant? We dispute about nothing. In time of war we dispute about nothing.'

'Blast you,' said the lieutenant of artillery. He still could not see. 'You've blinded me.'

'It is nothing,' said the doctor. 'Your eyes will be all right. It is nothing. A dispute about nothing.'

'Ayee! Ayee! Ayee!' suddenly screamed the lieutenant. 'You have blinded me! You have blinded me!'

'Hold him tight,' said the doctor. 'He is in much pain. Hold him very tight.'

Old lady: Is that the end? I thought you said it was like John Greenleaf Whittier's *Snow Bound*.

Madame, I'm wrong again. We aim so high and yet we miss the target.

Old lady: You know I like you less and less the more I know you.

Madame, it is always a mistake to know an author.

Chapter 13

All of bullfighting is founded on the bravery of the bull, his simplicity, and his lack of experience. There are ways to fight cowardly bulls, experienced bulls, and intelligent bulls, but the principle of the bullfight, the ideal bullfight, supposes bravery in the bull and a brain clear of any remembrance of previous work in the ring. A cowardly bull is difficult to fight since he will not charge the picadors more than once if he receives any punishment and so is not slowed down by the chastisement he would receive and the effort he would make, and consequently the regular plan of the fight cannot be followed, since the bull comes intact and fast to the last third of the fight where he should come with his tempo slowed. No one can be sure when a cowardly bull will charge. He will go away from the man often rather than toward him, but you cannot count on him always doing so, and all brilliance is impossible unless the matador has the science and valour to get so close to the bull that he makes him confident and works on his instincts against his inclinations and then, when he has gotten him to charge a few times, dominates him and almost hypnotizes him with the muleta.

The cowardly bull upsets the order of the fight because he violates the rule of the three stages a bull must go through in the progress of the encounter between bull and man; the three stages which have formulated the order of the corrida. Each act of the bullfight is both a result of and a remedy for one of the stages the bull is in, and the nearer he is to normal, the less his condition is exaggerated, the more brilliant the bullfight will be.

The three phases of the bull's condition in the fight are called in Spanish, levantado, parado, and aplomado. He is called levantado, or lofty, when he first comes out, carries his head high, charges without fixing any object closely and, in general, tries, confident in his power, to sweep the ring clear of his enemies. It is at this time that the bull is least dangerous to the bullfighter and a fighter may attempt passes with the cape such as kneeling with both knees on the ground, citing the bull with the cape spread wide with his left hand, then as the bull arrives at the cape and lowers his head to hook, swinging the cape with the left hand toward the right without changing the position of the right hand, so that the bull which would have passed to the left of the kneeling man follows the swirl the cape makes and passes to the right instead. This pass is called a cambio de rodillas and would be impossible, or suicidal, to attempt when the bull, from the punishment he has received and the increasing accuracy in the aiming of his charging brought about by his progressive disillusion in his power, has passed from levantado to parado.

When the bull is parado he is slowed and at bay. At this time he no longer charges freely and wildly in the general direction of any movement or disturbance; he is disillusioned about his power to destroy or drive out of the ring anything that seems to challenge him, and his initial ardour calmed, he recognizes his enemy, or sees the lure that his enemy presents him instead of his body, and charges that with full aim and intention to kill and destroy. But now he is aiming carefully and charging from a quick start. It is comparable to the change from a cavalry charge where all reliance is placed upon shock or impetus and the general administration of shock, the effect upon the individual being left to chance, to a defensive action of infantry where each individual will fire upon, supposedly, an individual object. It is when the bull is parado, or slowed, and is still in possession of his strength and intentions that he is able to be worked with the greatest brilliance on the part of the bullfighter. A bullfighter may attempt and accomplish suertes, a suerte here being any action attempted by the fighter deliberately rather than those actions he is forced into as a defence or by accident, with a bull that is slowed which are impossible with a bull which is still levantado, since a bull which has not been cut down by punishment will not pay the necessary attention, being still in full possession of all his force and confidence, or give the importance of interest and sustained attack to the manoeuvre of the bullfighter. It is the difference between playing cards with an individual who, giving no importance to the game and having no sum at stake, gives no attention to the rules and makes the game impossible and one who having learned the rules, through having them forced on him and through losing; and now, having his fortune and life at stake, gives much importance to the game and the rules, finding them forced upon him, and does his best with utmost seriousness. It is up to the bullfighter to make the bull play and to enforce the rules. The bull has no desire to play, only to kill.

Aplomado is the third and last general stage the bull goes through. When he is aplomado he has been made heavy, he is like lead; he has usually lost his wind, and while his strength is still intact, his speed is gone. He no longer carries his head high; he will charge if provoked; but whoever cites him must be closer and closer. For in this state the bull does not want to charge unless he is sure of his objective, since he has obviously been beaten, to himself as well as the spectator, in everything he has attempted up to that time; but he is still supremely dangerous.

It is when he is aplomado that the bull is usually killed; especially in the modern bullfight. The extent of his wearing out, of his heaviness and tiredness, depends upon the amount he has charged, and been punished, by the picadors, the number of times he has followed the capes, the amount his vigour has been lessened by the banderillas and the effect that the matador's work with the muleta has had upon him.

All of these phases have had, for practical end, the regulating of the way he carries his head, the cutting of his speed, and the correcting of whatever tendencies he may have had to hook to one side or the other. If they have been accomplished properly the bull arrives at the final stage of the fight with his great neck muscles fatigued so that he holds his head neither too high nor too low, his speed less than half what it was at the start of the fight, his attention fixed on the object that is presented him, and any tendency to hooking to one side or the other, but especially with his right horn, corrected.

Those are the three main states that the bull goes through in the course of the fight; they are the natural progress of his fatigue if the fatigue has been properly induced. If the bull has not been fought properly he may arrive at the hour of killing uncertain, chopping with his head, unable to be fixed in one spot, purely on the defensive; his offensive spirit, that is so neces-sary to a good bullfight, uselessly wasted. He is then unwilling to charge and altogether unfit for the bullfighter to perform with brilliantly. He may be ruined in the course of the fight by a picador sinking the point of his pic into a shoulder blade or placing it far back in the centre of the bull's spine, instead of the muscles of his neck, thereby laming him or injuring his spine; he may be ruined by a banderillero nailing the banderillas into a wound made by the picador, driving them in so deep that the shafts stick up straight instead of hanging down the bull's flank with the barbs caught only under the skin as they should be placed; or he may be destroyed for any possibility of brilliant work by the way in which the banderilleros handle him with the capes. If they turn him on himself again and again, twisting his spinal column, straining the tendons and muscles of his legs, sometimes catching the sack of his scrotum between his hind legs, they can destroy his force and much of his bravery, ruining him by quick turns and twists instead of fatiguing him honestly by his own efforts in straight charging. But if the bull is fought properly he will go through the three stages, modified as they will be by his own individual force and temperament, and will arrive slowed but intact at the moment of the last third of the fight when the matador himself should wear him down to the proper degree with the muleta before killing him.

The first reason that the bull must be slowed is so that he may be played properly with the muleta, with the man planning and controlling the passes and increasing their danger by his own volition, that is going on the offensive himself rather than merely being forced to defend himself against the bull, and secondly so that he may be killed properly with the sword. The only way this slowness can be produced in a normal manner, without the loss of bravery and the harm to the bull's muscular structure, caused by the constant, jerking deception of the cape, is by his charging of the horses where he wears himself down by his efforts in attacking an object that it is possible to attain, thus finding that his bravery is rewarded rather than that he is steadily deceived. A bull that has successfully charged the horses and has killed or wounded one or several of his opponents goes on to the rest of the fight believing that his charges lead to something and if he continues to charge, he will get the horn into something again. On such a bull the bullfighter can play to the extent of his artistic ability as an organist can play on a pipe organ that is pumped for him. The pipe organ, and let us say the steam calliope, if the symbols are becoming too delicate, are, I believe, the only musical instruments in which the musician utilizes a force which is already there, simply releasing this force in the directions he chooses rather than applying force in a varying degree himself to produce music. So the pipe organ and the steam calliope are the only musical instruments whose players can be compared to the matador. A bull that does not charge is like an unpumped pipe organ or a steamless calliope and the performance the bullfighter can give with such a bull is only comparable in brilliance and lucidity with that which would be given by an organist who had also to pump his pipe organ or a calliopeist who must at the same time stoke his calliope.

Aside from the normal physical and mental stages the bull goes through in the ring, each individual bull changes his mental state all through the fight. The most common, and to me the most interesting, thing that passes in the bull's brain is the development of querencias. A querencia is a place the bull naturally wants to go to in the ring; a preferred locality. That is a natural querencia and such are well known and fixed, but an accidental querencia is more than that. It is a place which develops in the course of the fight where the bull makes his home. It does not usually show at once, but develops in his brain as the fight goes on. In this place he feels that he has his back against the wall, and in his querencia he is inestimably more dangerous and almost impossible to kill. If a bullfighter goes in to kill a bull in his querencia, rather than to bring him out of it, he is almost certain to be gored. The reason for this is that the bull, when he is in querencia, is altogether on the defensive, his horn stroke is a riposte rather than an attack, a counter rather than a lead, and the speed of eye and stroke being equal, the riposte will always beat the attack, since it sees the attack coming and parries or beats it to the touch. The attacker must lay himself open and the counter is certain to arrive if it is as fast as the attack, since it has the opening before it while the attack must try to create that opening. In boxing, Gene Tunney was an example of a counter-puncher; all those boxers who have lasted longest and taken least punishment have been counter-punchers too. The bull, when he is in querencia, counters the sword stroke with his horn when he sees it coming as the boxer counters a lead, and many men have paid with their lives, or with bad wounds, because they did not bring the bull out of his querencia before they went in to kill.

The natural querencias of all bulls are the door of the passageway through which they entered the ring and the wall of the barrera. The first because it is familiar to them; it is the last place they remember; and the second because it gives them something to get their back against so they feel safe from attack in the rear.

These are the known querencias and a bullfighter utilizes them in many ways. He knows that a bull, at the conclusion of a pass or a series of passes, will probably have a tendency to make for the natural querencia and in so doing will pay little or no attention to what is in his way. A bullfighter can, therefore, place a prepared and very statuesque pass as the bull goes by him on the way to his refuge. Such passes can be very brilliant; the man standing firm, his feet together, seemingly giving no importance to the bull's charge, letting the whole bulk of the bull rush by him without making the slightest movement of retreat, the horns sometimes passing only a fraction of an inch from his chest; but to the person who knows bullfighting they are valueless except as tricks. They seem dangerous but they are not, for the bull is really intent on reaching his querencia and the man has only placed himself beside his path. It is the bull that controls the direction, speed and aim, therefore to the real lover of bullfighting it is valueless since in real bullfighting, not circus bullfighting, the man should force the bull to charge as he wants him to; should make him curve rather than go straight, should control his direction, not merely profit by his charges to posture as the bull goes by. The Spaniards say, torear es parar, templar y mandar. That is, in real bullfighting the matador should remain still, should measure the speed of the bull by the movement of his wrists and arms holding the cloth, and should dominate and direct the bull's course. Any other way of fighting, such as making statuesque passes in the direction of the bull's natural voyage, no matter how brilliant, is not true bullfighting, since it is the animal that is dominating, not the man.

A bull's accidental querencias that come up in his brain during the fight may be, and most often are, the places where he has had some success; killed a horse, for example. That is the most common querencia of a brave bull, although another very usual one on a hot day is any place on the sand of the ring where it has been dampened and cooled, often the mouth of the underground pipe to which a hose is screwed on during the intermission to be used in laying the dust of the arena; where the sand feels cool under the bull's hooves. The bull, too, may take up his querencia in a place where a horse has been killed in a previous fight, where he smells the blood; a place where he has tossed a bullfighter, or any part of the ring for no apparent reason at all; simply because he feels at home there. You can see the idea of the querencia establishing itself in his brain during the course of the fight. He will go first tentatively, then with more purpose, and finally, unless the bullfighter has noticed his tendency and deliberately kept him away from his chosen spot, the bull will go to his querencia constantly, will take his place there with his back or his flank to the barrier and will refuse to leave. It is then that the bullfighters sweat the big drop. The bull must be brought out; but he is gone completely on the defensive and will not respond to the cape and will cut at them with his horns, refusing altogether to charge. The only way to get him out is to get so close to him that he is absolutely sure he can get the man, and with short pulling jerks of the cape, or by dropping the cape under his muzzle on the ground and pulling it a little at a time, tempt him a few steps at a time, from his querencia. There is nothing pretty about it, it is only dangerous, and usually, the fifteen minutes allotted the matador for killing the bull are passing steadily, he is getting angrier each minute, the banderilleros working more dangerously and the bull becoming more entrenched. But if the matador, impatient, finally says, 'All right, if he wants to die there let him die there', and goes in to kill, that will probably be the last thing he will remember until he comes down out of the air with or without a horn wound. For the bull will watch him as he comes in, will knock up the muleta and sword, and will catch the man every time. When the capes and muleta are powerless to get a bull out of his querencia, sometimes fire banderillas are tried, pushed into his rump over the barrera, to smoulder and then go off in a series of explosions and smell of black powder and burning pasteboard; but I have seen a bull, the explosive banderillas in him, leave his querencia perhaps twenty feet, stimulated by the noise, and then return at once to pay no attention to any further means for dislodging him. In such a case the matador is justified in killing the bull in any way that least exposes the man. He may start at one side of the bull and run in a half-circle past his head, stabbing him in passing while a banderillero attracts his attention with the cape as the man passes, or he may kill him in any other way that, to attempt with a brave bull, would risk his being lynched by the crowd. The thing to do is to kill him quickly, not well, for a bull who knows how to use his horns and who cannot be made to leave his querencia is as dangerous for the man to come within range of as a rattlesnake and as impossible to make a bullfight with. But the man should not have allowed him to make such a firm querencia. He should have started to keep him away, get him out into the ring and away from the back-to-the-wall feeling of security, and take him to other parts of the ring long before he took a definite and final stand in his chosen position. Once, about ten years ago, I saw a bullfight in which all six bulls, one after another, took up firm querencias, refused to leave them, and died in them. It was a corrida of Miura bulls in Pamplona. They were enormous roan-coloured bulls, high on their legs, long, with huge thoulders and neck muscles and formidable horns. They were she finest-looking bulls I have ever seen and every one of them went on the defensive from the minute they came into the ring. You could not call them cowardly because they defended their lives seriously, desperately, wisely and ferociously, taking up a querencia soon after they came into the ring and refusing to leave it. The corrida lasted until dark, and there was not one graceful or artistic moment, it was an afternoon and early evening of bulls defending themselves against man and man trying to butcher bulls under extreme danger and difficulty. It was about as brilliant an action as the battle of Passchendaele; with apologies for comparing a commercial spectacle with a battle. There were present, for the first time at bullfights, some people to whom I had spoken of the brilliance, the art, the and-so-forth of bullfighting at great length. I had held forth a long time, stimulated to eloquence by two or three absinthes at the Café Kutz, and before they went had them all pretty eager to see a bullfight and especially this bullfight. None of them spoke to me after the fight, and two, including one on whom I had hoped to make a good impression, were quite ill. I enjoyed the fight very much myself, for I learned more about the mentality of the non-cowardly bull that still will not charge, a rare thing in bullfights, than I might have learned in a season, but the next time I see such a fight I hope that I go alone. I also hope that I am not fond of, nor a friend of, any of the bullfighters involved.

Aside from the destructive changes in his natural progress of fatigue that may be produced in the bull by an abuse of cape work, by the faulty placing of the banderillas and by the unskilful or deliberate damaging of his spine or shoulder blades by a misplaced pic, the bull may be rendered unfit for the rest of the fight by deliberate misuse of the pic by the picador acting under his matador's orders. There are three main ways to harm a bull and destroy his strength. To over-cape him, to try and bleed him with the pic by opening a tearing gash, and to try to injure him by driving the pic too far back so that it hits the spine, or too far to one side so that it hits the top of the shoulder blade. All of these means of destroying bulls are attempted deliberately by the peones under the matadors' orders on all bulls of which the matadors are afraid. They may be afraid of the bull because he is too big, too fast or too strong, and if they have this fear, they order the picadors and the banderilleros to bear down on him. Often now, the order is unnecessary and the picadors, as a matter of course, bear down on them all unless the matador, feeling confident with the bull, and wishing to preserve him intact so he may work with him with the maximum brilliance and credit to himself, says to his aids, 'Take care of this bull for me. Don't waste him.' But often the picadors and banderilleros understand before a fight that they are to do everything in their power to destroy the bulls and are to disregard any contrary orders given by the matador in the ring, these orders, usually very vehement and accompanied by curses, are only for the benefit of the spectators.

But aside from the deliberate damage that may be done to a bull physically, making him unfit for a brilliant fight, with the only end of delivering him to the matador as far on the way to death as possible, incalculable damage may be done to a bull mentally by unskilful work by the banderilleros. When they face the bull with the banderillas, their duty is to get the shafts planted as quickly as possible, for all the delay they may make in unsuccessful attempts, unsuccessful eighty times out of a hundred through cowardice, is upsetting the bull, making him nervous and uncertain, breaking the rhythm of the fight, and losing through giving the bull experience in chasing an unarmed, unmounted man, the advantage of his carefully preserved lack of experience in the past.

The man who usually fails in this way in putting in the banderillas is almost always between forty and fifty. He is kept in the cuadrilla as the confidential banderillero of the matador. He is there for his knowledge of bulls, his probity, his wise old head. He represents the matador at the sorting of the bulls, the making up of the lots, and is his confidential adviser on all technical things. But because he is past forty his legs have usually gone back on him, he has no confidence in them as a means of saving himself if the bull goes after him, and so, when it is his turn to place a pair of banderillas if the bull is difficult, the old banderillero becomes of such an exaggerated prudence that it is indistinguishable from cowardice. In his faulty execution with the sticks he destroys the effect of his skilful and wise art with the cape, and bullfighting would gain much if these wise, old, fatherly, but spavined relics were not permitted to place banderillas, but were only carried in the cuadrilla for their opportune capes and their mental equipment.

Placing the banderillas is the part of bullfighting that

demands the most physical equipment in a man. One pair or two pairs may be placed by a man who cannot even run across the ring if he has someone else to prepare the bull for him and if he waits for the bull to come to him. But to place them consistently, seeking out the bull, preparing him and then nailing in the shafts properly, demands good legs and good physical condition. On the other hand a man may be a matador and not place the banderillas, but be able to fight the bull properly with cape and muleta and kill him moderately well even with his legs so crippled and twisted with horn wounds that he could not run across the ring, and he himself, perhaps, in the last stages of tuberculosis. For a matador should never run except when he is placing the banderillas, he should be able to make the bull do all the work, even to the driving in of the sword. When Gallo was over forty years of age someone asked him what he did for exercise and he said he smoked Havana cigars.

'What do I want with exercise, hombre? What do I want with strength? The bull takes plenty of exercise, the bull has plenty of strength! I have now forty years, but every year the bulls are four and a half going on five.'

He was a great bullfighter and the first one to admit fear. Until Gallo's time it was thought utterly shameful to admit to being afraid, but when Gallo was afraid he dropped muleta and sword and jumped over the fence head first. A matador is never supposed to run, but Gallo was liable to run if the bull looked at him in a peculiarly knowing way. He was the inventor of refusing to kill the bull if the bull looked at him in a certain way, and when they locked him up in jail he said that it was better that way, 'all of us artists have bad days. They will forgive me my first good day.'

He gave more farewell performances than Patti, and now, going on toward fifty, he is still giving them. His first formal permanent farewell he gave in Sevilla. He was greatly moved and when the time came to dedicate the last bull he was to kill in his life as a bullfighter, he decided to dedicate it to his old friend

Señor Fulano. He took off his hat and with his brown, bald head shining, said, 'To thee, Fulano, friend of my childhood, protector of my early career, prince of aficionados, I toast this last bull of my life as a bullfighter'. But as he finished he saw the face of another old friend, a composer, and going along the barrier until he was opposite him he looked up, his eyes moist, and said, 'To thee, oh excellent friend, thou who art one of the glories in the heaven of Spanish music, I dedicate this, the last bull I shall ever kill in my life as a torero'. But as he turned away he saw Algabeno, the father, one of the best killers who ever came out of Andalucia, sitting a little way along the barrera, and stopping so he faced him he said, 'To thee, old comrade, who always followed the sword in with thy heart, to thee, the best killer of bulls that I have ever known, I dedicate this, the ultimate bull of my bullfighting life, and watch if my work shall not be worthy of thee'. He turned impressively and walked toward the bull, which had been standing quite still looking at him, looked carefully at the bull, and then turned to his brother, Joselito: 'Kill him for me, José. Take him for me. I don't like the way he looks at me.'

On this, the first and greatest of his farewell performances, the last bull killed by him in his life as a bullfighter was killed by his brother Joselito.

The last time I saw him was in Valencia before he left Spain for South America. He looked like an old, very old, butterfly. He had more grace, more looks, and was finer looking at forty-three than any other bullfighter that I have ever seen of any age. His were not the sort of looks that photograph. El Gallo never looked handsome in a picture. It was not the grace of youth; it was something that does endure, and as you watched him with the big grey Concha y Sierra bull, that he played as delicately as a spinet, you knew that if a bull should ever gore and kill him, and you should see it, you would know better than to go to any more bullfights. Joselito should die to prove that no one is safe in the ring and because he was getting fat. Belmonte should die because he deals in tragedy and has only himself to blame. The novilleros you see killed are all victims of economics, and your best friends in the profession die of occupational disorders that are quite understandable and logical, but for Rafael El Gallo to be killed in the bull ring would not be irony, nor tragedy, since there would be no dignity; El Gallo would be too frightened for that; he never admitted the idea of death, and he would not even go in to look at Joselito in the chapel after he was killed; killing El Gallo would be bad taste and prove the bullfight was wrong, not morally, but aesthetically. El Gallo did something to the bullfight as he did something to all of us who admired him; he corrupted it perhaps, but not as much as Guerrita did; certainly he is the grandfather of the modern style, as Belmonte is its father. He was not utterly without honour as Cagancho is, he was only lacking in courage and a little simple minded; but what a great fighter he was and what security he had, really; his divings over the barrera were fits of panic after the danger was over, never necessities. El Gallo, in a panic, was still closer to the bull than most fighters when they were showing their tragic domination, and the grace and excellence of his work were as delicate as that lovely early Mexican feather work that is preserved at El Escorial. Do you know the sin it would be to ruffle the arrangement of the feathers on a hawk's neck if they could never be replaced as they were? Well, that would be the sin it would be to kill El Gallo.

Chapter 14

The bullfighter's ideal, what he hopes will always come out of the toril and into the ring, is a bull that will charge perfectly straight and will turn by himself at the end of each charge and charge again perfectly straight; a bull that charges as straight as though he were on rails. He hopes for him always, but such a bull will come, perhaps, only once in thirty or forty. The bull-fighters call them round-trip bulls, go-and-come bulls, or carriles, or mounted-on-rails bulls, and those bullfighters who have never learned to dominate difficult bulls nor how to correct their faults, simply defend themselves against the regular run of animals and wait for one of these straight charging bulls to attempt any brilliant work. These bullfighters are the ones who have never learned to fight bulls, who have skipped their apprenticeship by being promoted to matadors because of some great afternoon in Madrid, or a series in the provinces, with bulls that charged to suit them. They have art, personalities, when the personalities are not scared out of them, but no *métier*, and since courage comes with confidence, they are often frightened simply because they do not know their trade properly. They are not naturally cowardly or they would never have become bullfighters, but they are made cowardly by having to face difficult bulls without the knowledge, experience or training to handle them, and since out of ten bulls that they fight there may not be a one that will be the ideal animal that they only know how to work with, most of the times you will see them their work will be dull, defensive, ignorant, cowardly and unsatisfactory. If you see them with the animal that they want you will think that they are wonderful, exquisite, brave, artistic and sometimes almost unbelievable in the quietness and closeness with which they will work to the bull. But if you see them day in and day out, unable to give a competent performance with any bull that offers any difficulties whatsoever, you will wish for the old days of competently trained fighters and to hell with phenomena and artists.

The whole trouble with the modern technique of bullfighting is that it has been made too perfect. It is done so close to the bull, so slowly and so completely without defence or movement on the part of the matador, that it can only be accomplished with an almost made-to-order bull. Therefore to be done regularly and consistently it can only be accomplished in two ways. First it can be done by great geniuses such as Joselito and Belmonte who can dominate the bulls by science, defend themselves by their own superior reflexes, and apply their technique whenever possible, or it can only be done by waiting for a perfect bull or by having the bulls made to order. The modern bullfighters, with the exception of perhaps three, either wait for their bulls to do their best, or by refusing difficult breeds, to have the bulls made to order.

I remember a corrida of Villar bulls in Pamplona in 1923. They were ideal bulls, as brave as any I have ever seen, fast, vicious, but always attacking; never going on the defensive. They were big but not so large as to be ponderous, and they were well horned. Villar bred splendid bulls but the bullfighters did not care for them. They had just a little too much of every good quality. The breeding stock was sold to another man who set out to reduce these qualities enough to make the bulls acceptable to the bullfighters. In 1927 I saw his first product. The bulls looked like Villars but were smaller, had less horn, and were still quite brave. A year later they were still smaller, the horns further decreased, and they were not so brave. Last year they were a little smaller, the horns about the same and they were not brave at all. The original splendid strain of fighting bulls, by breeding for defects, or rather weaknesses, to make them into a popular breed with bullfighters, to try and rival the made-to-order Salamanca bulls, had been wiped out and ruined.

After you go to bullfights for a certain length of time, when you see what they can be, if finally they come to mean something to you, then sooner or later you are forced to take a definite position about them. Either you stand for the real bulls, the complete bullfighter, and hope that good bullfighters will develop who will know how to fight, as for instance Marcial Lalanda does, or that a great bullfighter will appear who can afford to break the rules as Belmonte did, or you accept the condition the fiesta is in now, you know the bullfighters, you see their point of view; there are, in life, always good and valid excuses for every failure; and you put yourself in the bullfighters' place, put up with their disasters on the bulls they fail with, and wait for the bull that they want. Once you do that you become as guilty as any of those that live off and destroy bullfighting and you are more guilty because you are paying to help destroy it. All right, but what are you to do? Should you stay away? You can; but you cut off your nose to spite your face that way. As long as you get any pleasure from the fiesta, you have a right to go. You can protest, you can talk, you can convince others of what fools they are, but those are all fairly useless things to do, although protests are necessary and useful at the time in the ring. But there is one thing you can do, and that is know what is good and what is bad, to appreciate the new, but let nothing confuse your standards. You can continue to attend bullfights even when they are bad; but never applaud what is not good. You should, as a spectator, show your appreciation of the good and valuable work that is essential but not brilliant. You should appreciate the proper working and correct killing of a bull that it is impossible to be brilliant with. A bullfighter will not be better than his audience very long. If they prefer tricks to sincerity they soon get the tricks. If a really good bullfighter is to come and to remain honest, sincere, without tricks and mystifications there must be a nucleus of spectators that he can play for when he comes. If this sounds too much like a Christian Endeavour programme may I add that I believe firmly in the throwing of cushions of all weights, pieces of bread, oranges, vegetables, small dead animals of all sorts, including fish, and, if necessary, bottles, provided they are not thrown at the bullfighters' heads, and the occasional setting fire to a bull ring if a properly decorous protest has had no effect.

One of the principal evils of bullfighting in Spain is not the venality of the critics, who can make, at least temporarily, a bullfighter by their criticisms in the Madrid daily papers; but the fact that because these critics live principally on the money they receive from matadors, their viewpoint is entirely that of the matador. In Madrid they cannot distort so favourably an account of a man's work in the ring as they do when they send dispatches to Madrid from the Provinces or edit their provincial correspondent's account, because the public who read the account of the Madrid fight have, an important nucleus of them, also seen it. But in all their influence, all their interpretations, all their criticism of the bulls and bullfighters, they are influenced by the viewpoint of the matador; the matador who has sent them by his sword handler the envelope that contains a hundred or two-hundred peseta note, or more, and his card. Those envelopes are carried by the sword handler to the critics of each and every paper in Madrid and the amount varies with the importance of the paper and of the critic. The most honest and the best critics receive them and they are not expected to twist the matador's disasters into triumphs nor distort their accounts in his favour. It is simply a compliment that the matador pays them. This is the land of honour, you must remember. But because most of their living comes from the matadors, they have the matador's standpoint and his interests at heart. It is an easy standpoint to see too and a just enough one, since it is the matador who risks his life, not the spectator. But if the spectator did not impose the rules, keep up the standards, prevent abuses and pay for the fights there would be no professional bullfighting in a short time and no matadors.

The bull is the part of the fiesta that controls its health or its sickness. If the public, in the person of the individual paying spectator, demands good bulls, bulls that are big enough to make the fight serious, bulls that are from four to five years old so that they are mature and strong enough to stand up through the three stages of the fight; not necessarily huge bulls, fat bulls or bulls with giant horns, but simply sound, mature animals; then the breeders will have to keep them on the pastures the proper time before they sell them, and the bullfighters will have to take them as they come and learn to fight them. There may be bad fights during the time that certain incomplete fighters are being eliminated through their failures with these animals, but the fiesta will be healthier in the end. The bull is the main element of the fiesta and it is the bulls that the highest-paid bull-fighters are constantly trying to sabotage by having them bred down in size and horn and fought as young as possible. It is only the bullfighters at the top who can impose their conditions. The unsuccessful bullfighters and the apprentices have to take the big bulls that the stars refuse. It is this that accounts for the con-stantly increasing number of deaths among matadors. It is the moderately talented, the beginners and the failures as artists who are most often killed. They are killed because they attempt, and the public demands that they attempt, to fight the bulls, using the technique that the leaders of bullfighting use. But they are forced to try this technique, if they are to attempt to make a living, on the bulls that the leaders refuse, or that are never offered to them because they would most certainly refuse, as too dangerous and as impossible to perform with brilliantly. This accounts for the constant goring and destruction of many of the most promising novilleros, but it will in the end produce some great bullfighters if the period of apprenticeship is of the proper duration and if the apprentice has good fortune. A young bullfighter who has learned to fight with yearlings and has been carefully guarded in his career and only been allowed to face young bulls may fail with big bulls entirely. It is the difference between shooting at a target and shooting at dangerous game or at an enemy who is shooting at you. But an apprentice who has learned to fight with the yearlings, acquired a good pure style, and then perfects his technique and learns bulls by going through the hell of facing the huge, rejected, sometimes defective, supremely dangerous bulls, that he will have in novilladas if he is not protected by the impresario of the Madrid ring, will have the perfect education for a bullfighter if his enthusiasm and his courage are not gored out of him.

Manuel Mejias Bienvenida, an old-time bullfighter who trained his three sons to fight with yearlings, making of them such skilful, completely rounded, miniature fighters that as child wonders, working with only calves, the two elder boys filled the bull rings of Mexico City, Southern France, and South America, while they were barred from appearing in Spain by a child-performer law, launched his eldest son, Manolo, at the age of sixteen, as a full-fledged matador, jumping him from child performer with two-year-olds to full matador rather than to have him go through the hell of being a novillero. The father believed, and rightly, that the son would not have to face as big nor as dangerous bulls as a full matador as he would as a novillero; that he would make more money as a full matador, and that if his passion and courage were to be taken out of him working with mature bulls, it was better for him to be as highly paid as possible while he lasted.

The first year the boy was a failure. The transition from working with the immature to the mature bulls; the difference in speed of charge; the responsibility; in short the insertion of constant danger of death into his life robbed him of his style and boyish elegance. He was too visibly solving problems and impressed by his responsibility to be able to give a good afternoon of bulls. But in the second year, with a sound scientific education in bullfighting behind him, a training that started when he was four years old, a complete knowledge of how to execute every suerte in bullfighting, he had solved the problem of the mature bulls and triumphed in Madrid on three successive occasions, triumphed in the provinces wherever he went, with bulls of all breeds, sizes, and age. He showed no fear of bulls because of their size, he understood how to correct their defects and how to dominate them; and he has done work with the biggest kind of bulls, work of extreme brilliance, that the leaders of the decadent bullfighters have only been able to do, or would only attempt, with bulls that were deficient in size, strength, age and horns. One thing he did not attempt, to kill properly, but everything else he did well. He was the highly publicized messiah of the year 1930, but one thing is lacking before he can be judged; his first severe horn wound. All matadors are gored dangerously, painfully, and very close to fatally, sooner or later, in their careers, and until a matador has undergone this first severe wound you cannot tell what his permanent value will be. For no matter how much he may keep of his courage you cannot tell how it will affect his reflexes. A man may be brave as the bull himself to face any danger and still, by his nerves, be unable to face that danger coldly. When a bullfighter can no longer be calm and put danger away after the fight once starts, can no longer see the bull come calmly, without having to nerve himself, then he is through as a successful bullfighter. Nerved-up bullfighting is sad to watch. The spectators do not want it. They pay to see the tragedy of the bull; not the man. Joselito was only gored badly three times and killed fifteen hundred and fifty-seven bulls, but the fourth time he was gored he was killed. Belmonte used to be wounded several times each season and none of his wounds had any effect on his courage, his passion for bullfighting, nor his reflexes. I hope the young Bienvenida boy will never be gored, but if he has been by the time this book comes out and it has made no

difference to him, then it will be time to talk about the inheritance of Joselito. Personally I do not believe he will ever be the
inheritor of Joselito. Finished as his style is and with all his
facility in everything but killing, still, watching him in action, it
seems to me to smell of the theatre. Much of his work is tricked,
it is a more subtle trick than any we have seen yet, and it is a very
pretty trick to watch; seemingly very gay and lighthearted.
But I fear very much that the first big wound will take away his
lightness and that the trickiness will then be more visible.
Bienvenida, the father, deflated as badly as Niño de la Palma did
after his first horn wound, but in breeding bullfighters perhaps
it is the way it is with bulls, and the valour may come from the
mother, and the type from the father. It is unfriendly enough to
predict a coming lack of courage, but the last time I saw it the
much advertised Bienvenida smile was very forced, and all I
can say is that I do not believe in this particular messiah.

In 1930 Manolo Bienvenida was the local redeemer of bullfighting, but by 1931 there was a new one: Domingo Lopez
Ortega. The critics of Barcelona, where the most money had
been spent on his launching, wrote that Ortega began where
Belmonte left off; that he combined the best of Belmonte and
the best of Joselito, and that in all the history of bullfighting
there had never been such a case as Ortega, nor any man who so
combined the artist, the dominator and the killer. Ortega is not
as impressive as his eulogies. He is thirty-two years old, and has
been fighting for several years in the villages of Castilla, especially those around Toledo. He comes from a town of less than
five hundred people, in the dry country between Toledo and
Aranjuez, called Borox, and his nickname is the Hayseed of
Borox. In the fall of 1930 he had a good afternoon in the
second-rate Madrid ring of Tetuan de las Victorias, which was
then directed and promoted by Domingo Gonzales, called
Dominguin, a former matador. Dominguin took him to
Barcelona and rented the ring there after the season closed to
give a fight featuring Ortega and a Mexican fighter called

Carnicerito de Mexico. Fighting young bulls, they both had good days and filled the Barcelona ring three times in succession. Skilfully built up by Dominguin during the winter months with an elaborate press campaign and ballyhoo, Ortega was made a full matador at the opening of the 1931 season in Barcelona. I arrived in Spain immediately after the revolution and found him ranking with politics as a café topic. He had not yet fought in Madrid but every night the Madrid papers published notices of his triumphs in the provinces. Dominguin was spending much money on his publicity and Ortega cut ears and tails each night in all the evening papers. The nearest he had fought to Madrid was in Toledo and I found good aficionados who had seen him there did not agree in their judgements of him. All agreed he had certain details that were well executed, but the most intelligent aficionados said they were not convinced by his work. On the 30th of May, Sidney Franklin, who had just come to Madrid after a Mexican campaign, and I went out together to Aranjuez to see the great phenomenon. He was lousy. Marcial Lalanda made a fool of him, as did Vicente Barrera.

That day Ortega showed coolness and an ability to move the cape slowly and well, holding it low, provided the bull did the commanding. He showed an ability to cut the natural voyage of the bull and double him on himself with a two-handed pass with the muleta which was very effective in punishing and he made a good one-handed pass with his right. With the sword he killed quickly and trickily, profiling with great style, and then not keeping the promise of his very arrogant way of preparing to kill when he actually made the trip in. All the rest of him was ignorance, awkwardness, inability to use his left hand, conceit, and attitudes. He had, very obviously, been reading and believing his own newspaper propaganda.

In appearance he had one of the ugliest faces you could find outside of a monkey house, a good, mature, but rather thick-jointed figure, and the self-satisfaction of a popular actor. Sidney, who knew that he himself was capable of putting up a much better fight, cursed him all the way home in the car. I wanted to judge him impartially, knowing you cannot place a bullfighter by one performance, so I noted his good qualities and his defects and kept my mind open about him.

That night when we got to the hotel the papers were out and again we read of another great triumph for Ortega. Actually he had been hooted and jeered on the last bull, but in the *Heraldo de Madrid* we read that he had cut the bull's ear after a great triumph and been carried out of the ring on the shoulders of the crowd.

Next I saw him in Madrid in his formal presentation as a full matador. He was exactly as he had been at Aranjuez except that he had lost the knack of killing quickly. Twice again in Madrid he fought without showing anything to justify his propaganda, and in addition he was beginning to have spells of cowardice. At Pamplona he was so bad he was disgusting. He was being paid twenty-three thousand pesetas a fight and he did absolutely nothing that was not ignorant, vulgar and low.

Juanito Quintana, who is one of the best aficionados in the north, had written me to Madrid about Ortega, telling how pleased they were to have gotten him for Pamplona and about the price his manager was demanding to produce him. He was very eager to see him and my account of his dismal performances in and around Madrid only depressed him for a moment. After we had seen him once though he was very disillusioned and after we had seen him three times Juanito could not stand to have his name mentioned.

During the summer I saw him several times more and only once was he good even in his fashion. That was in Toledo with hand-picked bulls which were so small and inoffensive that anything he did needed to be discounted. What he has, when he is good, is lack of movement and a serenity which is phenomenal. The best pass he makes is the two-handed one designed to cut the voyage of the bull and turn him on himself, but because he does this best he does it again and again on every bull that he gets whether the bull needs this punishment or not and consequently unfits the animal for anything else. He makes a right-handed pass with the muleta, inclining his body toward the bull, very well, but he does not link it up with other passes and he is still quite incapable of making effective natural passes with his left. He is very good at spinning between the bull's horns, a very silly business, and he is a master of all the vulgarities which are substituted for the dangerous manoeuvres in bullfighting whenever the fighter knows that the public is ignorant enough to accept them. He has plenty of courage, strength, and health, and friends whom I trust tell me he was truly very good at Valencia, and if he were younger and less conceited he could undoubtedly become an excellent matador if he were able to learn to use his left hand; he may, like Robert Fitzsimmons, violate all standards of age and still do this, but as a messiah he is non-existent. I would not devote so much space to him except that he has had so many thousand columns of paid publicity; some of it is very skilful, that I know that if I had been away from Spain and only following the fights through the papers I would have probably taken him too seriously.

One bullfighter inherited the qualities of Joselito and lost his inheritance through venereal disease. Another died of bull-fighting's other occupational disorder, and a third became a coward through the first horn wound that came to test his valour. Of the two new messiahs, Ortega does not convince me nor does Bienvenida, but I wish Bienvenida much luck. He is a well-brought-up, pleasant, not conceited boy, and he is going through a hard time.

Old lady: You are always wishing people good luck and telling them about their mistakes, and it seems to me you criticize them very meanly. How is it, young man, that you talk so much and write so long about these bullfights and yet are not a bullfighter yourself. Why did you not take up this profession if you liked it so and think you know so much about it?

Madame, I tried it in its simplest phases, but without success. I was too old, too heavy, and too awkward. Also my figure was the wrong shape, being thick in all the places where it should be lithe, and in the ring I served as little else than target or punching dummy for the bulls.

Old lady: Did they not wound you in horrible fashion? Why are you alive today?

Madame, the tips of their horns were covered or blunted or I should have been opened up like a sewing basket.

Old lady: So you fought bulls with covered horns. I had thought better of you.

Fought is an exaggeration, madame. I did not fight them, but was merely tossed about.

Old lady: Did you ever have experience with bulls with naked horns? Did they not wound you grievously?

I have been in the ring with such bulls and was un-wounded though much bruised, since when I had com-promised myself through awkwardness I would fall on to the bull's muzzle, clinging to his horns as the figure clings in the old picture of the Rock of Ages and with equal passion. This caused great hilarity among the spectators.

Old lady: What did the bull do then?

If he were of sufficient force he threw me some distance. If this did not occur I rode a distance on his head, he tossing all the while, until the other amateurs had seized his tail.

Old lady: Were there witnesses to these feats you tell of? Or do you just invent them as a writer?

There are thousands of witnesses, although many may have died since from injuries to their diaphragms or other inner parts caused by immoderate laughter.

Old lady: Was it this that decided you against bullfighting as a profession?

My decision was reached on a consideration of my physical ineptitudes, on the welcome advice of my friends, and from the fact that it became increasingly harder as I grew older to enter the ring happily except after drinking three or four absinthes, which, while they inflamed my courage, slightly distorted my reflexes.

Old lady: Then I may take it that you have abandoned the bull ring even as an amateur?

Madame, no decision is irrevocable, but as age comes on I feel I must devote myself more and more to the practice of letters. My operatives tell me that through the fine work of Mr William Faulkner, publishers now will publish anything rather than to try to get you to delete the better portions of your works, and I look forward to writing of those days of my youth which were spent in the finest whorehouses in the land amid the most brilliant society there found. I had been saving this background to write of in my old age when with the aid of distance I could examine it most clearly.

Old lady: Has this Mr Faulkner written well of these places?

Splendidly, madame. Mr Faulkner writes admirably of them. He writes the best of them of any writer I have read for many years.

Old lady: I must buy his works.

Madame, you can't go wrong on Faulkner. He's prolific too. By the time you get them ordered there'll be new ones out.

Old lady: If they are as you say, there cannot be too many.

Madame, you voice my own opinion.

Chapter 15

The cape in bullfighting was the original means of defence against the danger of the animal. Later, when the fiesta became formalized, its uses were to run the bull when he first came out, to take the bull away from the fallen picador, and to place him before the next picador who was to receive his charge, to place him in position for the banderillas, to place him in position for the matador, and to distract his attention when any bullfighter had gotten himself into a compromising position. The whole aim and culmination of the bullfight was the final sword thrust, the moment of truth, and the cape was in principle only an adjunct used to run the bull and help towards preparing that moment.

In modern bullfighting the cape has become increasingly important and its use increasingly dangerous, and the original moment of truth, or of reality, the killing, has become a very tricky business indeed. The matadors take turns in being responsible for taking the bull away from the picador and his mount and protecting the man and the horse after the bull's charge. This act of taking the bull out into the ring away from the man and horse and then, supposedly, placing him in position to charge the next picador is called the quite or removing. The matadors stand in line on the left of the horse and rider and the one who takes the bull out and away from the fallen man and horse goes to the rear of the line when he comes back from making the quite. The quite, pronounced key-tay, from being merely an act of protection for the picador, performed as quickly, as valiantly and as gracefully as possible has now become an obligation on the matador performing it after he has taken the bull out to pass the bull with the cape in whatever style he elects, but usually in veronicas, at least four times as closely, as quietly and as dangerously as he is able. A bullfighter is now judged, and paid, much more on the basis of his ability to pass the bull quietly, slowly, and closely with the cape than on his ability as a swordsman. The increasing importance and demand for the style of cape work and work with the muleta, that was invented, or perfected, by Juan Belmonte; the expectation and demand that each matador pass the bull, giving a complete performance with the cape, in the quites; and the pardoning of deficiency in killing of a matador who is an artist with the cape and muleta, are the main changes in modern bullfighting.

The present quite, as a matter of fact, has become almost as much a moment of truth as the killing ever was. The danger is so real, so controlled, and selected by the man, and so apparent, and the slightest tricking or simulating of danger shows so clearly, that the modern quites in which the matadors rival with each other in invention and in seeing with what purity of line, how slowly, and how closely they can make the horns of the bull pass their waists, keeping him dominated and slowing the speed of his rush with the sweep of the cape controlled by their wrists; the whole hot bulk of the bull passing the man, who looks down calmly where the horns almost touch, and sometimes do touch, his thighs, while the bull's shoulders touch his chest, with no move of defence against the animal and no means of defence against the death that goes by in the horns except the slow movement of his arms and his judgement of distance; these passes are finer than any cape work of the past and as emotional as anything can be. It is to have an animal that they can do this with, increasing the closeness of the horns until they touch actually the man, that the bullfighters pray for a straight-charging bull, and it is the modern cape work, supremely beautiful, supremely dangerous and supremely arrogant, that has kept bullfighting popular and increasingly prosperous through a period when all was decadence and the cape the only real moment of truth. Matadors torear with the cape now as never before, the good ones have taken Belmonte's invention of working close in the bull's territory, keeping the cape low, and using only the arms and made it even better than Belmonte did, better than Belmonte if they have a bull that suits them. There has been no decadence in bullfighting in the use of the cape. There has been not a renaissance, but a constant, steady, and complete improvement.

I will not describe the different ways of using the cape, the gaonera, the mariposa, the farol, or the older ways, the cambios de rodillas, the galleos, the serpentinas in the detail I have described the veronica, because a description in words cannot enable you to identify them before you have seen them as a photograph can. Instantaneous photography has been brought to such a point that it is silly to try and describe something that can be conveyed instantly, as well as studied, in a picture. But the veronica is the touchstone of all cape work. It is where you can have the utmost in danger, beauty, and purity of line. It is in the veronica that the bull passes the man completely and, in bullfighting, the greatest merit is in those manoeuvres where the bull passes the man in his charge. Nearly all other passes with the cape are picturesque variations of the same principle or else are more or less tricks. The one exception to this is the quite of the mariposa, or the butterfly, invented by Marcial Lalanda. This, the photograph shows clearly what it is, partakes more of the principle of the muleta than of the cape. Its merit is when it is done slowly and when the folds of the cape that correspond to the butterfly wings swing back from the bull, moved suavely rather than snatched away, while the man shifts backward from side to side. When it is done properly each backward swing of the wings of the cape is like a pase natural with the muleta and is as dangerous. I have seen no one but Marcial Lalanda do it well. The imitators, especially the steel-sinewed, leg-jittering, eagle-nosed Vicente Barrera of Valencia, do the mariposa as though they snatched the cape from under the bull's nose by electricity. There is a good reason why they do not do it slowly. If you do it slowly there is danger of death.

Originally quites were made, preferably, by the use of largas. In these the cape was fully extended and one end offered to the bull who was drawn away following the extended cape and then turned on himself to fix him in place by a movement made by the matador who would swing the cape over his shoulder and walk away. These could be executed with great elegance. Many variations were possible. Largas could be done while the man knelt and the cape could be so swung that it would wind in the air like a snake making the so-called serpentinas and other fantasies that Rafael El Gallo did so well. But in all largas the principle was that the bull followed the loose length of the cape and was finally turned on himself and fixed by a movement of the cape's end imparted to it by the man who held the opposite extremity. Their advantage was that they turned the bull less brusquely than the two-handed passes with the cape and so kept the animal in better condition to attack during the final act.

The amount of cape work that is now done with the bull by the matadors alone is, of course, very destructive to him. If the object of the fight had remained, as it was originally, simply to put the bull in the best condition for the killing, the amount that the matadors use the cape, using both hands, would be indefensible, but as bullfighting has progressed or decayed so that the killing is now only a third of the fight rather than the whole end, and the cape work and the muleta work a large two-thirds, the type of bullfighter has changed. Rarely, extremely rarely, do you get a matador who is both a great killer and a great artist with either cape or muleta. As rarely as you would get a great boxer who was also a first-rate painter. To be an artist with the cape, to use it as well as it can be used, takes an aesthetic sense that can only be a handicap to a great killer. A great killer must love to kill. He must have extraordinary courage and ability to perform two distinctly different acts with two hands at the same time, much more difficult than patting your head with one hand and rubbing your stomach with the other: he must have a primitive and all-controlling sense of honour, for there are many ways to trick the killing of bulls without going straight in on them; but above all he must love to kill. To most of the bull-fighters who are artists, starting with Rafael El Gallo and going on down through Chicuelo, the necessity to kill seems almost regrettable. They are not matadors but toreros, highly developed, sensitive manipulators of cape and muleta. They do not like to kill, they are afraid to kill, and ninety times out of a hundred they kill badly. Bullfighting has gained greatly by the art they have brought to it, and one of the great artists, Juan Belmonte, learned to kill well enough. Although he was never a great killer, he had enough of the natural killer in him to develop it and such a great pride in doing everything perfectly that he finally became acceptable and secure as a killer after being deficient for a long time. But there was always a wolf look about Belmonte, and there is nothing of the wolf in any of the other aestheticians that have developed since his time, and since they cannot kill honestly, since they would be driven out of bullfighting if they had to kill bulls as they should be killed, the public has taken to expecting and wanting the maximum they can give with the cape and the muleta, regardless of its final fitting of the bull for killing, and the structure of bull-fighting has been changed accordingly.

Madame, does all this writing of the bullfights bore you?

Old lady: No, sir, I cannot say it does, but I can only read so much of it at one time.

I understand. A technical explanation is hard reading. It is like the simple directions which accompany any mechanical toy and which are incomprehensible.

Old lady: I would not say your book is that bad, sir.

Thank you. You encourage me, but is there nothing I can do to keep your interest from flagging?

Old lady: It does not flag. It is only that I get tired sometimes.

To give you pleasure then?

Old lady: You give me pleasure.

Thank you, madame, but I mean in the way of writing or conversation.

Old lady: Well, sir, since we have stopped early today why do you not tell me a story?

About what, madame?

Old lady: Anything you like, sir, except I would not like another one about the dead. I am a little tired of the dead.

Ah, madame, the dead are tired too.

Old lady: No tireder than I am of hearing of them and I can speak my wishes. Do you know any of the kind of stories Mr Faulkner writes?

A few, madame, but told baldly, they might not please you.

Old lady: Then do not tell them too baldly.

Madame, I will tell you a couple and see how short and how far from bald I can make them. What sort of story would you like first?

Old lady: Do you know any true stories about those unfortunate people?

A few, but in general they lack drama as do all tales of abnormality, since no one can predict what will happen in the normal, while all tales of the abnormal end much the same.

Old lady: Just the same I would like to hear one. I have been reading of these unfortunate people lately and they are very interesting to me.

All right, this is a very short one, but well written it could be tragic enough, but I will not try to write it but only to tell it quickly. I was eating at the Anglo-American Press Association lunch in Paris and sat next to the man who told this story. He was a poor newspaperman, a fool, a friend of mine, and a garrulous and dull companion and he lived at a hotel too expensive for his salary. He still held his job because the circumstances which were later to demonstrate how poor a newspaperman he was had not yet arisen. He told me at lunch that he had slept very badly the night before because there had been a row going on the whole night in the room next to his at the hotel. About two o'clock someone had knocked on his door and begged to be let in. The newspaperman had opened the door and a dark-haired young man about twenty, in pyjamas and a new-looking dressing-gown came into the room crying. At first he was too hysterical to make much sense except to give the newspaperman the impression that something horrible had been narrowly averted. It seemed this young man had arrived with his friend in Paris on that day's boat train. The friend, who was a little older, he had met only recently, but they had become great friends and he had accepted his friend's invitation to come abroad as his guest. His friend had plenty of money and he had none, and their friendship had been a fine and beautiful one until tonight. Now everything in the world was ruined for him. He was without money, he would not see Europe, at this point he sobbed again, but nothing on earth would induce him to go back into that room. He was firm on this point. He would kill himself first. He really would. Just then there was another knock on the door and the friend, who was also a fine, clean-cut-looking American youth wearing an equally new and expensive-looking dressing-gown, came into the room. On the newspaperman asking him what this was all about he said it was nothing; his friend was overwrought from the trip. At this the first friend commenced crying again and said nothing on earth would make him go back in that room. He would kill himself, he said. He would absolutely kill himself. He went back, however, finally, after some very sensible reassuring pleading by the older friend and after the newspaperman had given them each a brandy and soda and advised them to cut it all out and get some sleep. The newspaperman did not know what it was all about, he said, but thought it was something funny all right, and anyway, he went to sleep himself and was next awakened by what sounded like fighting in the next room and someone saying, 'I didn't know it was that. Oh, I didn't know it was that! I won't! I won't!' followed by what the newspaperman described as a despairing scream. He hammered on the wall and the noise ceased, but he could hear one of the friends sobbing. He took it to be the same one who had sobbed earlier.

'Do you want any help?' the newspaperman asked. 'Do you want me to get someone? What's the matter in there?'

There was no answer except the sobbing by the one friend. Then the other friend said, very clearly and distinctly, 'Please mind your own business'.

The newspaperman was angry at this and thought he would call the desk and have them both thrown out of the hotel, and he would have too if they had said anything more. As it was he told them to cut it out and went back to bed. He could not sleep very well because the one friend sobbed for quite a long while but finally ceased sobbing. The next morning he saw them at breakfast outside the Café de la Paix, chatting together happily, and reading copies of the Paris *New York Herald*. He pointed them out to me a day or two later riding together in an open taxi, and I frequently saw them, after that, sitting on the terrace of the Café des Deux Magots.

Old lady: And is that all of the story? Is there not to be what we called in my youth a wow at the end?

Ah, madame, it is years since I added the wow to the end of a story. Are you sure you are unhappy if the wow is omitted?

Old lady: Frankly, sir, I prefer the wow.

Then, madame, I will not withhold it. The last time I saw the two they were sitting on the terrace of the Café des Deux Magots, wearing well-tailored clothes, looking clean-cut as ever, except that the younger of the two, the one who had said he would kill himself rather than go back in that room, had had his hair hennaed.

Old lady: This seems to me a very feeble wow.

Madame, the whole subject is feeble and too hearty a wow would overbalance it. Would you like me to relate another story?

Old lady: Thank you, sir. But this will be enough for today.

Chapter 16

You read of bulls in the old days accepting thirty, forty, fifty, and even seventy pics from the picadors, while today a bull that can take seven pics is an amazing animal, and it seems as though things were very different in those days and the bullfighters must have been such men as were the football players on the high-school team when we were still in grammar school. Things change very much and instead of great athletes only children play on the high-school teams now, and if you sit with the older men at the café you know there are no good bull-fighters now either; they are all children without honour, skill or virtue, much the same as those children who now play football, a feeble game it has become, on the high-school team and nothing like the great, mature, sophisticated athletes in canvas-elbowed jerseys, smelling vinegary from sweated shoulder pads, carrying leather headguards, their moleskins clotted with mud, that walked on leather-cleated shoes that printed in the earth along beside the sidewalk in the dusk, a long time ago.

There were always giants in those days and the bulls really did accept that many pics, the contemporary accounts prove, but the pics were different. In the oldest old days the pic had a very small steel triangular tip so wrapped and protected that only that small tip could go into the bull. The picadors received the bull with their horse straight toward him, drove the pic at him and as they held him off pivoted the horse to the left, free-ing him from the charge and letting the bull go by. A bull, even a modern bull, could accept a large number of those pics since the steel did not cut into him deeply and it was a move of address on the part of the picador rather than a deliberately sought shock and punishment.

Now, after many modifications, the pic is as the illustration represents it.* There is always dispute between bull breeders and picadors as to its form, since the form determines its deadliness and the amount of times the bull may charge against it without being ruined, both physically and in bravery.

The present pic is very destructive even though properly placed. It is especially destructive since the picador does not place it, shoot the stick it is called, until the bull has reached the horse. The bull must then make the effort of lifting the horse at the same time the man is leaning his weight on the shaft and driving the steel into the bull's neck muscle or his withers. If all of the picadors were as skilful as a few are there would be no need to let the bull reach the horse before shooting the stick. But the majority of the picadors, because it is a poorly paid occupation that leads only to concussion of the brain, are not even capable of sinking the pic into a bull properly. They rely on a lucky drive and the certain effort the bull must make in tossing horse and rider to tire the bull's neck muscles and do the work that a real picador could accomplish without losing either his horse or his seat in the saddle. The wearing of protective mattresses by the horses has made the picador's work much more difficult and hazardous. Without the mattress the bull's horn can get into the horse and he can lift him, or, sometimes, satisfied with the damage he is doing with his horn, be held off by the man's pic; with the mattress he butts into the horse, there is nothing for his horn to go into and he crashes horse and rider over in a heap. The use of the protective mattress has led to another abuse in bullfighting. Horses that are no longer killed in the ring may be offered by the horse contractor again and again. They are so afraid of the bulls and become so panic-stricken on smelling them that they are almost impossible to

* See Glossary, p. 326.

manage. The new government regulation provides that the picadors may refuse such horses and that they must be marked so that they cannot be used or offered by any horse contractor, but since the picador is so poorly paid, this regulation, too, will probably be destroyed by the propina, or tip, which makes up a regular part of the picador's income and which he accepts from the contractor for riding the animals he is given the right and duty by the government regulations to refuse.

The propina is responsible for almost every horror in bull-fighting. The regulations provide for the size, sturdiness, and fitness of the horses used in the bull ring and if proper horses are used and the picadors well trained there would be no need for any horses to be killed except accidentally and against the will of the riders as they are killed, for instance, in steeplechasing. But the enforcing of these regulations for his own protection are left to the picador as the most interested party and the picador is so poorly paid for the danger he undergoes that, for a small addition to this pay, he is willing to accept horses that make his work even more difficult and dangerous. The horse contractor must furnish or have available thirty-six horses for each fight. He is paid a fixed sum no matter what happens to his horses. It is to his interest to furnish the cheapest animals he can get and see that as few of them are used as possible.

This is about how it works out; the picadors arrive the day before the fight or in the morning of the fight at the corrals of the bull ring to choose and test the horses they are to ride. There is a piece of iron set in the stone wall of the corral that marks the minimum height at the shoulder that a horse must have to be accepted. A picador has the big saddle put on a horse, mounts, tests whether the horse minds bit and spur, backs, wheels, and riding toward the corral wall drives against it with the shaft of a pic to see if the horse is sound and solid on his feet. He then dismounts and says to the contractor, 'I wouldn't risk my life on that lousy skate for a thousand dollars'.

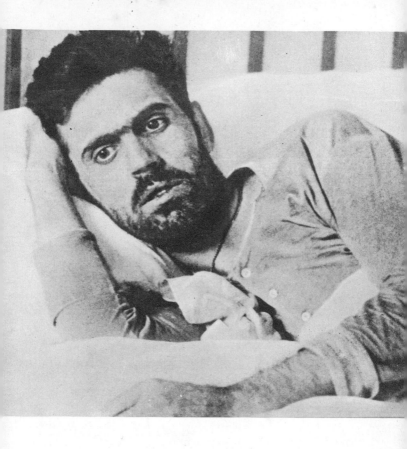

And of this. After the cornada. Varelito in the hospital.

And of these. Bull of Vicente Martinez that went alive out of the Madrid ring in 1923 when Chicuelo was unable to kill him.

These took his place. Manolo Bienvenida, Domingo Ortega, and
Marcial Lalanda making the paseo in the ring at Aranjuez. Ortega when
this photograph was taken was still an unknown novillero and acted as
sobresaliente or substitute matador for the other two.

Marcial Lalanda making the quite of the mariposa or butterfly.
Moving backward across the ring, the folds of the cape swing lightly.
It takes great skill and knowledge of bulls to do properly or at all.

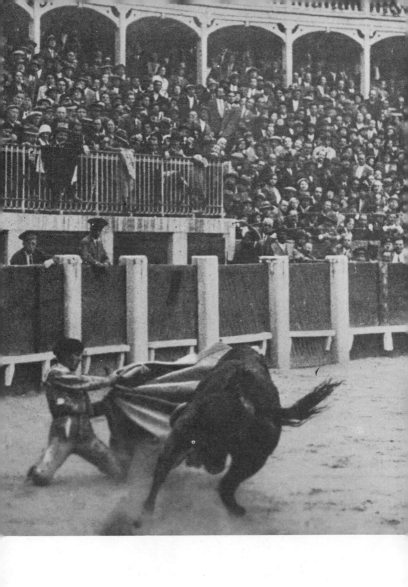

Marcial Lalanda in a cambio de rodillas made when the bull first comes into the ring.

Marcial Lalanda, most scientific and able of present fighters, watching the bull go down after an estocade.

The highly paid Cagancho often kills like this from cowardice, while in Navarra amateurs do this for fun.

Amateur fight in Pamplona.

[left] Sidney Franklin killing on the day of his debut in Sevilla and [above] the same Franklin making a veronica in the ring at Cadiz.

Good and bad killing. [left] Varelito has gone in over the horn, kept the bull's head down as he crossed with his left hand guiding the bull after the muleta and is coming out with the sword in and the bull already dead from the thrust. [above] Manolo Bienvenida is coming out before he has ever gone in and is stabbing at the bull in passing without ever bringing his body within range of the horn.

[above] Zurito killing – see how the man's whole
body will pass over the horn, the sword seems
going in an inch at a time – the bull's front legs are
doubling under him. [top right] Luis Freg killing –
his sword hand tight up against the bull – the bull's
eye controlled by the swing of the cloth at the tip
of the muleta. [right] El Espartero killing – both
the bull's front legs are off the ground – notice how
he is crossing with the left hand.

[above] What happens when the bull raises his head from the muleta when the sword is in. The horn is lifting Varelito by the neck. No man going in to kill can be certain the bull may not raise his head from the cloth while the man's body is passing the horn no matter how well controlled the muleta may be. It is this moment that gives the bull his chance at the man and it is when the man avoids this moment that he is said to assassinate the bull rather than to kill him according to rule.

[right] This, for movement, is Felix Rodriguez in a pase natural on a fast charging bull.

This, for instruction, with a certain amount of movement still, is a picador ruining a bull by pic-ing him in the ribs instead of placing the pic in the hump of muscle over his neck and shoulders.

This, to remove all tragedy, is El Gallo dedicating the last bull of his life as a bull fighter. The story is in the text.

Four of the type of incidents El Gallo avoided so assiduously while fighting bulls for thirty years as a full matador.

Half-bred bull killed in an amateur fight or capea near Madrid, but not without, first, having wet his left horn. The amateur bullfight is as unorganized as a riot and all results are uncertain, bulls or men may be killed; it is all chance and the temper of the populace. The formal bullfight is a commercial spectacle built on the planned and ordered death of the bull, and that is its end. Horses are killed incidentally. Men are killed accidentally, and in the case of full matadors, rarely. All are wounded; many of them severely and often. But in a perfect bullfight no men are wounded nor killed and six bulls are put to death in a formal and ordered manner by men who expose themselves to the maximum of danger over which their ability and knowledge will allow them to triumph without casualties. In a perfect bullfight, it may be admitted frankly, some horses will be killed as well as the bulls, since the power of the bull will allow him to reach the horse sometimes even though the picadors were completely skilful and

honourable – which they are not. But the death of the horses in the ring is
an unavoidable accident and affords pleasure to no one connected with or
viewing the fight except the bull, who derives supreme satisfaction from
it. The only practical good the death of the horse gives is in showing the
spectator the danger the man is constantly exposed to, and keeping him
reminded that the spectacle, which the grace and skill of the men engaged
in makes him take lightly, or for granted, is one of great physical peril.
Writers on the peninsula who tell of the public applauding the death of
the horses in the ring are wrong. The public is applauding the force and
bravery of the bull, which has killed those horses, not their death, which
is incidental and, to the public, unimportant. The writer is looking at the
horses and the public is looking at the bull. It is the lack of understanding
of this view-point in the public which has made the bullfight unexplain-
able to non-Spaniards.

And finally El Gallo in one of the series of delicate formal compositions that the happier part of his life in the ring consisted of. The bull, as he should be, is dead. The man, as he should be, is alive and with a tendency to smile.

[left] Maera citing the bull for the second of four pairs of banderillas he placed at Pamplona in 1924; citing for each pair from such an increasingly dangerous and seemingly impossible terrain that after the second pair the audience were all shouting together 'No! No! No! No!' begging him not to take such risks. He placed all four pairs perfectly in the manner and terrain that he chose, performed a brilliant faena, and killed the bull as well as a bull could be killed. He had not been to bed the night before, and had taken part in the amateur fight at seven o'clock that same morning.

[above] Maera in his characteristic right-handed pass made in the manner of a pase de pecho.

Ignacio Sanchez Mejias, Maera's only rival as a banderillero in difficult and impossible terrains, placing a pair and letting the bull's horn come so close that it is ripping the gold embroidery from his right trouser leg.

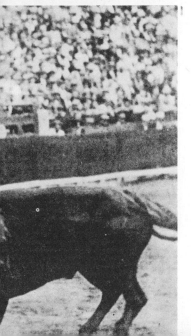

Ignacio Sanchez Mejias cheating in the placing of a pair of banderillas through having a number of capes flopping to take the bull away from the man as he places the sticks. Note, however, how well all the banderillas are placed together.

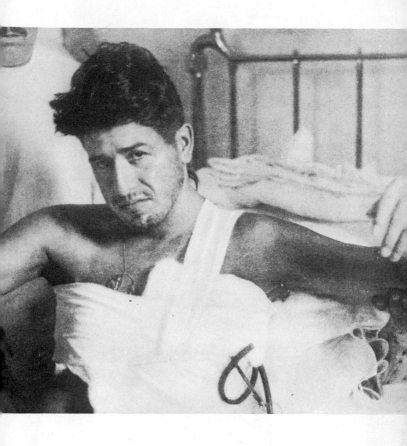

[left] The beginning of the faena. Luis Freg in the
pase de la muerte in Madrid.
[above] The end of the faena. Luis Freg in the
hospital with a cornada in his chest. Note the scar
in the left armpit, and the unplaited lock of hair
that when braided makes the pigtail that was
formerly the caste mark of a bullfighter.

Rafael Gomez y Ortega, called El Gallo, standing in the entrance to the Madrid ring with his young brother, Jose, called Joselito or Gallito, at the start of Joselito's career as a matador. El Gallo is on the left, Joselito

beside him. Fourth from the left is Enrique Berenguet, called Blanquet, the confidential banderillero of Joselito. The matador on the right is Paco Madrid of Malaga.

[left] Joselito in a pase natural at the start of his career. Note how, without any contortions, with complete naturalness, with no cork-screwing or faking, he is passing the horn past his belly; bringing the bull around controlled by the swinging end of the cloth that the man is keeping before his far eye.

[above] Joselito, at eighteen, watching a Miura bull that he has killed swaying on his legs before going over on his back, four legs in the air.

Joselito working with a difficult bull, provoking the charge with his leg; then doubling the bull on himself with the muleta, making him attempt to turn in a shorter space than his own length to tire him.

Joselito at the height of his career, working close, dominating the bull with absolute security, knowing just how much swing of the cloth will move him, controlled a step at a time, and how much more will provoke the full charge. His intelligence and security and the closeness with which he worked made all the bulls look easy to handle. Blanquet, standing by the white-marked burladero, knowing as much about bulls as Joselito, is the only one in all the audience who looks worried.

Joselito, the spring he was killed, fat and out of condition after a winter in Lima, Peru, citing an uncertain bull to charge. The bull is slow to start, and Joselito, reluctant to rise from his knees and admit his proposal to pass the bull with both knees on the ground was a failure, has just taken out his pocket handkerchief and thrown it at the bull to start him.

The bull comes and Joselito passes him with the muleta without rising from his knees or having to sway back, having calculated exactly the angle the bull will take in his charge.

Joselito taking a bull out a step at a time from the querencia or position he has taken by the barrera; talking to the bull, working on the eye farthest away from the man with the end of the cloth that he imparts a swinging, flicking motion to with his wrist; exposing his own body to give the bull confidence that there is something to charge and yet keeping the animal's point of vision on the cloth and controlling his

impulse to charge with that wrist movement. A brave bull is easy to work with if the man is brave and technically sound; it is the cowardly bull and the uncertain bull that call for most intelligent and careful handling since they will charge as fast as the brave bull but there is no way of knowing when the charge may come.

Here are the naturals of Joselito and Belmonte; the touchstones of their art. Joselito [above] is healthy, sound, natural, his physique and knowledge enabling him to keep the bull well controlled in the muleta. Belmonte [left] is natural in that there is no distortion of his body by himself, but he takes the bull from a more dangerous angle, he emphasizes his peril at the same time as his domination, and he has a sinister delicacy of movement that Joselito lacks.

Joselito dead.

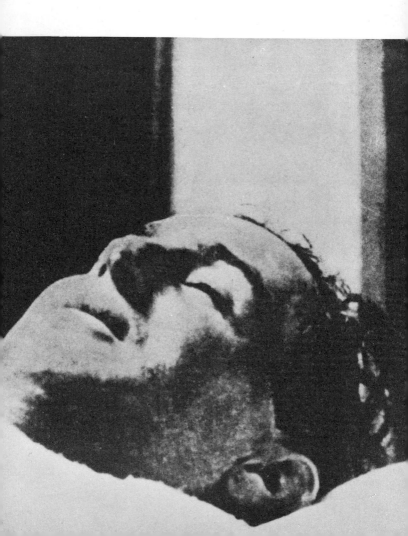

Juan Belmonte.

Last view of Juan Belmonte.

First view of Chicuelo.

Chicuelo. Who could do this.

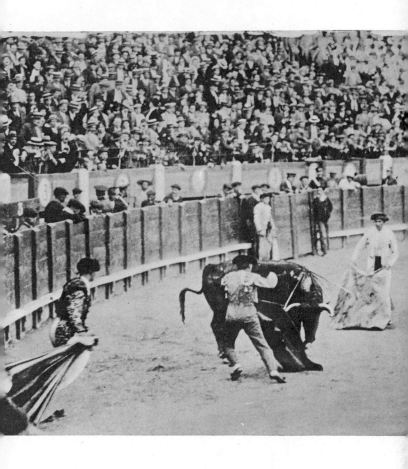

[left] Chicuelo. Who hated to kill.
[above] Chicuelo. Of the disasters.

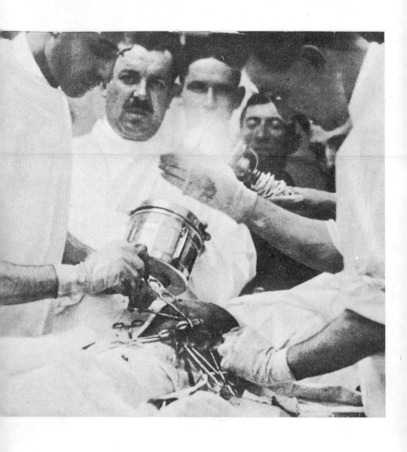

Afraid of this. Opening a cornada in the Madrid Infirmary.

Afraid of this. Vallencia II, called Chato, with a cornada in the right thigh.

And of this. Manuel Granero killed in the Madrid ring.

And of this. Granero dead in the infirmary. Only two in the crowd are thinking about Granero. The others are all intent on how they will look in the photograph.

And of this. Vicente Pastor killing in the ring at Burgos. The horn has caught him as he put in the sword because the wind has blown the muleta up and towards the man.

The seed bull. At twenty-two years the horns are splintered; the eyes are slow and all the weight has gone forward and away from where eight hundred and twenty-two sons came from to the ring so that in the end the hind-quarters are light as a calf's but all the rest is built into the bull's own monument.

The ox. While here we have the ox built for beef and for service who might have been president with that face if he had started in some other line of work. He differs from the fighting bull in this, as well as in his general shape; his hoofs are large and broad, his tail is thick and the hairs are flaxy, not silky; he is built high instead of low and there is no hump of muscle that runs from just behind his horns until the middle of his back. He may work hard all his life or he may be made into beef early in his career, but he will never kill a horse. Nor will he ever want to. Hail to the useful ox; a friend and contemporary of man.

Two fighting bulls. The hump of muscle in the neck rises in a crest when the bull is disturbed. It is his tossing muscle and when the bull carries his head as high as this one in the picture a man could not reach over the horns with a sword. This muscle must be tired for the man to kill the bull properly, and it is in the process of tiring this muscle so that a man may kill him by putting a sword in from in front high up between the bull's shoulder blades that the bullfight consists.

Zurito, from Cordoba, one of the greatest picadors who ever lived, shooting the stick a little back of where it should go, having let the bull get the horn in so he may be well pegged. The style is perfect, the execution is cynical, and the horse, who will be dead very shortly (if you look closely you may assure yourself of this), is not panicky because those knees have convinced him that he is being properly ridden. The horses, incidentally, mostly come from the United States where they are bought at the St Louis and Chicago markets at five dollars or less a head and shipped through Newport News, a shipload at a time, to Spain. The bull is rather cowardly, otherwise Zurito would not have thrown his hat to provoke a charge. Knowing the charges will be few may account for him pegging the bull farther back than would be necessary ordinarily.

Veneno, killed in the Madrid ring, pic-ing a brave bull, leaning forward on to the stick, the matadors (standing on the right) watching to see where and how the picador will fall and how the bull will turn since they must take him out and away with the capes.

This is what happens when the saddle girth breaks and the picador falls on to the horns. Chicuelo, the matador, whose face is partly hidden by the hat, seems a little late in starting in, but photographs are very tricky, and the fact the picador's hat is still on shows he has just arrived on the horns, which are unusually short. Only the right horn has penetrated.

The other matador is Juan Anllo, Nacional II, and the chances are that he will make the quite, although if the man falls from the horn when tossed and the bull sees the horse before his horn finds the man, the horse will make the quite.

Here every one is coming in to make the quite; even El Gallo, the farthest on the left, whose face shows that he does not like the look of things at all. The bull, trying to gore too fast, is bumping with his nose.

Veronica by Juan Belmonte. Having taken the bull out away from the fallen picador, the matador passes him with the cape.

Veronica to the right made by Gitanillo de Triana. This is the second movement in the process of passing the bull by veronicas.

Veronica to the left by Enrique Torres. This is the third movement in passing a bull by veronicas and the three matadors shown making the passes are, with the addition of Felix Rodriguez, the finest artists with the cape the ring has known. Belmonte has not the complete suavity and the low, slow swing of the other three, but his is the original style on which they have improved.

Gathering the cape toward him at the end of a series of veronicas to wind the bull around him like a belt, his right leg pushed toward the bull in that bent slant, which will be copied but never made truly until another genius comes in the same twisted body – the media veronica of Juan Belmonte. This pass is the end of a series of veronicas and serves to fix the bull in place and allow the man to walk away.

Juan Belmonte.

Cagancho sculpturing with the cape. Finishing a series of veronicas with a rebolera, he has turned the bull so short that he has brought him to his knees.

The gaonera as performed by its inventor, Rodolfo Gaona.

[above] Bulls fighting on the range at Colmenar.
[below] Bulls in the corral. Five sons of Diano the seed bull.

Vicente Barrera in a pase de pecho. This picture and the one opposite show the basis of the emotion in bull fighting. The emotion is given by the closeness with which the matador brings the bull past his body and it is prolonged by the slowness with which he can execute the pass.

This is Vicente Barrera in the same pass as in the photograph opposite, except that here instead of letting the horn go by his chest he has pulled away prudently so that with the danger removed man and bull do not form one group but are separate entities held together neither by emotion nor by plastic line. A position which would be artistically correct becomes ridiculous without the danger of the horns and the necessary bulk of the bull to give it dignity.

Grace and the lack of it in the ring are in this picture of Cagancho and the following one of Nicanor Villalta performing the same pass, an ayudado por alto, in their respective fashions.

Nicanor Villalta, in the pass Cagancho has made in the photograph
opposite. Villalta can be much more anti-aesthetic than this, but this
is a fair example of his praying-mantis manner.

Villalta kills, though in a way no gypsy ever killed, and it would be unfair to show how silly he looks with his feet apart and not show him leaning in after the sword.

While when he gets his feet together he will do things like this that you see here; the bull is coming by his legs, and as you watch he will spin with him so close the blood from the bull's shoulder will come off on to Villalta's belly. There is great demand for this, and only Nicanor can do it.

Here you have him spinning, and if there is no blood on his belly afterwards you ought to get your money back.

[left] Manuel Garcia, Maera. The year before he died.

[above] Maera in a pair of banderillas. Notice how the arms are raised and how straight the body is held. The straighter the body and the higher the arms the closer the bull's horn can come to the man.

'What's the matter with that horse?' says the contractor. 'You'll go a long way before you'll find a horse like that.'

'Too long a way,' says the picador.

'What's the matter with him? That's a handsome little horse.'

'He's got no mouth,' the picador says. 'He won't back. Besides he's short.'

'He's just the right size. Look at him. Just the right size.'

'Just the right size for what?'

'Just the right size to ride.'

'Not me,' says the picador turning away.

'You won't find a better horse.'

'I believe that,' says the picador.

'What's your real objection?'

'He's got glanders.'

'Nonsense. That isn't glanders. That's just dandruff.'

'You ought to spray him with flit,' says the picador. 'That would kill him.'

'What's your real objection?'

'I have a wife and three children. I wouldn't ride him for a thousand dollars.'

'Be sensible,' the contractor says. They talk in low tones. He gives the picador fifteen pesetas.

'All right,' says the picador. 'Mark up the little horse.'

So, in the afternoon you see the picador ride out the little horse, and if the little horse gets ripped, and instead of killing him, the red-jacketed bull-ring servant runs with him toward the horse gate to get him back where he can be patched up so the contractor can send him in again, you may be sure the bull-ring servant has received or been promised a propina for every horse he can bring alive out of the ring, instead of killing them mercifully and decently when they are wounded.

I have known some fine picadors, honest, honourable, brave, and in a bad business, but you may have all the horse contractors I have ever met, although some of them were nice fellows. If you wish and will take them, you may have all the bull-ring servants too. They are the only people I have found in bull-fighting that are brutalized by it and they are the only ones who take an active part who undergo no danger. I have seen several of them, two especially that are father and son, that I would like to shoot. If we ever have a time when for a few days you may shoot anyone you wish I believe that before starting out to bag various policemen, Italian statesmen, government functionaries, Massachusetts judges, and a couple of companions of my youth, I would shove in a clip and make sure of that pair of bull-ring servants. I do not want to identify them any more closely because if I ever should bag them this would be evidence of premeditation. But of all the filthy cruelty I have ever seen they have furnished the most. Where you see gratuitous cruelty most often is in police brutality; in the police of all countries I have ever been in, including, especially, my own. These two Pamplona and San Sebastian monosabios should be, by rights, policemen, and policemen on the radical squad, but they do the best they can with their talents in the bull ring. They carry on their belts puntillas, broad-headed knives, with which they can give the gift of death to any horse that is badly wounded, but I have never seen them kill a horse that could possibly be gotten on his feet and made to move toward the corrals. It is not only a question of the money they could make by salvaging horses to be taxidermed while alive so they may be reintroduced into the ring, for I have seen them refuse to kill, until forced to by the public, a horse there was no hope of getting on to his feet or of bringing back into the ring purely from pleasure in exerting their power to refuse to perform a merciful act as long as possible. Most bull-ring servants are poor devils that perform a miserable function for a mean wage, and are entitled to pity if not sympathy. If they save a horse or two that they should kill they do it with fear that outruns any pleasure and earn their money as well as the men do who pick up cigar butts, say. But these two that I speak of are both fat, well-fed, and arrogant.

I once succeeded in landing a large, heavy, one-peseta-fifty rented, leather cushion alongside the head of the younger one during a scene of riotous disapproval in a bull ring in the north of Spain and I am never at the ring without a bottle of Manzanilla which I hope yet I will be able to land, empty, on one or the other at any time rioting becomes so general that a single bottle stroke may pass unperceived by the authorities. After one comes, through contact with its administrators, no longer to cherish greatly the law as a remedy in abuses, then the bottle becomes a sovereign means of direct action. If you cannot throw it at least you can always drink out of it.

In bullfights now a good pic is not one in which the picador, pivoting, protects his horse completely. That is what it should be, but you might go a long time and never see one. All you can expect in a good pic now is that the picador will place his stick properly, that is, drive the point into the morrillo, or hump of muscle that rises from the back of the bull's neck to his shoulders, that he will try to hold the bull off and that he will not twist his pic or turn it to try and make a deep wound in the bull in order that he may lose blood and so weaken, to make the danger less for the matador.

A bad pic is one that is placed anywhere else but in the morrillo, one which rips or opens a big wound, or one in which the picador lets the bull reach the horse, then when the horn is in, pushes, drives, and twists on the pic which is in the bull and tries to give the impression he is protecting his horse when he is really only injuring the bull to no good purpose.

If picadors had to own their own horses and were well paid they would protect them and the horse part of the bullfighting would become one of the most brilliant and skilful of all rather than a necessary evil. For my own part if horses are to be killed the worse the horses are the better. For the picadors' part an old horse with big feet is much more useful to them in the way they pic now than would be a thoroughbred in good condition.

To be useful in the bull ring a horse must be either old or well-tired. It is as much to tire the horses as to provide transportation for the picadors that the animals are ridden from the ring into town to the picadors' boarding-house and back. In the provinces the bull-ring servants ride the horses in the morning to tire them. The role of the horse has become that of providing something the bull will charge so that his neck muscles will be tired and of supporting the man who receives the charge and places his pic in such a manner as to force the bull to tire those muscles. His duty is to tire the bull rather than to weaken him by wounds. The wound made by the pic is an incident rather than an end. Whenever it becomes an end it is censurable.

Used for this purpose the worst horses possible, that is those past any other usefulness, but which are solid on their feet and moderately manageable, are the best. I have seen thoroughbreds killed in their prime in other places than the bull ring, and it is always a sad and disturbing business. The bull ring is a death's business for horses and the worse horses they are the better.

As I say, having the picadors own their own horses would change the whole spectacle. But I would rather see a dozen old worthless horses killed on purpose than one good horse killed by accident.

What about the Old Lady? She's gone. We threw her out of the book, finally. A little late you say. Yes, perhaps a little late. What about the horses? They are what people always like to talk about in regard to the bullfight. Has there been enough about the horses? Plenty about the horses, you say. They like it all but the poor horses. Should we try to raise the general tone? What about higher things?

Mr Aldous Huxley, writing in an essay entitled 'Foreheads Villainous Low', commences: 'In (naming a book by this writer) Mr H. ventures, once, to name an Old Master. There is a phrase, quite admirably expressive (here Mr Huxley inserts a compliment), a single phrase, no more, about "the bitter nail-holes" of Mantegna's Christs; then quickly, quickly, appalled by his own temerity, the author passes on (as Mrs Gaskell might hastily have passed on, if she had somehow been betrayed into mentioning a water-closet), passes on, shamefacedly, to speak once more of Lower Things.

'There was a time, not so long ago, when the stupid and uneducated aspired to be thought intelligent and cultured. The current of aspiration has changed its direction. It is not at all uncommon now to find intelligent and cultured people doing their best to feign stupidity and to conceal the fact that they have received an education' – and more; more in Mr Huxley's best educated vein, which is a highly educated vein indeed.

What about that, you say? Mr Huxley scores there, all right, all right. What have you to say to that? Let me answer truly. On reading that in Mr Huxley's book I obtained a copy of the volume he refers to and looked through it, and could not find the quotation he mentions. It may be there, but I did not have the patience nor the interest to find it, since the book was finished and nothing to be done. It sounds very much like the sort of thing one tries to remove in going over the manuscript. I believe it is more than a question of the simulation or avoidance of the appearance of culture. When writing a novel a writer should create living people; people not characters. A *character* is a caricature. If a writer can make people live there may be no great characters in his book, but it is possible that his book will remain as a whole; as an entity; as a novel. If the people the writer is making talk of old masters; of music; of modern painting; of letters, or of science then they should talk of those subjects in the novel. If they do not talk of those subjects and the writer makes them talk of them he is a faker, and if he talks about them himself to show how much he knows then he is showing off. No matter how good a phrase or a simile he may have if he puts it in where it is not absolutely necessary and irreplaceable he is spoiling his work for egotism. Prose is architecture, not interior decoration, and the Baroque is over. For a writer to put his own intellectual musings, which he might sell for a low price as essays, into the mouths of artificially constructed characters which are more remunerative when issued as people in a novel is good economics, perhaps, but does not make literature. People in a novel, not skilfully constructed *characters*, must be projected from the writer's assimilated experience, from his knowledge, from his head, from his heart and from all there is of him. If he ever has luck as well as seriousness and gets them out entire they will have more than one dimension and they will last a long time. A good writer should know as near everything as possible. Naturally he will not. A great enough writer seems to be born with knowledge. But he really is not; he has only been born with the ability to learn in a quicker ratio to the passage of time than other men and without conscious application, and with an intelligence to accept or reject what is already presented as knowledge. There are some things which cannot be learned quickly, and time, which is all we have, must be paid heavily for their acquiring. They are the very simplest things and because it takes a man's life to know them the little new that each man gets from life is very costly and the only heritage he has to leave. Every novel which is truly written contributes to the total knowledge which is there at the disposal of the next writer who comes, but the next writer must pay, always, a certain nominal percentage in experience to be able to understand and assimilate what is available as his birthright and what he must, in turn, take his departure from. If a writer of prose knows enough about what he is writing about he may omit things that he knows and the reader, if the writer is writing truly enough, will have a feeling of those things as strongly as though the writer had stated them. The dignity of movement of an iceberg is due to only one-eighth of it being above water. A writer who omits things because he does not know them only makes hollow places in his writing. A writer who appreciates the seriousness of writing so little that he is anxious to make people see he is formally educated, cultured or well-bred is merely a popinjay. And this too remember: a serious writer is not to be confounded with a solemn writer. A serious writer may be a hawk or a buzzard or even a popinjay, but a solemn writer is always a bloody owl.

Chapter 17

There is no part of the fiesta that appeals to the spectator seeing bullfights for the first time as docs the placing of the banderillas. The eye of a person unfamiliar with the bullfight cannot really follow the cape work; there is the shock of seeing the horse struck by the bull and no matter how this affects the spectator he will be liable to continue to watch the horse and miss the quite that the matador has made. The work with the muleta is confusing; the spectator does not know which passes are difficult to make and, it all being new, his eye is hardly competent to distinguish one move from another. He watches the muleta as something picturesque and the killing may be done so suddenly that unless the spectator has very trained eyes he will not be able to break up the different figures and see what really happens. Often enough, too, the killing will be done so without style or sincerity, the matador making as little of it as he can in order to decrease its importance, that the spectator will have no idea of the emotion and the spectacle that a properly killed bull will give. But the placing of the banderillas he sees clearly, he follows it easily in all its details and almost invariably, when it is well done, he enjoys it.

In the banderillas he sees a man walk out carrying two slender sticks with barbed points; the first man he has seen go toward the bull without a cape in his hands. The man attracts the bull's attention, I am describing the simplest way of planting banderillas, runs toward him as the bull charges, and as bull and man come together and the bull lowers his head to hook, the man puts his feet together, raises his arms high and drives the shafts straight down into the lowered neck of the bull. That is as much of it as the spectator's eye can follow.

'Why doesn't the bull get him?' someone seeing their first fight, or even after many fights, will ask. The answer is this, the bull cannot turn in a shorter space than his own length. Therefore, if the bull charges, once the man has passed the horn he is safe. He may pass the horn by taking a course which brings him at an angle toward the bull's course, judging the moment of encounter when he puts his feet together so that the bull's head is down, sinking the sticks and pivoting on them past the horn. This is called placing them poder a poder or force to force. The man may start from a position so that he makes a quarter of a circle as he crosses the bull's charge, thus placing them al cuarteo, the commonest way, or he may stand still and await the bull's charge, the finest way of planting them, and as the bull reaches him in his charge and is about to lower his head to hook, the man lifts the right foot and sways to the left so that the bull follows the lure of his body, then sways back, brings his right foot down, and drives down the sticks. This is called placing the banderillas al cambio. It may be done, of course, to either the right or left. The way I have described it the bull would pass to the left.

There is another variation of this called al quiebro in which the man is not supposed to lift either foot, deceiving the bull and giving him the false direction with a movement of his body, the feet kept still; but I have never seen this done. I have seen many pairs of banderillas that the critics called al quiebro, but I have never seen one placed without the man raising either one foot or the other.

In all these ways of placing the banderillas there are two men with capes in different parts of the ring, in general a matador in the centre and another, either matador or banderillero, in the rear of the bull, so that when the man has planted the banderillas and passed the bull's horn, by whatever means he has chosen, the bull, as he turns to pursue him, will see a cape before he has made his turn and taken out after the man. There is a definite place in the ring that each of the two or three men with capes occupies in all of the various ways of placing banderillas. The ways I have described, the cuarteo or quarter of a circle, power-to-power and its variations, in both of which the man and bull are both running, and the cambio and its variations, in which the man stands still and awaits the bull's charge, are the usual ways of placing banderillas in which the man seeks to perform brilliantly. They are usually the ones used by the matador when he takes the banderillas himself and their effect depends upon the grace, cleanness, decision and domination that the man puts into them and the proper placing of the shafts. They should be placed high up on the top of the shoulders, well back behind the bull's neck, they should be sunk together, not spread apart, and they should not be placed where they will interfere with the sword thrust. Banderillas should never be placed in the wounds made by the picadors. A banderilla properly placed pierces the hide only and the weight of the shaft causes it to hang down the bull's flank. If it is driven in too deep it stands straight up, makes it impossible to work brilliantly with the bull with the muleta, and instead of a sharp prick that has no lasting effect it makes a painful wound that discom poses the bull and makes him un-certain and difficult. There is no manoeuvre in the bullfight which has, as object, to inflict pain on the bull. The pain that is inflicted is incidental, not an end. The object of all the man-oeuvres, in addition to giving the most brilliant spectacle, is to try to tire the bull and slow him in preparation for the killing. I believe that part of the bullfight which inflicts most pain and suffering, some of it useless, on the bull is the placing of the banderillas. Yet it is the part of the fight which causes least repugnance to American and British spectators. I believe this is because it is the easiest to follow and to understand. If all of the bullfight were as easy to follow, appreciate, understand and see the danger of as is the placing of the banderillas, the attitude of the non-Spanish world toward the bullfight might be very different. In my own time I have seen the attitude of American newspapers and popular magazines changed greatly toward bullfighting by some presentation of it, as it is, or an honest attempt at this presentation in fiction; and this before the son of a Brooklyn policeman had become a capable and popular matador.

There are, in addition to the three ways of placing banderillas that I have described, at least ten others, some of which have become obsolete, such as the man who is to place the banderillas citing the bull with a chair in one hand, seating himself as the bull charges, rising from the chair to lure the bull to one side with a feint, driving in the banderillas and then sitting again in the chair. This is almost never seen now, nor are various other ways of placing banderillas which were invented by certain bullfighters, and, being rarely executed well except by their inventors, passed into disuse.

Bulls that take up a querencia against the barrera cannot be banderilla-ed by the use of the quarter-or the half-circle method of running across the line of the bull's charge, placing the sticks as the man's line of movement crosses that of the bull's, since the man after passing the horn would be caught between the bull and the barrier, and such bulls must be banderilla-ed on this bias or al sesgo. In this manoeuvre, the bull being against the barrera, one man should be in the passageway with a cape to attract the bull's attention until the man who is to place the banderillas starts at an angle, from farther down the barrera, plants his banderillas as he passes the bull's head, without stopping, as best he can. Often he has to vault the barrera if the bull takes after him. There is a man farther out in the ring with a cape to try to pick the bull as he turns but, since bulls that necessitate this manoeuvre are usually those that are liable to make for the man rather than the lure, often the man with the cape is comparatively useless.

Bulls which will not charge, or in charging cut in on the man, or those which are nearsighted, are banderilla-ed by what is called the media-vuelta or half-turn. In this way of placing, the banderillero comes close behind the bull, calls the bull's attention and, as the bull revolves toward the man and drops his head to hook, the man, who is already in motion, drives in the banderillas.

This is only an emergency method of placing them, since it violates the principle of the bullfight that the man should, in accomplishing any manoeuvres with the bull, approach him from the front.

Another way of placing the banderillas that you still sometimes see is what is called a relance; that is when the bull is still running and tossing after the placing of a pair of banderillas the man takes advantage of this running, as distinct from a charge he has provoked deliberately, to cut in on it in a half-or quarter-circle and place another pair.

The matador usually takes the banderillas himself when he thinks the bull is one that he can perform brilliantly with. In former times a matador took the banderillas only when the crowd asked him to. Now placing the banderillas is a part of the regular repertoire of all matadors who have the necessary physique and who have taken the time to learn to banderillear well. In the preparation of the bull alone, sometimes drawing the bull on by running backwards in zig-zags, these sudden shifts of direction being the defence of a man on foot against the bull, seeming to play with him while they place him where they want him, then challenging him arrogantly, walking steadily and slowly toward him and then when the charge comes either awaiting it or running in to meet it, a matador has an opportunity to impress his personality and his style on all that he does in this third of the fight. A banderillero, however, even though he might be more skilful than his master, has only one instruction, aside from advice as to where to place them in the animal, to put them in quickly and properly so that the bull will be delivered as soon and in the best condition possible to his master, the matador, for the last and final act. Most banderilleros are good at placing the sticks from either one side or the other. It is very rarely that a man is able to banderillear properly from both sides. For this reason a matador will carry one banderillero who is best on the right and another who is good on the left.

The best banderillero I have ever seen was Manuel Garcia Maera. He, with Joselito and Rodolfo Gaona, the Mexican, were the greatest of modern times. A peculiar thing is the overwhelming excellence of all Mexican bullfighters with the banderillas. For the last few years, each season there have come to Spain from three to six unknown Mexican apprentice bullfighters, any one of whom is as good as or better than the best artists with the banderillas in Spain. They have a style in their preparation and execution and an emotional quality that comes from the unbelievable chances they take, that are, except for the Indian coldness of the rest of their work, the mark and characteristics of Mexican bullfighting.

Rodolfo Gaona was one of the greatest bullfighters that ever lived. He was produced under the régime of Don Porfirio Diaz, and worked in Spain exclusively during the years when the fights were suspended while Mexico was in revolution. He modified his early style in imitation of Joselito and Belmonte and competed with them on almost equal terms during the season of 1915; on equal terms in 1916, but after that a horn wound and an unfortunate marriage ruined his career in Spain. He was steadily worse in his performances as a fighter while Joselito and Belmonte improved. The pace, he was not as young as they were, the new style, and his loss of morale caused by domestic difficulties were too much for him and he returned to Mexico where he dominated all other bullfighters and served as a model for all the present crop of elegant Mexicans. Most of the youngest Spanish bullfighters have never seen either Joselito or Belmonte, only their imitators, but the Mexicans have all seen Gaona. In Mexico he was also the master of Sidney Franklin and Franklin's style with the cape, which so puzzled and amazed Spaniards when he first appeared, was formed and influenced by Gaona. Mexico is producing now, during another period without civil war, a quantity of bull-fighters who may become great if the bulls leave anything of them. The arts never flourish much in wartime, but with Mexico at peace the art of bullfighting is flourishing now to a greater degree in Mexico than in Spain. The difficulty is the difference in size, temperament, and nerve of the Spanish bulls which, when the young Mexicans come to Spain, they are not used to, and so are, often after the most brilliant work, caught and gored not through any defects in their technique, but simply because they are working with animals more nervous, powerful, and difficult to judge than those of their own country. You cannot have a great bullfighter that is not gored sooner or later, but if you gore him too early, too often and too young he will never be the bullfighter he might have been if the bulls had respected him.

When you judge the placing of a pair of banderillas the thing to notice is how high the man raises his arms when he puts in the sticks, since the higher he raises them the closer he lets the bull come to his body. Notice too the amount of circle or cuarteo he uses to cut across the bull's charge, the more he cuarteos the safer it is. In a really good pair the man puts his feet together as he raises his hands, and in the cambios and so-called quiebros you should watch how well he waits and how close he lets the bull come before he shifts his feet. The merits of banderillas placed from the barrera depend entirely on whether the man-oeuvre is tricked or not by capes flung over from behind the barrera to attract the bull's attention. When working in the centre of the ring the man, when he comes toward the bull, has two men with capes some distance away on each side, but they are to distract the bull if he pursues the man after the sticks are planted. When placing banderillas from against the barrera it may be necessary to flop a cape over after the banderillas have been placed, to protect the man if he has gotten into an impossible position. But a cape flopped over each time at the moment of placing means that it is only a trick.

Among the actual matadors the best performers with the banderillas are Manolo Mejias ('Bienvenida'), Jesús Solorzano, José Gonzalez ('Carnicerito de Mexico'), Fermin Espinosa ('Armillita II'), and Heriberto Garcia. Antonio Márquez, Félix Rodríguez, and Marcial Lalanda are very interesting with the banderillas. Lalanda sometimes puts in excellent pairs, but he usually makes much too big a quarter of a circle past the bull's head, Márquez has difficulty dominating and placing the bull, and when he puts the banderillas in close to the barrera almost always has the bull tricked into driving his horns against the wood to make him shy of the barrier and, at the time he is driving in his pair, has a peon flop a cape over the barrier to distract the bull while he makes his escape. Félix Rodríguez is a splendid banderillero, but has been ill and lacks the necessary physical strength to banderillear well. When he is at his best he is perfect.

Fausto Barajas, Julián Saiz ('Saleri II'), and Juan Espinoza ('Armillita') were excellent banderilleros, but are on the decline. Saleri may have retired by the time this is published. Ignacio Sanchez Mejias was a very great banderillero, who has also retired as a matador, but his style was heavy and graceless.

There are half a dozen young Mexicans who are as good as any of these matadors who by the time this book is published, may be dead, ruined or famous.

Of banderilleros working as peons under the orders of matadors the best with the sticks that I know are Luis Suárez, 'Magritas', Joachim Manzanares, 'Mella', Antonio Duarte, Rafael Valera, 'Rafaellillo', Mariano Carrato, Antonio Garcia, 'Bombita IV', and with the cape Manuel Aguilar, 'Rerre', and Bonifacio Perea, 'Boni', Bienvenida's peon de confianza or confidential banderillero. The greatest peon with the cape that I ever saw was Enrique Berenguet, 'Blanquet'. The best banderilleros are often men who have wanted to be matadors, but

having failed in their trials with the sword have resigned themselves to the position of working for wages in a cuadrilla. They
often know more about bulls than the matador they are working for, and often have more personality and style, but they are
in a servile position and must be careful not to take away any
of the attention from their chief. The only man in bullfighting
who really makes money is the matador. This is right in that he
takes the responsibility and runs the greatest danger of death,
but good picadors, who receive only two hundred and fifty
pesetas, and banderilleros who are paid two hundred and fifty
to three hundred, are ridiculously underpaid if the matador is
receiving ten thousand pesetas and over. If they are not good at
their trade they are a definite liability to the matador and are
expensive at any price, but as it is, no matter how good they
become at their profession, they cannot become more than
day labourers compared to the matadors. The very best banderilleros and picadors are in great demand and a half-dozen
of each may have as many as eighty fights in a season, but there
are many good and capable ones who make a bare living. They
are organized into a syndicate and matadors must pay them a
minimum wage; this varies depending on the matador's ranking; they are divided into three categories according to the
price they receive for fighting; but there are many more banderilleros than there are opportunities to fight and a matador
may get them at any price he wishes, if he is mean enough, by
making them sign a note for a certain amount of the money
they should receive and holding out this amount when he pays
them. In spite of how badly paid a profession it is these men
keep on, living always close to hunger, from the illusion that
they may make a living from the bulls and from the pride of
being fighters.

Banderilleros are sometimes lean, brown, young, brave, skilful, and confident; more of a man than their matador, perhaps
deceiving him with his mistress, making what seems to them a
good living; enjoying the life; other times they are respectable

fathers of families, wise about bulls, fat but still fast on their feet, small business men with the bulls as their business; other times they are rough, unintelligent, but brave and capable, lasting like ballplayers, as long as their legs hold out; others may be brave but unskilful, eking out a living, or they may be old and intelligent but with their legs gone, sought out by young fighters for their authority in the ring and their skill at placing bulls correctly.

Blanquet was a very small man, very serious and honourable, with a Roman nose and an almost grey face, who had the greatest intelligence of the bullfight I have ever seen and a cape that seemed magic in correcting the faults of a bull. He was the confidential peon of Joselito, Granero, and Litri, all of whom were killed by bulls, and to none of whom his cape, so providential always when needed, was of any use on the days when they were killed. Blanquet himself died of a heart attack coming on in a hotel room after he had left the ring and before he had changed his clothes to bathe.

Of the banderilleros working now, the one with the most style with the sticks is probably Magritas. There is no one with the cape who has the style Blanquet had. He handled the cape with one hand with the same sort of delicacy that Rafael El Gallo did, but with the skilful, self-effacing modesty of a peon. It was watching the interest and activities of Blanquet at moments when nothing particular seemed to be happening that I learned the profundity of unseen detail in the fighting of any single bull.

Do you want conversation? What about? Something about painting? Something to please Mr Huxley? Something to make the book worth while? All right, this is the end of a chapter, we can put it in. Well, when Julius Meier-Graefe, the German critic, came to Spain he wanted to see the Goyas and Velasquezes to have publishable ecstasies about them, but he liked the Grecos better. He was not content to like Greco better; he had to like him alone, so he wrote a book proving what poor painters Goya and Velasquez were in order to exalt Greco, and the yardstick that he chose to judge these painters by was their respective paintings of the crucifixion of Our Lord.

Now it would be hard to do anything stupider than this because of the three only Greco believed in Our Lord or took any interest in His crucifixion. You can only judge a painter by the way he paints the things he believes in or cares for, and the things he hates; and to judge Velasquez, who believed in costume, and in the importance of painting as painting, by a portrait of a nearly naked man on a cross who had been painted, Velasquez must have felt, very satisfactorily in the same position before, and in whom Velasquez took no interest at all, is not intelligent.

Goya was like Stendhal; the sight of a priest could stimulate either of those good anti-clericals into a rage of production. Goya's crucifixion is a cynically romantic, wooden oleograph that could serve as a poster for the announcement of crucifixions in the manner of bullfight posters. A crucifixion of six carefully selected Christs will take place at five o'clock in the Monumental Golgotha of Madrid, government permission having been obtained. The following well-known, accredited and notable crucifiers will officiate, each accompanied by his cuadrilla of nailers, hammerers, cross-raisers, and spade-men, etc.

Greco liked to paint religious pictures because he was very evidently religious and because his incomparable art was not then limited to accurate reproducing of the faces of the noblemen who were his sitters for portraits, and he could go as far into his other world as he wanted, and, consciously or unconsciously, paint saints, apostles, Christs, and Virgins with the androgynous faces and forms that filled his imagination.

One time in Paris I was talking to a girl who was writing a fictionalized life of El Greco, and I said to her, 'Do you make him a maricón?'

'No,' she said. 'Why should I?'

'Did you ever look at the pictures?'

'Yes, of course.'

'Did you ever see more classic examples anywhere than he painted? Do you think that was all accident or do you think all those citizens were queer? The only saint I know who is universally represented as built that way is San Sebastian. Greco made them all that way. Look at the pictures. Don't take my word for it.'

'I hadn't thought of that.'

'Think it over,' I said, 'if you are writing a life of him.'

'It's too late now,' she said. 'The book is done.'

Velasquez believed in painting in costume, in dogs, in dwarfs, and in painting again. Goya did not believe in costume, but he did believe in blacks and in greys, in dust and in light, in high places rising from plains, in the country around Madrid, in movement, in his own cojones, in painting, in etching, and in what he had seen, felt, touched, handled, smelled, enjoyed, drunk, mounted, suffered, spewed-up, lain-with, suspected, observed, loved, hated, lusted, feared, detested, admired, loathed, and destroyed. Naturally no painter has been able to paint all that but he tried. El Greco believed in the city of Toledo, in its location and construction, in some of the people who lived in it, in blues, greys, greens and yellows, in reds, in the Holy Ghost, in the communion and fellowship of saints, in painting, in life after death and death after life, and in fairies. If he was one he should redeem, for the tribe, the prissy exhibitionistic, aunt-like, withered old maid moral arrogance of a Gide; the lazy, conceited debauchery of a Wilde who betrayed a generation; the nasty, sentimental pawing of humanity of a Whitman and all the mincing gentry. Viva El Greco, el Rey de los Maricónes.

Chapter 18

The ability of a bullfighter with the muleta is what, in the end, determines his ranking in the profession, for it is the most difficult of all the phases of modern bullfighting to dominate and is the part of the bullfight where the genius of a matador has greatest latitude for expression. It is with the muleta that a reputation is made, and it is by the extent of this ability to give a complete, imaginative, artistic, and emotional performance with the muleta, granted that he has a good bull, that a bullfighter is paid much or little. To draw a brave bull in Madrid, have him come in ideal condition to the final act and then, through a limited repertoire, not be able to take advantage of his bravery and nobility to make a brilliant faena finishes a bullfighter's chance of a successful career. For bullfighters are now categoried, classed, and paid, strangely enough, not by what they actually do, for the bull may upset their performance, they themselves may be ill, they may not be altogether recovered from a horn wound, or they may simply have offdays; but by what they are capable of doing under most favourable conditions. If the spectators know the matador is capable of executing a complete, consecutive series of passes with the muleta in which there will be valour, art, understanding and, above all, beauty and great emotion, they will put up with mediocre work, cowardly work, disastrous work because they have the hope sooner or later of seeing the complete faena; the faena that takes a man out of himself and makes him feel immortal while it is proceeding, that gives him an ecstasy that is, while momentary, as profound as any religious ecstasy; moving all the people in the ring together and increasing in emotional intensity as it proceeds, carrying the bullfighter with it, he playing on the crowd through the bull and being moved as it responds in a growing ecstasy of ordered, formal, passionate, increasing disregard for death that leaves you, when it is over, and the death administered to the animal that has made it possible, as empty, as changed, and as sad as any major emotion will leave you.

A bullfighter who can do a great faena is at the top of his profession as long as he is believed capable of still doing it, if the conditions are favourable; but a bullfighter who has shown his inability to do a great faena with the conditions right, who is lacking in artistry and genius with the muleta even though he be brave, honourable, skilful, and not lacking in knowledge of his work, will always be one of the day labourers of bullfighting and paid accordingly.

It is impossible to believe the emotional and spiritual intensity, and pure, classic beauty that can be produced by a man, an animal, and a piece of scarlet serge draped over a stick. If you do not choose to believe it possible and want to regard it all as nonsense you may be able to prove you are right by going to a bullfight in which nothing magical occurs; and there are many of them; enough always so you will be able to prove it to your own satisfaction. But if you should ever see the real thing you would know it. It is an experience that either you will have in your life or you will never have. However, there is no way you can be sure you will ever see a great faena in bullfighting unless you go to many bullfights. But if you ever do see one, finished by a great estocada, you will know it, and there will be many things you will forget before it will be gone.

Technically, the muleta is used to defend the man from the charge of the bull, to regulate the carriage of the bull's head, to correct a tendency he may have to hook to one side or the other, to tire him and place him in position for killing, and, in killing, to furnish an object for him to charge in place of the man's body as the matador goes in on him with the sword.

The muleta is, in principle, held in the left hand and the sword in the right, and passes made with the muleta in the left hand are of greater merit than those made with it in the right, since when it is held in the right hand, or in both hands, it is spread wide by the sword, and the bull having a larger lure to charge may pass farther from the man's body and also, by the swing of the larger lure, be sent away to a greater distance before recharging; thus allowing the man more time to prepare his next pass.

The greatest pass with the muleta, the most dangerous to make and the most beautiful to see, is the natural. In this the man faces the bull with the muleta held in his left hand, the sword in his right, the left arm hanging naturally at his side, the scarlet cloth dropping in a fold over the stick that supports it, and which the man holds as you see in the picture. The man walks toward the bull and cites him with the muleta and as he charges the man simply sways with the charge, swinging his left arm ahead of the bull's horns, the man's body following the curve of the charge, the bull's horns opposite his body, the man's feet still, he slowly swings his arm holding the cloth ahead of the bull and pivots, making a turn of a quarter-circle with the bull. If the bull stops the man may cite him again, and describe another quarter of a circle with him, and again, and again, and again. I have seen it done six successive times; the man seeming to hold the bull with the muleta as though by magic. If the bull instead of stopping with the charge, and what stops him is a final flick the man gives the lowest end of the cloth at the end of each pass, and the great twist that has been given his spinal column through the curve the matador has forced him to describe in bending him around, turns and recharges, the man may get rid of him by a pase de pecho, or pass past the chest. This is the reverse of the pase natural. Instead of the bull coming from in front and the man moving the muleta slowly before his charge, in the pase de pecho the bull, having turned, comes from behind or from the side, and the man swings the muleta forward, lets the bull go past the man's chest and sends him away with the sweep of the folds of scarlet cloth. The chest pass is the most impressive when it completes a series of naturals or when it is forced by an unexpected return and charge of the bull and is used by the man to save himself rather than as a planned manoeuvre. The ability to execute a series of naturals and then to finish them off with the chest pass mark a real bullfighter.

First it takes courage to cite the bull for a true natural when there are so many other passes in which the bullfighter exposes himself less; it takes serenity to await the arrival of the bull with the unspread muleta low in the left hand, knowing that if he does not take the small lure offered he will take the man, then it takes great ability to move the muleta ahead of his charge, keeping him well centred in it, the elbow straight as the arm moves, swinging straight, and to follow the curve with the body without moving the location of the feet. It is a difficult pass to make properly four times in succession before a mirror in a drawing-room without any bull being present, and if you make it seven times you will be dizzy enough. There are many bullfighters who never learn to make it presentably at all. To do it well, without contortion, keeping the lines of the figure with the horn of the bull so close to the man's waist that they would only have to move up an inch or two to gore, controlling the bull's charge by the movement of arm and wrist and keeping him centred in the cloth, stopping him with the wrist flick at just the proper moment, repeating this three or four or five times takes a bullfighter and an artist.

The natural can be tricked by doing it with the right hand, the muleta spread wide with the sword and the man gyrating on his feet so that the bull follows a sort of half spin made by man and muleta rather than a slowly moved arm and wrist. There are many passes made with the right hand that are of positive merit, but in almost all the sword with its point pricked into the cloth and the hilt held in the same hand with the stick enlarges the spread of the muleta, and by giving it greater extent enables the bullfighter to pass the bull farther from his body if he wishes. He may pass him close, but he has a means of passing him farther away in case of necessity that the man working with the muleta in his left hand does not possess.

Aside from the natural and the pecho, the principal passes with the muleta are the ayudados, passes made with sword pricked into the muleta and the two held in both hands. These passes are either called por alto or por bajo, depending on whether the muleta passes over the bull's horns or is swung below the bull's muzzle.

All passes and half passes, that is those in which the bull does not completely pass the man, made with the muleta have a definite purpose. Nothing so punishes a bull that is strong and willing to charge as a series of naturals which at the same time that they are twisting and tiring him make him follow the lure and the man with his left horn, training him to take the direction the man wants him to take as he later goes in to kill. A bull whose neck muscles have not been sufficiently tired and who carries his head high, will after a series of ayudados por alto – passes made with the muleta and sword held in both hands and the muleta held high so that the bull drives up after it as he goes by the man – have his muscles tired so the head will be much lower. If he is tired and carries his head too low the matador can bring it up, temporarily, with the same pass if he modifies it and does not wait for the carriage of the head to fall again before he goes in to kill. The low passes, made with a swing and a sharp twist of the muleta, sometimes a slow-drawing swing and flip of the lower part of the cloth, and the quick chops back and forth are for bulls that are still too strong on their feet or difficult to fix in one spot. They are made from in front of bulls that will not pass, and the merit of the bullfighter consists in his foot-work in never losing his place at the head of the animal, never retreating more than he needs to, and with the movements of his muleta dominating the animal, making him turn sharply on himself, wearing him down quickly, and fixing him in position. A bull that will not pass, that is charge from a certain distance with sufficient force so that if the man remains still and moves the muleta properly the bull will pass him entirely, is either a cowardly bull or a bull who has been so used in the fight that he has lost all buoyancy and will no longer attack. A skilful matador can by a few passes that he forces at close range and is careful to keep suave, not turning the bull too much on himself or twisting his legs, make the cowardly bull believe that the muleta is not a punishment; that he will not be hurt if he charges and convert the cowardly bull into the semblance of a brave bull by giving him confidence. In the same way, by working delicately and wisely, he can light up the bull that has lost his charging ability and bring him out of his defence and into the offensive again. To do this a bullfighter must take great chances, as the only way to give a bull confidence, to force him to charge when he is on the defensive and to master him, is to work as close to him as you can get, leave him just enough of his own terrain to stand on, as Belmonte puts it, and in provoking the charge from such close range the bullfighter has no way to avoid being caught if he guesses wrong and no time to prepare his passes. His reflexes must be perfect and he must know bulls. If at the same time he is graceful you may be sure that grace is an altogether inherent quality and not a pose. You may be able to pose as the horns approach from a distance, but there is no time to pose when you are between them, or shifting back and forth to a little place of safety at the corner of his neck, as by giving him the muleta on one side and then withdrawing it, pricking him with the point of the sword or the muleta stick to make him turn, you wear him down, or light him up when he does not want to charge.

There is a whole school of bullfighting in which grace is developed until it is the one essential, and the passing of the horn past the man's belly eliminated as far as possible, which was inaugurated and developed by Rafael El Gallo. El Gallo was too great and sensitive an artist to be a complete bullfighter, so he gradually avoided, as much as possible, those parts of the bullfight which had to do with or were capable of bringing on death, either of the man or the bull, but most especially of the man. In this way he developed a way of working with the bull in which grace, picturesqueness, and true beauty of movement replaced and avoided the dangerous classicism of the bullfight as he found it. Juan Belmonte took such of Gallo's inventions as he wanted and combined them with the classic style and then developed the two into his own great revolutionary style. Gallo was as much of an inventor as was Belmonte, he had more grace, and if he would have had the cold, passionate, wolf-courage of Belmonte there could never have been a greater bullfighter. The nearest you come to that combination was Joselito, his brother, and his only fault was that everything in bullfighting was so easy for him to do that it was difficult for him to give it the emotion that was always supplied by Belmonte's evident physical inferiority, not only to the animal he was facing but to everyone who was working with him and most of them who were watching him. Watching Joselito was like reading about D'Artagnan when you were a boy. You did not worry about him finally because he had too much ability. He was too good, too talented. He had to be killed before the danger ever really showed. Now the essence of the greatest emotional appeal of bullfighting is the feeling of immortality that the bullfighter feels in the middle of a great faena and that he gives to the spectators. He is performing a work of art, and he is playing with death, bringing it closer, closer, closer, to himself, a death that you know is in the horns because you have the canvas-covered bodies of the horses on the sand to prove it. He gives the feeling of his immortality, and, as you watch it, it becomes yours. Then when it belongs to both of you, he proves it with the sword.

When you have a bullfighter to whom bullfighting is as easy

as it was to Joselito he cannot give the feeling of danger that Belmonte gave. Even if you saw him killed it would not be you who would be killed, it would be more like the death of the gods. Gallo was something entirely different. He was pure spectacle. There was no tragedy in it, but no tragedy could replace it. But it was only good if he did it. His imitators only showed how unsound it all was.

One of Gallo's inventions was the pase de la muerte or the pass of the dead one. He used this pass to start his faenas and it has been adopted by most bullfighters as the first pass in almost any faena. It is the one pass in bullfighting that any person who could dominate his nerves enough to see the bull approach could learn to make, yet it is tremendously effective to see. The matador goes out toward the bull and cites him, standing in profile, the muleta, spread by the sword, held in both hands, at the height of his waist somewhat as a baseball player holds his bat when facing the pitcher. If the bull does not charge the matador advances two or three strides and again stands still, his feet together, the muleta spread wide. When the bull charges the man stands still as though he were dead until the bull reaches the muleta, then he raises it slowly and the bull goes by him, usually going up in the air after the muleta, so that you see the man standing straight still and the bull going up into the air at an angle, his impetus then carrying him away from the man. It is easy and safe to make because it is usually given in the direction of the natural querencia of the bull, so that he goes by as though going to a fire, and because, instead of a small lure of scarlet cloth as in the natural on which the man must focus the bull's attention, a great spread like a jib is offered to the bull and he sees it instead of the man. He is not dominated and controlled, his charge is merely taken advantage of.

Gallo, too, was a master of gracious passes made before the bull's horns, passes made with both hands, changing the muleta from one hand to the other, sometimes behind his back, passes that started as though they were to be naturals and instead, the man spinning round, the muleta wrapping itself around him and the bull following the spinning loose end of it; others in which the man turned on himself, getting close to the bull's neck and winding him around him, passes made kneeling, using both hands on the muleta to swing the bull around in a curve; all passes that needed a great knowledge of the bull's mentality and great confidence to make safely, but that, with that knowledge and confidence, were beautiful to see and very satisfactory to Gallo to make although they were the negation of true bullfighting.

Chicuelo is a present-day bullfighter who possesses much of Gallo's repertoire of working before the face of the bull. Vicente Barrera does them all too, but his nervous footwork and his electric speed of execution give no idea of the pure grace of Gallo or the skill of Chicuelo, although Barrera is improving his style and execution greatly.

All this flowery work is for bulls that will not pass or for the second part of a faena, for the matador to show his domination of a bull and his inventive grace. To work only at the head of a bull that will pass, no matter how effectively, gracefully or with what invention it is done, is to deprive the spectators of the real part of bullfighting, the man deliberately passing the bull's horns as close and as slowly as he can past his own body and to substitute a series of graceful tricks, valuable as ornaments to a faena, for the sincere danger of the faena itself.

The present-day bullfighter who dominates the bulls most completely with his muleta, who masters them quickest whether they are brave or cowardly and then executes most often all the classic and dangerous passes, the natural with the left hand and the pase de pecho which are the base of sincere bullfighting, and yet is excellent in the picturesque and graceful work before the bull's horns is Marcial Lalanda. At the start of his career his style was faulty, he twisted and corkscrewed with the cape, and his naturals were not at all natural but forced, made very much on the bias, and affected looking. He has steadily improved his style, until it is now excellent with the muleta, he has become much more robust in health, and with his great knowledge of bulls, and his very great intelligence he can give an adequate and interesting performance with any bull that comes out of the toril. He has lost most of the apathy that was his first characteristic, he has been gored severely three times, and it has given him more rather than less courage, and his seasons of 1929, 1930, and 1931 were those of a great bullfighter.

Manuel Jiminez, Chicuelo, and Antonio Márquez are each capable of giving a complete, pure, and classical faena with the muleta when the bull is without difficulty and the man able to conquer his nerves. Félix Rodríguez and Manolo Bienvenida are both masters with the muleta, able to reduce a difficult bull and profit by the candour and bravery of an easy bull, but Rodríguez has not been well and Bienvenida, as I explained in another chapter, should not really be judged until his ability to dominate his nerves and reflexes after his first serious wounding has been proven. Vicente Barrera is an able dominator of bulls with a tricky style in all of the passes in which the bull goes completely by the man, but he is steadily improving his way of working, and he may, if he keeps on, become a very satisfactory performer. He has in him the ability to be a great bullfighter. He has talent, a natural sense of bullfighting, and ability to see the fight as a whole, extraordinary reflexes, and a good physique, but he had for a long time such an overwhelming conceit that it was easier for him to subsidize a press to praise his defects than it was for him to face those defects and correct them. He is at best in the picturesque work at the face of the bull and especially in one particular ayudado por bajo in which he imitates Joselito, where the sword and muleta are held together pointed straight down and the man turns the bull with a slightly ridiculous but delicate lifting motion as though he were with extended hands together stirring a great kettle of soup with a furled umbrella.

Joaquín Rodríguez, called Cagancho, is a gipsy who is the

inheritor of Gallo as far as grace, picturesqueness and panics go, but in no sense inherits Gallo's great knowledge of bulls and of the principles of bullfighting. Cagancho has statuesque grace, majestic slowness and suavity of movement, but faced by a bull which will not allow him to put his feet together and prepare his passes he shows he has no resources and if the bull deviates at all from mechanical perfection, the gipsy becomes panic stricken and will get no closer to the animal than the tip of his muleta held at the greatest distance possible from his body. He is a bullfighter who, if you should happen to see him with a bull he had confidence in, could give you an afternoon you would not forget, but you might see him seven successive times and have him act in a way that would disgust you thoroughly with bullfighting.

Francisco Vega de los Reyes, called Gitanillo de Triana, is a cousin of Cagancho who can be very good with the cape, and while he lacks Cagancho's grace with the muleta is much more able and courageous with it, although his work is fundamentally unsound. While he is doing a faena he seems unable to get rid of the bull properly, to send him far enough with each pass so that, as he turns, he does not cut back in too quickly and so is constantly getting the bull on top of him when he wants him least and has been gored many times through his own awkwardness. Like Chicuelo and Márquez he is not well nor strong, and while there is no reason for the public to excuse a highly paid performer on the grounds of his health, since there is no law which requires him to fight bulls unless he is in condition to do so, yet the physical condition of a bullfighter is one of the things that must be taken into account in judging his work critically even though he has no right to evoke it as excuse to the paying spectator. Gitanillo de Triana is cheerfully brave and naturally honourable in the ring, but the confident unsoundness of his technique gives you a feeling that he may be gored at any time while you are watching him.

Since writing that about Gitanillo de Triana I saw him

destroyed by a bull in Madrid on Sunday afternoon, 31st May 1931. It had been over a year since I had seen him fight and on the way to the ring in a taxi I wondered if he would be changed and how much I should have to revise what I had written about him. He came out in the paseo with long-legged easy swing, dark-faced, better looking than he had been before and smiling at everyone he recognized as he came up to the barrera to change capes. He looked healthy, his skin clear tobacco brown, his hair that had been discoloured by the peroxide they had used to soak out the clotted blood after a motor-car accident in which he had been severely hurt in the last year I had seen him, was ebony black again and shining, and he wore a silver bullfighting suit to emphasize all this black and brown, and seemed very pleased with things.

With the cape he was confident, managing it beautifully and slowly; the style of Belmonte, except that it was being done by a long-legged, thin-hipped, dark gipsy. His first bull was the third of the afternoon and after being very good with the cape he watched the banderillas placed; then, before he went out with sword and muleta, he motioned to the banderilleros to bring the bull closer in to the barrera.

'Watch him; he hooks a little to the left,' said the sword handler as he handed him the sword and the cloth.

'Let him hook as he wants; I can handle him.' Gitanillo drew the sword out of the leather sheath that went limp as the stiffness was gone, and strode, long legging toward the bull. He let him come once and go by for the pase de la muerte. The bull turned very quickly and Gitanillo turned with the muleta to let him come by on the left, raised the muleta and then rose himself into the air, his legs wide spread, his hands still holding the muleta, his head down, the bull's left horn in his thigh. The bull turned him on the horn and threw him against the barrera. The bull's horn found him, picked him up once more and threw him against the wood again. Then as he lay there the bull drove the horn through his back. All of this did not take three seconds and from the instant the bull first lifted him Marcial Lalanda was running toward him with the cape. The other bullfighters had their capes wide spread, flopping them at the bull. Marcial went in at the bull's head, shoving his knee into the bull's muzzle, slapping him across the face to make him leave the man and come out in a rush; Marcial running out into the ring backwards, the bull following the cape. Gitanillo tried to get to his feet, but couldn't, the bull-ring servants picked him up and ran with him, his head swaying, toward the infirmary. A banderillero had been gored by the first bull and the doctor had him still on the operating table when they came in with Gitanillo. He saw there was no tremendous haemorrhage, the femoral artery had not been severed, finished with the banderillero and then went to work. There was a horn wound in each thigh and in each wound the quadriceps and abductor muscles had been torn loose. But in the wound in the back the horn had driven clean through the pelvis and had torn the sciatic nerve and pulled it out by the root as a worm may be pulled out of the damp lawn by a robin.

When his father came to see him, Gitanillo said, 'Don't cry, little papa. You remember how bad the automobile thing was, and they all said we wouldn't get over it? This is going to be the same way.' Later he said, 'I know I can't drink, but tell them to moisten my mouth. Just moisten my mouth a little.'

Those people who say they would pay to go to a bullfight if they could see the man gored, not just always the bulls killed by the men, should have been at the ring, in the infirmary, and later in the hospital. Gitanillo lived through the heat of June and July and the first two weeks of August, dying finally then of meningitis from the wound at the base of the spine. He weighed one hundred and twenty-eight pounds when he was gored and he weighed sixty-three pounds when he died, and during the summer suffered three different ruptures of the femoral artery, weakened by ulcers from the drainage tubes in his thigh wound and rupturing when he coughed. While he was in the hospital

Félix Rodríguez and Valencia II came in with almost identical thigh wounds, and were both discharged as able to fight, although their wounds were still open, before Gitanillo died. Gitanillo's bad luck was that the bull threw him against the base of the wooden fence so that he was against something solid when the horn made that chop at his back. Had he been lying on the sand in the open ring, the same horn stroke that wounded him fatally would probably have thrown him into the air rather than driven through his pelvis. The people who say they would pay to see a bullfighter killed would have had their money's worth when Gitanillo became delirious in the hot weather with the nerve pain. You could hear him in the street. It seemed a crime to keep him alive, and he would have been much luckier to have died soon after the fight while he still had control of himself and still possessed his courage rather than to have gone through the progressive horror of physical and spiritual humiliation that the long enough continued bearing of unbearable pain produces. To watch and to hear a human being in this time should, I suppose, make one more considerate about the horses, the bulls, and other animals, but there is a quick pull forward on a horse's ears to tighten the skin over the vertebrae at the base of the skull, and an easy stroke by the puntilla between the vertebrae that solves all a horse's problems and drops him dead without a twitch. The bull gets death within fifteen minutes of when the man starts to play him, and all wounds he receives are in hot blood, and if they do not hurt any more than the wounds a man receives in hot blood they cannot hurt much. But as long as man is regarded as having an immortal soul, and doctors will keep him alive through times when death would seem the greatest gift one man could give another, then the horses and the bulls will seem well taken care of and man to run the greatest risk.

Heriberto Garcia and Fermin Espinoza, Armillita Chico, are two Mexicans who are complete and capable artists with the muleta. Heriberto Garcia can equal the very best, and his work does not have the cold Indian quality that takes away emotion from most Mexicans' work in the bull ring. Armillita is cold; a brown little chinless Indian with an odd collection of teeth, a beautiful build for a fighter, more length in legs than torso, and is one of the really great artists with the muleta.

Nicanor Villalta, when he has a bull that charges straight enough so that the matador can put his feet together, works closer to the bull, becomes more exalted, more excited, curving on himself so he thrusts his waistline at the horns, and with his amazing wrist controlling the muleta brings the bull around him in circles, again and again, passes him so close before his chest that the bull's shoulder sometimes jostles him and the horns so close to his belly that you can see welts on his abdomen afterwards at the hotel. No exaggeration; I've seen the welts, but I thought they might have come from the shafts of the ban-derillas that struck him as he passed the bulk of the bull by him so close that it covered his shirt with blood; but they might have come from the flat of the horns, the horns were so close I did not want to watch them too closely. When he does a great faena it is all valour; valour and that magic wrist, and it makes you put up with the greatest awkwardness you could see on all bulls which will not allow him to get his feet together. You may see a great faena of Villalta's in Madrid; he has drawn more good bulls there than any matador who ever lived. You are certain to see him as awkward-looking as a praying mantis any time he draws a difficult bull, but remember that his awkward-ness is caused by his physical structure, not cowardliness. Because of the way he is built he can only be graceful if he can put his feet together, and where awkwardness on the part of a naturally graceful bullfighter is a sign of panic, in Villalta it only means that he has drawn a bull which he must spread his legs apart to work with. But if you can ever see him when he can put his feet together, see him bend like a tree in a storm before the bull's charge, see him wind the bull around him again, and again, and again; see him get so excited that he will kneel in front of the bull after he has dominated him and bite the horn, then you will forgive him the neck God gave him, the muleta the size of a bed sheet that he uses, and his telephone-pole legs, because his strange mixture of a body contains enough valour and pundoner to make a dozen bullfighters.

Cayetano Ordonez, Niño de la Palma, could manage the muleta perfectly with either hand, was a beautiful performer with a great artistic and dramatic sense of a faena, but he was never the same after he found the bulls carried terms in the hospital, inevitable, and death, perhaps, in their horns as well as five-thousand pesetas notes between their withers. He wanted the notes, but he was unwilling to approach the horns to get them when he found the forfeit that was collectable from their points. Courage comes such a short distance; from the heart to the head; but when it goes no one knows how far away it goes; in a haemorrhage, perhaps, or into a woman, and it is a bad thing to be in bullfighting business when it is gone, no matter where it went. Sometimes you get it back from another wound, the first may bring fear of death, and the second may take it away, and sometimes one woman takes it away and another gives it back. Bullfighters stay in the business relying on their knowledge and their ability to limit the danger, and hope the courage will come back, and sometimes it does and most times it does not.

Neither Enrique Torres nor Victoriano Roger, Valencia II, has any real ability with the muleta, and it is that which limits them in their profession, for they are both, at their best, fine artists with the cape. Luis Fuentes Bejarano, and Diego Mazquarian, Fortuna, are two bullfighters, very brave, very sound in their knowledge of their profession, able to reduce difficult bulls and give competent performance with any, but with heavy undistinguished styles. Fortuna's is more old-fashioned than Bejarano's, whose style is simply bad modern tricks, but they are alike in their bravery, their competence, their very good luck, and their lack of genius. They are matadors to see with ordinary or difficult bulls. Where the stylists would attempt nothing they will give you a competent bullfight with all the cheap thrills and theatricalisms intermixed with one or two moments of true emotion. Of the three best killers, in bullfighting, Antonio de la Haba, Zurito, Martín Aguero, and Manolo Martínez, only Martínez can give a semblance of a faena with the muleta, and his success, when he has it, is entirely due to his courage and the chances he takes rather than any true ability in managing the serge.

Of the thirty-four other full matadors in active service only a few are worth mentioning. One, Andrès Merida, from Málaga, is a tall, thin, vacant-faced gipsy who is a genius with cape and muleta and is the only bullfighter I have ever seen who had a completely absent-minded air in the ring as though he were thinking of something very distant and very different. He is liable to attacks of fear so complete that there is no word for them, but if he becomes confident with a bull he can be wonderful. Of the three real gipsies, Cagancho, Gitanillo de Triana, and Merida I like Merida the best. He has the grace of the others with an added grotesque which, with his absent-mindedness, makes him, for me, the most appealing of all the gipsies after Gallo. Cagancho is, of all of them, the most talented; Gitanillo de Triana the bravest and most honourable. Last summer I heard from several people from Málaga that Merida was not really a gipsy. If this is true then he is even better as an imitation than a real one.

Saturio Toron is an excellent banderillero, very valiant, with the worst, most ignorant, most dangerous manner of working as a matador that I have ever seen. After being a banderillero he took the sword as an apprentice bullfighter in 1929 and he had an excellent season forcing success through valour and good luck. He was made a formal matador in 1930 by Marcial Lalanda at Pamplona, and was severely gored in his first three fights. If his taste improves he can possibly rid himself of some of his small-town vulgarities of style, and learn to fight bulls, but from what I saw of him in 1931 his case looked hopeless, and I can only hope the bulls do not destroy him.

In this list of those who started as though they might be good matadors and end in varying degrees of failure and tragedy the two great causes of failure, eliminating bad luck, are lack of artistic ability, which of course cannot be overcome by valour, and fear. The two really brave matadors who have nevertheless failed to hold any place because of the shortness of their repertoires are Bernard Munoz, Carnicerito, and Antonio de la Haba, Zurito. Another who is really brave and has more of a repertoire than Carnicerito and Zurito and may amount to something, although handicapped by lack of stature, is Julio Garcia, Palmeno.

Besides Domingo Ortega, whom I have written about in another place in this book, the new matadors of any reputation include José Amoros, who has a peculiar rubbery style, seeming to stretch away from the bull as though he were made of elastic bands, and is completely second rate, except, of course, in his unique rubberyness; José Gonzalez called Carnicerito of Mexico, a Mexican Indian belonging to the gutful-wonder school who eats them alive, and while very brave, a good banderillero and a capable and very emotional performer will not be with us very long if he takes the same chances with the real bulls that he does with the young ones, and, since he has accustomed his public to such strong sensations, will almost certainly cease to interest if he stops taking these chances; and, most promising of all the new fighters, Jesús Solorzano. Jesús, called Chucho, in case you don't know the diminutive for that Christian name, is a non-Indian Mexican who is a perfect bullfighter, brave, artistic, intelligent, and dominating every department of his art completely except the very minor one of administering the descabello or *coup de grâce*, and yet is completely without personality. This lack of personality is difficult to analyse, but so far it seems to consist of a sort of apologetic, slinking, faulty, hump-backed way of carrying himself when he is not directly involved with the bull. Bullfighters say that fear of a bull takes the type away from a bullfighter, that is, if he is arrogant and bossy, or easy and graceful, fear removes these characteristics; but Solorzano seems to have no type to lose. Yet when he is working with a bull that he is confident with he is perfect in everything he does, and he placed the finest pair of banderillas, walking slowly, foot by foot toward the bull in the style of Gaona, did the best and slowest work with the cape, and the closest and most emotional faena with the muleta that I saw in all the season of 1931. The negative part of his work is that he performs beautifully with the bull, and then as soon as he steps away from the animal lapses into that hump-backed, frozen-faced apathy, but personality or not he is a wonderful bull-fighter with knowledge and great art and valour.

Two other new matadors are José Mejias, called Pepe Bien-venida, the younger brother of Manolo, who is braver and more excitable than his elder brother, had a varied and picturesque repertoire and a very attractive personality, but is lacking in Manolo's artistic ability and knowledge of how to dominate bulls safely, although this may come with time, and David Liceaga, a young Mexican fighter, who is enormously skilful with the muleta and without style or ability with the cape, and, oddly enough for a Mexican, mediocre with the banderillas. I write this about Liceaga without having seen him on the reports of those people whose opinion I trust who have watched him work. He fought only twice in Madrid in 1931; once as a novillero on the day I went out to Aranjuez to see Ortega and again in October, to be made a full matador, after I had left Spain. But he is very popular in Mexico City and anyone who wants to check up on him will probably be able to see him in Mexico during the winter.

I have omitted all phenomena from this listing, rating no one who has not proved his right to be judged. There are always new phenomena in bullfighting. There will be newer ones by the time this book comes out. Watered by publicity they sprout each season on the strength of one good afternoon in Madrid with a bull that was kind to them; but the morning glory is a floral monument of lasting endurance compared to these one-triumph bullfighters. Five years from now, eating only occasionally, but keeping their one suit neat to wear to the café, you will be able to hear them tell how, on their presentation in Madrid, they were better than Belmonte. It may be true, too. 'And how were you the last time?' you ask. 'I had a little bad luck killing. Just a little bad luck,' the ex-phenomenon says, and you say, 'That's a shame. A man can't have luck killing them all,' and in your mind you see the phenomenon, sweating, white-faced, and sick with fear, unable to look at the horn or go near it, a couple of swords on the ground, capes all around him, running in at an angle on the bull, hoping the sword will strike a vital spot, cushions sailing down into the ring and the steers ready to come in. 'Just a little bad luck killing.' That was two years ago, and he hasn't fought since except in bed at night when he wakes up wet with sweat and fear and he will not fight again unless hunger makes him and then, because everyone knows he is a coward and worthless, he may have to take some bulls that no one else will take and if he nerves himself up to do something, since he is out of training, the bulls may kill him. Or else he may have, 'Just a little bad luck killing,' again.

There are seven hundred and sixty-some unsuccessful bull-fighters still attempting to practise their art in Spain; the skilful ones unsuccessful through fear, and the braves ones through lack of talent. You sometimes see the brave ones killed if you are unlucky. In the summer of 1931 I saw a fight with very big, very fast, five-year-old bulls and three apprentice matadors. The oldest in point of service was Alfonso Gomez, called Finito de Valladolid, well over thirty-five, once handsome, a failure in his profession, yet very dignified, intelligent, and brave, who had been fighting in Madrid ten years without ever interesting the public enough to justify a move from novillero to full matador. Next oldest in service was Isidoro Todo, called Alcalareno II, thirty-seven years old, only a little over five feet tall, a chunky, cheerful little man who supported four children, his widowed sister and the woman he lived with on the little money he made from the bulls. All he had as a bullfighter was great bravery and the fact that he was so short that this defect, which made it impossible for him to succeed as a matador, made him an attraction as a curiosity in the ring. The third fighter was Miguel Casielles, a complete coward. But it is a dull and ugly story, and the only thing to remember was the way Alcalareno II was killed, and that was too ugly, I see now, to justify writing about when it is not necessary. I made the mistake of telling my son about it. When I came home from the ring he wanted to know all about the fight and just what had happened, and like a fool I told him what I'd seen. He didn't say anything except to ask if he had not been killed because he was so small. He himself was small. I said yes he was small, but also because he had not known how to cross with the muleta. I hadn't said he was killed – only hurt; I'd had that much sense, although it was not much. Then somebody came in the room, Sidney Franklin I think it was, and said in Spanish, 'He's dead.'

'You didn't say he was dead,' the boy said.

'I didn't know for sure.'

'I don't like it that he's dead,' the boy said.

The next day he said, 'I can't stop thinking about that man who was killed because he was so small.'

'Don't think about it,' I said, wishing for the thousandth time in my life that I could wipe out words that I'd said. 'It's silly to think about that.'

'I don't try to think about it, but I wish you hadn't told me, because every time I shut my eyes I see it.'

'Think about Pinky,' I said. Pinky is a horse in Wyoming. So we were very careful about death for a while. My eyes were too bad to read and my wife was reading Dashiell Hammett's bloodiest to date, *The Dain Curse*, out loud, and every time that Mr Hammett would kill a character or a set of characters she would substitute the word umpty-umped for the words killed, cut the throat of, blew the brains out of, spattered around the room, and so on, and soon the comic of umpty-umped so appealed to the boy that when he said, 'You know the one who was umpty-umped because he was so small? I don't think about him now,' I knew it was all right.

There have been four new matadors promoted in 1932, two of whom deserve mention as possibilities, one as a curiosity, and one could probably be omitted as a phenomenon. The two possibilities are Juanito Martín Caro, called Chiquito de la Audiencia and Luis Gomez, called El Estudiante. Chiquito, at twenty, has been fighting young bulls as a child prodigy since he was twelve. Elegant in style, very graceful, sound, intelligent, and competent, he has the pretty pretty look of a young girl, but in the ring he is domineering and serious, and has nothing effeminate about him except his girl's face, and certainly none of the feeble, whipped look of Chicuelo. His drawback is that his work while intelligent and beautiful is cold and passionless; he has been fighting so long that he seems to have the caution and protective resources of a matador at the end of his career rather than to be a boy who must risk everything to arrive. But he has great artistic ability and intelligence, and his career will be very interesting to follow.

Luis Gomez, El Estudiante, is a young medical student with a keen, brown, good-looking face and a good figure that might serve as a model for a formalized young matador type who possesses a good sound classic modern style with cape and muleta, and kills quickly and well. After three seasons of fighting in the provinces in the summer and studying medicine in Madrid in the winter, he made his début last fall in Madrid as a novillero and had a great success. He became a full matador at Valencia in the corridas of San José in March of 1932, and according to aficionados whom I trust, he was very good and showed great promise, although, occasionally with the muleta, his valour and desire to make a faena led him into compromising situations which he was unconscious of and from which he was saved only by luck and good reflexes. On the surface it seemed he dominated the bulls, but in reality luck saved him more than once; but with intelligence, valour, and a good style, he is a legitimate hope as a matador if his luck holds during his first full campaign.

Alfredo Corrochano, son of Gregorio Corrochano, the very influential bullfight critic of the Madrid monarchist daily, *A.B.C.*, is a matador made to order by his father under the influence of Ignacio Sanchez Mejias, the brother-in-law of Joselito, whom Corrochano attacked so bitterly and virulently during the season that saw his death. Alfredo is a dark, slight, contemptuous, and arrogant boy with a rather Bourbonic face, a little like that of Alfonso XIII as a child. He was educated in Switzerland, and trained as a matador at the testings of the calves and brood stock of the bull ranches around Madrid and Salamanca by Sanchez Mejias, his father, and all those who toady to his father. For about three years he has fought as a professional, first with the Bienvenida boys as a child performer, then last year as a full novillero. Due to his father's position, his presentation in Madrid aroused much feeling, and he was made to feel the bitterness of all the enemies his father's often excellent and extremely well-written sarcasms had made, as well as those who hated him as a son of the middle-class royalist and believed he was depriving boys who needed bread to eat of the chance to earn it in the ring. At the same time he profited by the publicity and curiosity all this feeling aroused, and through his three appearances as a novillero in Madrid he bore himself insolently, arrogantly, and very much like a man. He showed he was a good banderillero, an excellent dominator with the muleta, with much intelligence and vista in handling of the bull, but with a lamentably bad style with the cape and an utter inability to kill properly or even decently. In 1932 he took the alternativa in Castellón de la Plana in the first corrida of the year, and according to my informants he was not changed since I had seen him except that he was trying to remedy his vulgar way of making the veronica by substituting various picturesque tricks with the cape for that one irreplaceable test of a fighter's serenity and artistic ability. As a curiosity his career will be extremely interesting, but I believe that unless he acquires security in killing he will soon cease to interest the public, once his novelty as a son of his father has been thoroughly exploited.

Victoriano de la Serna was a young novillero who had that necessity for the production of a phenomenon, a great afternoon in Madrid, in September of 1931. He was taken up, exploited, shown near Madrid, with hand-picked, small bulls, where a disaster could be minimized and a triumph made much of by the Madrid critics paid to attend, then at the very end of the season he was presented for his second Madrid appearance as a full matador. He showed that the elevation was premature, that he was green, insufficiently grounded in his profession, and needed much more seasoning and experience before being able to handle the mature bulls securely. This season he has a certain amount of contracts signed last year before his failure in Madrid, but in spite of his undoubtedly phenomenal natural ability, his too early elevation to a matador would seem to have started him on the quick descent to oblivion, well greased as it is by all those other phenomena who have slid along it before him. As always, I hope for the performer, who is less guilty than his exploiters, that I am wrong, and that he may miraculously learn his trade while practising it as a master, but it is such a defrauding of the public to do so that even when a matador does so learn his craft, the public rarely forgives him, and when he is secure enough to satisfy them they have no wish to see him.

Chapter 19

There are only two proper ways to kill bulls with the sword and muleta and as both of them deliberately invoke a moment in which there is unavoidable goring for the man if the bull does not follow the cloth properly, matadors have steadily tricked this finest part of the fight until ninety of one hundred bulls that you will see killed will be put to death in a manner that is only a parody of the true way to kill. One reason for this is that rarely will a great artist with the cape and muleta be a killer. A great killer must love to kill; unless he feels it is the best thing he can do, unless he is conscious of its dignity and feels that it is its own reward, he will be incapable of the abnegation that is necessary in real killing. The truly great killer must have a sense of honour and a sense of glory far beyond that of the ordinary bullfighter. In other words he must be a simpler man. Also he must take pleasure in it, not simply as a trick of wrist, eye, and managing of his left hand that he does better than other men, which is the simplest form of that pride, and which he will naturally have as a simple man, but he must have a spiritual enjoyment of the moment of killing. Killing cleanly and in a way which gives you aesthetic pleasure and pride has always been one of the greatest enjoyments of a part of the human race. Because the other part, which does not enjoy killing, has always been the more articulate and has furnished most of the good writers, we have had a very few statements of the true enjoyment of killing. One of its greatest pleasures, aside from the purely aesthetic ones, such as wing shooting, and the ones of pride, such as difficult game stalking, where it is the disproportionately increased importance of the fraction of a moment that it takes for the shot that furnishes the emotion is, the feeling of rebellion against death which comes from its administering. Once you accept the rule of death thou shalt not kill is an easily and a naturally obeyed commandment. But when a man is still in rebellion against death he has pleasure in taking to himself one of the Godlike attributes – that of giving it. This is one of the most profound feelings in those men who enjoy killing. These things are done in pride, and pride, of course, is a Christian sin, and a pagan virtue. But it is pride which makes the bullfight and true enjoyment of killing which makes the great matador.

Of course these necessary spiritual qualities cannot make a man a good killer unless the man has all the physical talent for the performance of the act – a good eye, a strong wrist, valour, and a fine left hand to manage the muleta. He must have all of these to an exceptional degree or his sincerity and pride will only put him in the hospital. There is not, in Spain today, one really great killer. There are successful matadors who can kill perfectly though without great style when they wish, luck being with them, but who do not attempt it often because they do not need to in order to hold their public; there are matadors who might have been great killers in the old days, who started in their careers killing bulls as well as it could be done, but who, through their lack of ability with cape and muleta, early ceased to interest the public, and so have few contracts, and lack the opportunity to develop their art with the sword or even to keep in practice; and there are matadors who are starting their careers who still kill well, but are not yet proven or tested by time. But there is no outstanding matador who day in and day out kills well, easily, and with pride. The leading matadors have developed a facile and tricky way of killing which has robbed what should be the culmination of the emotion of the bullfight of all emotion except that of disappointment. The emotion now is given by the cape, by, occasionally, the banderillas, most surely by the work with the muleta, and the best you can hope for from the sword is a quick ending that will not spoil the effect of what has gone before. I believe I saw more than fifty bulls killed with various degrees of facility before I consciously saw one killed well. I had no complaint about the bullfight as it was, it was interesting enough, better than anything I had seen up to that time; but I thought the sword business was a not particularly interesting anticlimax. Still, knowing nothing about it, I thought perhaps it was really an anticlimax and that the people who spoke and wrote highly of the killing of the bull in bullfighting were merely liars. My own standpoint was quite simple; I could see the bull had to be killed to make the bullfight; I was pleased that he was killed with a sword, for anything to be killed with a sword was a rare enough business; but the way that he was killed looked like a trick and gave me no emotion at all. This is the bullfight, I thought; the end is not so good, but perhaps that is part of it and I do not understand it yet. Anyway it is the best two dollars' worth I have ever had. Still, I remembered, at the first bullfight I ever saw, before I could see it clearly, before I could even see what happened, in the new, crowded, confused, white-jacketed beer-vendor passing in front of me, two steel cables between my eyes and the ring below, the bull's shoulders smooth with blood, the banderillas clattering as he moved, and a streak of dust down the middle of his back, his horns solid-looking like wood on top, thicker than my arm where they curved; I remembered in the midst of this confused excitement having a great moment of emotion when the man went in with the sword. But I could not see in my mind exactly what happened, and when, on the next bull, I watched closely the emotion was gone and I saw it was a trick. I saw fifty bulls killed after that before I had the emotion again. But by then I could see how it was done, and I knew I had seen it done properly that first time.

When you see a bull killed for the first time, if it is the usual run of killing, this is about how it will look. The bull will be standing square on his four feet facing the man who will be standing about five yards away with his feet together, the muleta in his left hand and the sword in his right. The man will raise the cloth in his left hand to see if the bull follows it with his eyes; then he will lower the cloth, hold it and the sword together, turn so that he is standing sideways toward the bull, make a twist with his left hand that will furl the cloth over the stick of the muleta, draw the sword up from the lowered muleta and sight along it toward the bull, his head, the blade of the sword, and his left shoulder pointing toward the bull, the muleta held low in his left hand. You will see him draw himself taut and start toward the bull, and the next thing you will see is that he is past the bull and either the sword has risen into the air and gone end over end or you will see its red-flannel-wrapped hilt, or the hilt and part of the blade, sticking out from between the bull's shoulders or from his neck muscles and the crowd will be shouting in approval or disapproval, depending on the manner in which the man has gone in and the location of the sword.

That is all you will see of the killing; but the mechanics of it are these. Bulls are not killed properly by a sword thrust in the heart. The sword is not long enough to reach the heart, if driven in where it should go high up between the shoulder blades. It goes past the vertebrae between the top of the ribs and, if it kills instantly, cuts the aorta. That is the end of a perfect sword thrust and to make it the man must have the good luck that the sword point should not strike either the spine or the ribs as it goes in. No man can go toward a bull, reach over the top of his head if it is carried high, and put a sword in between his shoulders. The instant the bull's head is up the sword is not long enough to reach from his head to his shoulders. For it to be possible for the man to put the sword into the place where it is designed to go to kill the bull, he must have the bull's head down so that this place is exposed, and even then the man must lean forward over the bull's lowered head and neck to get the sword in. Now, if when the bull raises his head as the sword goes in the man is not to go up in the air, one of two things must be happening; either the bull must be in motion past the man, guided by the muleta on the man's left arm as he shoves the sword in with his right, or else the man must be in motion past the bull who is guided away from the man by the muleta held by the left hand which is crossed low in front of and to the left of the man's body as he goes in over the bull's head and comes out along his flank. Killing can be tricked by having both the man and bull in motion.

These are the mechanical principles of the two ways to kill bulls properly; either the bull must come to and pass the man, cited, drawn on, controlled and going out and away from the man by a movement of the muleta while the sword is being inserted between his shoulders; or else the man must fix the bull in position, his front feet together and his hind feet square with them, his head neither too high nor too low, must test him by raising and lowering the cloth to see if he follows it with his eyes, and then, with the muleta in his left hand making a cross in front of him so that if the bull follows it he will pass to the man's right, go in toward the bull and as he lowers his head after the cloth which is to guide him away from the man, put the sword in and come out along the bull's flank. When the man awaits the charge of the bull it is called killing recibiendo. When the man goes in on the bull it is called a volapié or flying with the feet. Preparing to go in, left shoulder toward the bull, sword pointed along the man's body, muleta held furled in the left hand, is called profiling. The closer it is done to the animal the less chance the man has to deviate and escape if the bull does not follow the cloth as the man goes in. The movement made to swing the left arm holding the muleta, which is crossed in front of the body, out and past the right side to get rid of the bull is called crossing. Any time the man does not make this cross he will have the bull under him. Unless he swings him far enough out, the horn is certain to catch him. To make this cross successfully necessitates a wrist movement which will swing the folds of the furled muleta out and to the side as well as a simple arm movement across and away from the body. Bullfighters say that a bull is killed more with the left hand which controls the muleta and guides the animal than with the right which shoves in the sword. There is no great force needed to put in the sword if the point does not strike bone; properly guided by the muleta, if the man leans after the blade, the bull will seem sometimes to pluck the sword out from his hand. Other times, hitting bone, it will seem as though he had struck a wall of rubber and cement.

In the old days bulls were killed recibiendo, the matador provoking and awaiting the final charge, and those bulls which were too heavy on their feet to charge were ham-strung with a half-moon-shaped blade attached to a long pole and then killed with a dagger stroke between the vertebrae of the neck after they were helpless. This repugnant business was made unnecessary by the invention of the volapié by Joachín Rodríguez, called Costillares, toward the end of the eighteenth century.

The killing of a bull recibiendo; the man now standing still and erect his feet only a little apart after he has provoked the charge by bending one leg forward and swinging the muleta toward the bull, letting the bull come until man and bull become one figure as the sword goes in; then the figure broken by the shock of the encounter, there coming a moment when they are joined by the sword that seems to slip in an inch at a time, is the most arrogant dealing of death, and is one of the finest things you can see in bullfighting. You may never see it because the volapié, dangerous enough when properly executed, is so much less dangerous than the suerte de recibir that only very rarely does a fighter ever receive a bull in our times. I have seen it properly completed only four times in over fifteen hundred bulls I have seen killed. You will see it attempted but unless the man really waits out the encounter and gets rid of the bull with an arm-and-wrist movement, rather than by tricking with a side-stepping at the end, it is no receiving. Maera did it, Niño de la Palma did it once in Madrid, and faked it several times, and Luis Freg did it. Few bulls come now to the end of a fight in proper condition to be received, but there are even fewer fighters to receive them. One reason for the decadence of this form of killing is that if the bull leaves the cloth as he reaches the man the horn wound will be in the chest. In fighting with the cape the first wound or catching will usually be in the lower leg or thigh. Where the second one is, if the bull passes the man from one horn to another, is a matter of luck. In the muleta or in killing by the volapié the wound is nearly always in the right thigh as that is where the bull's horn passes when it is lowered, although a man who has gone well over the horn may be caught under the arm or even at the neck if the bull raises his head before the man has passed him. But in killing recibiendo if anything goes wrong the horn chop hits the chest and so you hardly ever see it attempted any more except by someone who has drawn such a fine bull and done such a splendid faena that at the end he wants to make a super-emotional climax so he tries to kill recibiendo, and usually he has used his bull up with the muleta or else the man lacks the experience to receive properly, and the faena ends in an anticlimax or in a goring.

The volapié, if properly executed, that is slowly, closely and well-timed, is a fine enough way to kill. I have seen bullfighters gored in the chest, have heard the rib crack, literally, with the shock, and seen a man turn on the horn with the horn in him and out of sight, muleta and sword in the air, then on the ground, the bull thrusting head and man high and the man not leaving the horn when he is tossed, to come off the next toss into the air and be caught by the other horn and come down, try to get up, put his hands where he was breathing through his chest, and be carried with his teeth knocked out to die within an hour in the infirmary still in his clothes, the wound too big to do anything with. I have seen that man's, Isidoro Todo's, face while he was in the air, he being fully conscious all of the time on the horn and after, and able to talk in the infirmary before he died, although the blood in his mouth made his words unintelligible, so I see the bullfighters' viewpoint about killing recibiendo when they know the cornada comes in the chest.

According to historians, Pedro Romero, who was a matador in Spain at the time of the American revolution, killed five thousand six hundred bulls recibiendo between the years of 1771 and 1779, and lived to die in his bed at the age of ninety-five. If this is true we live in a very decadent time indeed, when it is an event to see a matador even attempt to receive a bull, but we do not know how many bulls Romero would have lived to receive if he had tried to pass them as close as Juan Belmonte with the cape and mulcta. Nor do we know how many of those five thousand he received well, waiting quietly and getting the sword in high up between the shoulders or how many he received badly; side-stepping and letting the sword go into the neck. Historians speak highly of all dead bullfighters. To read any history of the great fighters of the past it would seem impossible that they ever had bad days or that the public was ever dissatisfied with them. It may be that they never were dissatisfied with them before 1873, because I have not had time to read the contemporary accounts any farther back than that, but since that time bullfighting has always been considered by contemporary chroniclers to be in a period of decadence. During what you now hear referred to as the golden age of all golden ages, that of Lagartijo and Frascuelo, which was really a golden age, there was a generally expressed opinion that things were in a bad way; the bulls were much smaller and younger, or else they were big and they were cowardly. Lagartijo was no killer; Frascuelo, yes; but he was mean as dirt to his cuadrilla and impossible to get along with; Lagartijo was chased from the ring by the crowd on his final performance in Madrid. When in the accounts we come to Guerrita, another golden-age hero, who corresponds to the period just before, during and after the Spanish–American war, you read that the bulls are small and young again; gone are the giant animals of phenomenal bravery of the days of Lagartijo and Frascuelo. Guerrita is no Lagartijo we read, it is sacrilege to compare the two, and this florid monkey business makes those who remember the serious honesty (no longer ugly meanness) of Frascuelo turn in their graves; El Espartero is no good and proves it by getting killed; finally Guerrita retires and everyone is relieved; they have had enough of him, although once the great Guerrita is gone bullfighting is in a profound depression. The bulls, oddly enough, have gotten smaller and younger, or if they are big they are cowardly; Mazzantini is no good, he kills still, yes, but not recibiendo, and he cannot get out of his own way with a cape and is at a loss with the muleta. Fortunately he retires, and once the great Don Luis Mazzantini is gone the bulls get smaller and younger although there are a few huge cowardly ones more fit to draw carts than for the ring, and with that colossus of the sword disappeared, gone alas with Guerrita, the master of masters, such newcomers as Ricardo Bombita, Machaquito, and Rafael El Gallo, none of them anything but a fake, dominate the bull business. Bombita masters bulls with the muleta and has a pleasant smile, but he cannot kill as Mazzantini killed; Gallo is ridiculous, an insane gipsy, Machaquito is brave but ignorant, only his luck saves him and the fact that the bulls are so much younger and smaller than those giant, always brave, animals of the time of Lagartijo and Salvador Sanchez, Frascuelo, now always called the Negro affectionately rather than as an insult and beloved for his kindness to all. Vicente Pastor is honourable and brave in the ring, but he gives a little jump when killing and is frightened sick before he goes in to fight. Antonio Fuentes is still elegant, a beautiful performer with the sticks and with a nice style of killing, and that lets him out, since who wouldn't be elegant working with the bulls that are nowadays so much younger and smaller than in the time of those faultless colossi Lagartijo, Frascuelo, the heroic Espartero, the ruler of masters Guerrita, and that pinnacle of swordsmanship Don Luis Mazzantini. In this epoch incidentally when Don

Indalecio Mosquera promoted the Madrid Ring and cared nothing about bullfights but only about the size of the bulls, statistics show the bulls were consistently the biggest that were ever fought in Madrid.

Along about this time Antonio Montes got himself killed in Mexico, and it was at once realized that he had been the real fighter of his era. Serious and masterly, always giving them their money's worth, Montes was killed by a hollow-flanked, long-necked, little Mexican bull that lifted his head instead of following the muleta when the sword went in, and as Montes turned and tried to swing out of the cradle of the horns the bull's right horn caught him between the cheeks of his rump, lifted him and carried him, as though he were seated on a stool (the horn had gone in out of sight), for four yards and then fell dead from the sword thrust. Montes lived four days after the accident.

Then comes Joselito, who, when he appeared, was called Pasos-Largos or big jumps, and was attacked by all the admirers of Bombita, Machaquito, Fuentes, and Vicente Pastor, who fortunately all retired and at once became incomparable. Guerrita said if you want to see Belmonte, see him in a hurry because he won't last; no man can work so close to bulls. When he kept working closer and closer, it was discovered that the bulls were, of course, parodies of the giant animals he, Guerrita, had killed. Joselito was admitted to be very good in the press, but it was pointed out that he was only able to place banderillas on one side, the right (the bulls of course were very small), he insisted on that; that he killed holding the sword so high that some said he pulled it out of his hat and others that he merely used it as a prolongation of his nose, and, this is Christ's truth: he was hooted, whistled at, and had cushions thrown at him the last day he fought in Madrid, the 15th of May 1920, while he was working his second bull, after having cut the ear of his first, and was hit in the face by a cushion while the crowd shouted 'que se vaya! que se vaya!' which can be translated, 'May he get the hell out of here and stay!' The next day, the 16th of May, he was killed in Talavera de la Reina, gored through the lower abdomen so his intestines came out (and he was unable to hold them in with both hands, but died of traumatic shock from the force of the cornada while the doctors were working on the wound, and his face composed very peacefully on the operating-table after he was dead, with his brother-in-law having his picture taken holding a handkerchief to his eyes and a crowd of wailing gipsies outside with more coming, and Gallo wandering around outside very pitiful, afraid to go in to see his brother dead, and Alamendro the banderillero saying, 'If they can kill this man I tell you none of us is safe! None of us!') and at once became, in the press, and remains, the greatest bullfighter of all time; greater than Guerrita, Frascuelo, Lagartijo, according to the same men who, while he lived, attacked him. Belmonte retired and became greater than José even, returned after Maera died, and was discovered to be an exploiter of a formerly great name avid for money (he did have his bulls selected that year), fought one more year; I swear this was the best he ever had; he fought all bulls, made no specifications on size, and triumphed along the whole line, including killing, which he had never truly mastered before, and was attacked the whole season in the press. He retired again after a nearly mortal horn wound, and all contemporary accounts agree he is the greatest living bullfighter. So there you have it, and I will not know how Pedro Romero was until I shall have read the contemporary accounts before, during, and after, and I doubt very much if enough of these exist, even in letters, to enable a true judgement to be formed.

From all the different sources I have read and all contemporary accounts, the epoch of biggest bulls and true golden age in Madrid was that of Lagartijo and Frascuelo, who were the greatest bullfighters of the last sixty years until Joselito and Belmonte. Guerrita's was no golden age, and he was responsible for introducing younger and smaller bulls (I've looked up the weights and the photographs), and in the twelve years that he fought he had only one truly great year as a fighter, that of 1894. Big bulls were brought back during the epoch of Machaquito, Bombita, Pastor, and Gallo, and the size of the bulls was sensibly decreased during the golden age of Joselito and Belmonte although they fought the biggest kind of bulls many times. At present the bulls are big and old for the matadors without influence and small and young whenever the bullfighter is powerful enough to have any hand or influence in their selection. Bulls are always as big as they can be bred at Bilbao in spite of the matadors, and usually the Andalucian breeders send their biggest and finest bulls to the July fair at Valencia. I have seen Belmonte and Marcial Lalanda triumph in Valencia with bulls as large as any ever fought in the history of the ring.

This historical summary started with regrets for the disappearance of the killing of the bulls recibiendo, which, to recapitulate, disappeared because it is not taught nor practised, since the public does not demand it, and since it is a difficult thing which must be practised, understood, and dominated, and is much too dangerous to be improvised. If it were practised it could be performed readily enough if the bulls were allowed to reach the end of the fight in proper condition for it. But any suerte which can be approximated in bullfighting by another almost equal in public appeal, and with less chance of death if its execution goes wrong, will surely die out in bullfighting unless the public demands that fighters perform it.

The volapié to be properly executed demands that the bull be heavy on his feet and that he have his two front feet on a line and together. If he has one foot farther forward than the other, the top of one shoulder blade will be moved forward, and the opening through which the sword must go, and which is shaped rather like that between the palm of your hands if you place them with finger-tips touching and wrists a little way apart, will be closed just as that between your hands will close if you bring the wrist of one hand forward. If the bull's feet are spread wide this opening is narrowed by the shoulder blades being forced together and if the feet are not together it is closed entirely. It is through this opening that the point of the sword must enter to penetrate into the body cavity, and it will only continue on in if it does not strike a rib or the spine. In order to make it have a better chance of going in and taking a downward course in the direction of the aorta, the tip of the sword is curved so that it dips down. If the man goes in to kill the bull from in front with his left shoulder forward, if he puts the sword in between the shoulder blades, he will automatically come within reach of the bull's horns; in fact his body must pass over the horn at the moment of putting in the sword. If his left hand, crossed in front of him and holding the muleta almost to the ground, does not keep the bull's head down until the man has passed over the horn and come out along the bull's flank, the man will be gored. To avoid this moment of very great danger to which the man exposes himself each time he kills a bull according to the rules, bullfighters who wish to kill without exposition profile at a considerable distance from the bull, so that the bull, seeing the man coming in, will be in motion himself, and the man running across the line of the bull's charge with his right arm forward rather than his left shoulder tries to drive the sword in without ever letting his body come within range of the horn. The way that I have just described is the most flagrant form of bad killing. The farther forward in the bull's neck the sword is put in and the lower down at the side, the less the man exposes himself and the surer he is of killing the bull, since the sword is driven into the chest cavity, the lungs, or cuts the jugular or other veins, or the carotid or other arteries of the neck, all of which can be reached by the point of the sword without the man exposing himself to the slightest danger.

It is for this reason that a killing is judged by the place in which the sword is put in and by the manner in which the man goes in to kill, rather than by the immediate results. To kill the bull with a single sword thrust is of no merit at all unless the sword is placed high between the bull's shoulders and unless the man passed over and had his body within reach of the horn at the moment he went in.

Many times in Southern France and occasionally in provinces in Spain where they have a few bullfights, I have seen a matador applauded enthusiastically because he killed his bull with a single entry when the killing was no more than a riskless assassination, the man having never exposed himself at all, but merely slipped the sword into an unprotected and vulnerable spot. The reason the man is required to kill the bull high up between the shoulders is because the bull is able to defend that place, and will only uncover it and make it vulnerable if the man brings his body within range of the horn, provided he enters according to the rules. To kill a bull in his neck or his flank, which he cannot defend, is assassination. To kill him high up between the shoulders demands risk by the man and studied ability if great danger is to be avoided. If the man uses this ability to make the proper execution of the entry with the sword as secure as possible, exposing his body but protecting it through his skill with his left hand, then he is a good killer. If he uses his ability merely to trick the killing, so that he gets enough of the sword into the correct place to kill without ever exposing his body, then he is an able remover of bulls but, no matter how quickly or securely he kills them off, he is no killer.

The truly great killer is not the man who is simply brave enough to go in straight on the bull from a short distance and get the sword in somehow high between the shoulders, but is a man who is able to go in from a short distance, slowly, starting with the left foot and being so skilful in the management of his left hand that as he goes in, left shoulder forward, he makes the bull lower his head and then keeps it down as he goes over the horn, pushes in the sword, and, as it is in, goes out along the bull's flank. The great killer must be able to do this with security and with style, and if, as he goes in left shoulder first, the sword strikes bone and refuses to penetrate, or if it strikes ribs or the edge of the vertebrae and is deviated so that it goes in only a third of the way, the merit of the attempt at killing is as great as though the sword had gone all the way in and killed, since the man has taken the risk and the result has only been falsified by chance.

A little over a third of a sword, properly placed, will kill a bull that is not too big. Half a sword will reach the aorta on any bull there is, if the sword is directed properly and placed high enough up. Many bullfighters, therefore, do not follow the sword all the way with their body but only try to slip in half of the blade, knowing it will account for the bull if in the right spot, and realizing they themselves are much safer if they do not have to push in that last foot and a half. This practice of skilfully administering half estocadas, originated by Lagartijo, is what has robbed killing of its emotion, since the beauty of the moment of killing is that flash when man and bull form one figure as the sword goes all the way in, the man leaning after it, death uniting the two figures in the emotional, aesthetic, and artistic climax of the fight. That flash never comes in the skilful administering of half a blade to the bull.

Marcial Lalanda is the most skilful of present matadors at getting the sword in, holding it high up on a level with his eyes, as he sights, taking one or more backward steps before he starts the voyage in, and with the point of the blade tilted up, he enters, avoids the horns skilfully, and leaves the sword nearly always perfectly placed yet without there having been the least exposition or emotion in the killing. He can kill well, too. I have seen him execute the volapié perfectly; but he gives them their money's worth in the other departments of the fight, and relies on his ability to remove the bull from in front of him speedily so that the memory of how good he was with cape, banderillas, and muleta will not be spoiled. His ordinary manner of killing, as I have described it, is a sorry parody of what killing can be. From much reading of contemporary accounts I believe Marcial Lalanda's case, not his early trials, but his present continuous mastery, his philosophy of the bullfight and his manner of killing, are very comparable to the middle period of the great Lagartijo, although Lalanda certainly cannot compare with the grace, style, and naturalness of the Cordoban; but no one can be the present Lalanda's superior in mastery. I believe ten years from now people will be referring to the years 1929, 1930, 1931 as the golden age of Marcial Lalanda. Now he has as many enemies as any great bullfighter attracts, but he is unquestionably the master of all present fighters.

Vicente Barrera kills in worse style than Lalanda, but he has a different system. Instead of having a skilful way of placing half a blade in the correct spot he relies on a tricky entry to place part of a blade anywhere above the neck, thus complying with the law which requires at least one entry by the matador, in order that, having gone in once, he may kill the bull with a descabello. He is the living virtuoso of the descabello, which is a push with the point of the sword between the cervical vertebrae to cut the spinal cord, supposedly for use as a *coup de grâce* on a bull which is dying and is too far gone to follow the muleta with his eyes, thus preventing the matador from going in another time to kill. Barrera uses his first entry, required by law of every matador, according to the regulations of bullfighting, simply to try his luck at getting the sword in without exposing himself in any way. No matter what the effect of this sword thrust, Barrera plans to kill the live bull with a descabello. He relies on his footwork, tricks the bull with the muleta into lowering his muzzle and exposing the spot between the vertebrae at the base of his skull while he raises the sword slowly from behind him, bringing it high over his head, keeping it carefully out of sight of the bull, and then, with its poised point down, controlled by the wrist and with the precision of a juggler he drives it down and severs the spinal marrow, dropping the bull dead as suddenly as an electric light is extinguished by the pushing of a button. Barrera's method of killing, while it keeps within the letter of the rules, is the negation of the whole spirit and tradition of the bullfight. The descabello which is administered by surprise as a *coup de grâce* designed to avoid the suffering of an animal which can no longer defend itself, is used by him to assassinate live bulls that he is supposed to expose his body to in killing with the sword. He has developed such a deadly precision in its use, and the public know from experience that nothing will influence him to expose a hair in killing, that they have come to tolerate his abuse of the descabello and even sometimes to applaud it. To applaud him for cheating in the killing because he performs a trick with skill, assurance, and security that is made safe by his sureness in his foot-work before the bull, and ability to make a live bull lower his head as though he were dying, is about as low as the mentality of a bull-ring public can go.

Manolo Bienvenida is the worst at killing of any of the first series of matadors except Cagancho. Both of these make no pretence of observing the rules in killing and usually go in running on a bias to stab the bull with the sword with less exposing of themselves than a banderillero suffers in putting in the banderillas. I have never seen Bienvenida kill a bull well, and only twice in twenty-four times, in 1931, did I see him kill a bull even decently. His cowardice at the moment of killing is disgusting. Cagancho's cowardice when he has to kill is more than disgusting. It is not the sweating, dry-mouthed fear of the nineteen-year-old boy who cannot kill properly, having been too frightened of it with big bulls ever to take the chances necessary to attempt it in order to learn to dominate it properly, and so is sick afraid of the horn. It is a cold-blooded gipsy defrauding of the public by the most shameless, anger-arousing obtainer of money under false pretences that ever went into a bull ring. Cagancho can kill well, he has height, which makes killing much easier, and any time he wants to he can kill competently, well, and with good style. But Cagancho never takes a chance on performing anything that he thinks might cost him a horn wound. Killing is admittedly dangerous, even to a great killer, therefore Cagancho, sword in hand, will not let his body come within range of the bull's horn unless he has become convinced that the bull is candid and inoffensive and will follow the cloth as though his muzzle were glued to it. If Cagancho has proved to his satisfaction that the bull offers him no danger he will kill with style, grace, and absolute security. If he believes there is the faintest danger he will not let his body approach the horn. His cynical cowardice is the most disgusting negation of bullfighting that can be seen; worse even than the panic of Niño de la Palma, for Niño de la Palma no longer can execute his passes correctly, he is altogether unnerved by his fear, while nearly everything that Cagancho does when he is confident could serve as a model and illustration of perfection in artistic bullfighting. He only performs, however, if he is certain that there is no danger to a man working with the bull; not that the chances are all in the man's favour; that is not enough for him. He does not take chances. He must be certain in his own mind that danger does not exist or he will flop a cape from two yards away, wave the spike end of a muleta, and assassinate with a side-running stab. He will do this to bulls which are not criminal or even particularly dangerous to a matador with average ability and good courage. He has not the courage of a louse, since his amazing physical equipment, his knowledge, and his technique permit him to be much safer in the bull ring than anyone is crossing a street in traffic provided he attempts nothing close to the bull. A louse takes chances in the seams of your garments. It may turn out that you are in a war and eventually be de-loused, or you may hunt the louse down with a thumb nail, but you cannot de-louse Cagancho. If there were any commission to regulate bullfighters and suspend matadors as faking boxers are occasionally deprived of their licences, when their political protection is inadequate, Cagancho might be eliminated from the bull rings or he might, through fear of the commission, become a great bullfighter.

The one really great fight that Manolo Bienvenida made in all of 1931 was the last day at Pamplona when he was more afraid of the public and their anger at his previous cowardly performances than he was of the bulls. He had asked the governor for troops to protect him before the fight and the governor told him if he went into the ring and performed well he would need no protection. Each night at Pamplona Manolo had been on the long-distance telephone hearing news of the chopping down of trees on his father's ranch by the peasant jacquerie in Andalucia; groves of trees being cut down and charcoal burnings started, pigs and chickens killed, cattle driven off; the ranch, which was not yet paid for and which he was fighting bulls to complete the payment on, being gradually pillaged in the sound Agrarian sabotage plan of the Andalucian revolt, and being nineteen years old and hearing his world destroyed over the telephone each night, he was worried enough. But the boys at Pamplona and the peasants from the country around who were spending their savings to see bull-fights and not seeing them, through the cowardice of matadors, could not go into the economic causes of a matador's abstraction and lack of interest in his work, and they rioted against Manolo so violently and so scared him that finally, afraid of being lynched, he gave a splendid afternoon on the last day of the fair.

If there was a penalty of suspension from his profitable business operations, Cagancho might give a good afternoon oftener. His excuse is that he runs danger and the spectator does not, but one is being paid proportionately and the other is paying, and when the spectators protest is when Cagancho refuses to run danger. True, he has been gored, but each time through an accident such as a sudden gust of wind that left him uncovered when he was working close to a bull that he believed safe. There is the one chance he cannot eliminate and after he comes back to the ring from the hospital he will not even come close to a bull he believes to be harmless since there is no guarantee the wind will not blow up while he is working, or the cape get between his legs, or that he might not step on the cape or even that the bull may not go blind. He is the only bullfighter I have been glad to see gored; but goring him is no solution since he behaves much worse on coming out of the hospital than before he went in. Yet he keeps on having contracts and robbing the public because they know that when he wishes he can do a complete and splendid faena, a model of perfect execution, and end it by killing beautifully.

The best killer today is Nicanor Villalta who started in by tricking his killing, using his height to lean over the bull as he blinded him with his huge muleta and has now so purified, so mastered, and so perfected the art that, in Madrid at least, he kills nearly every bull he faces closely, confidently, correctly, securely and emotionally, having learned the way to profit by his magic left wrist really to kill instead of merely tricking. Villalta is an example of the simple man that I spoke of at the beginning of this chapter. In intelligence and in conversation he is not as smart as your twelve-year-old sister if she is a backward child, and he has a sense of glory and belief in his greatness that you could reach high enough to hang your hat upon. Added to this he has a semi-hysterical bravery that no cold valour can compete with in intensity. Personally I find him insufferable, although he is pleasant enough if you do not mind conceited hysteria, but with sword and muleta in Madrid he is the bravest, most secure, and most consistent and emotional killer in Spain today.

The best swordsmen in my time were Manuel Vare, called Varelito, probably the best killer of my generation; Antonio de la Haba, called Zurito; Martín Aguero, Manolo Martínez, and Luis Freg. Varelito was of moderate stature, simple, sincere and a consistently great killer. Like all killers of only moderate height he took much punishment from the bulls. Not yet recovered from the effects of a horn wound received the year before, he was unable to kill with his old style in the April fair in Sevilla in 1922, and, his work unsatisfactory, the crowd jeered and insulted him all through the fair. Turning his back on a bull after he had put the sword in, the bull caught him and gave him a terrific wound near the rectum that perforated the intestines. It was almost the same wound that Sidney Franklin received and recovered from in the spring of 1930, and it was the same sort of wound that killed Antonio Montes. He, Vare-lito, being gored late in April, lived until 13th May. As they were carrying him down the passageway around the ring to the infirmary, the crowd, which had been hooting him a minute before, now murmuring with the rush of talk that always follows a serious cogida, Varelito kept saying, looking up at them, 'Now you've given it to me. Now I've got it. Now you've given it to me. Now you've got what you wanted. Now I've got it. Now you've given it to me. Now I've got it. Now I've got it. I've got it.' He had it although it took nearly four weeks for it to kill him.

Zurito was the son of the last and one of the greatest of the old-time picadors. He was from Cordoba, dark and rather thin; his face very sad in repose; serious and with a deep sense of honour. He killed classically, slowly and beautifully, with a sense of honour that forbade him to use any advantage, or trick, or to deviate from a straight line as he went in. He was one of four novilleros who were sensations in their class in 1923 and 1924, and when the other three, who were all much riper than he, though none of them were very ripe, became matadors he became one himself at the very end of the season although his apprenticeship, in the sense that an apprenticeship should continue until the craft has been mastered, was not finished.

None of the four had served a proper apprenticeship. Manuel Baez, called Litri, the most sensational of the four, was a prod-igy of valour and wonderful reflexes, but insensate in his bravery, and very ignorant in his fighting. He was a brown-faced, bow-legged little boy with black hair, a face like a rabbit, and a nervous tic of vision which made his eyelids wink as he watched the bull come; but for a year he substituted bravery, luck, and reflexes for knowledge, and while he was tossed, literally, hundreds of times he was often so close to the horn that it could not get a good chop at him and his luck saved him from all but one serious horn wound. We all spoke of him as carne de toro, or meat for the bulls, and it really did not make much difference when he took the alternativa since he fought on a nervous valour that could not last, and with his faulty technique he was certain to be destroyed by a bull, and the more money he made before it happened the better. He was fatally wounded in the first fight of the year in Málaga early in February of 1926, after he had been a matador one full season. He need not have died of that wound if it had not become infected with gaseous gangrene and his leg amputated too late to save his life. The bullfighters say, 'If I must be gored let it be in Madrid,' or if they are Valencian they substitute Valencia for Madrid, since it is in those two cities that there are most serious bullfights; therefore most horn wounds, and consequently, two of the greatest specialists in that surgery. There is no time for a specialist to come from one city to another for the most vital part of a wound treatment which is the opening and cleaning to avoid the possibility of infections of all the multiple trajectories a horn wound makes. I have seen a horn wound in the thigh with an opening no larger than a silver dollar which, when probed and opened inside, had as many as five different trajectories, these being caused by the man's body revolving on the horn, and, sometimes, by the end of the horn being splintered. All of these inner wounds must be opened and cleaned, and at the same time all incisions in the mucles must be made so that it will heal in the minimum of time and with the least possible loss of mobility. A bull-ring surgeon has two aims: to save the man, the aim of ordinary surgery; and to place the torero back in the ring as soon as possible in order that he may fulfil contracts. It is his ability to get the fighter back to work rapidly that makes a horn-wound specialist able to command high fees. It is a very special sort of surgery, but its simplest form, which is the caring for the ordinary wound, which comes oftenest between knee and groin or between knee and ankle, since that is where the bull's lowered horns catch the man in goring, is to ligate the femoral artery with promptness if it has been opened, and then find, with the finger usually, or with a probe, open and clean all the various trajectories which a horn wound may have, at the same time keeping the patient's heart going with camphor injections and replacing the lost blood with injections of normal salt solution and so forth. Anyway, Litri's leg infected in Málaga and they amputated it, having promised him, when he was anaesthetized, it was only to clean the wound; and when he was conscious and found the leg gone he did not want to live and was in great despair. I was very fond of him and wished he might have died without the amputation since he was marked to die anyway, when he took the alternativa, and was certain to be destroyed as soon as his luck ran out.

Zurito never had any luck. His apprenticeship uncompleted, he had the shortest kind of repertoire with cape and muleta, the latter consisting principally of passes por alto and the easily learned trick of the molinete and the excellence of his swordsmanship, and the purity of his style with the sword, were obscured by the hair-raising campaign Litri was making and the great seasons Niño de la Palma had. Zurito had two good seasons after Litri's death, but before he ever had a chance to really become a dominating figure his work was old-fashioned, since he made no improvement with the cape and muleta, and, as he always aimed the sword for the very top of the opening between the shoulder blades and going in so high with his left shoulder forward it was difficult to keep the muleta low enough to get rid of the bull completely, he took much punishment from the bulls; especially those terrible blows from the flat of the horn against the chest with which the bulls lifted him off his feet nearly every time he killed. Then he almost lost a season from internal injuries and a growth of some sort that came on his lip where it had been hurt. In 1927 he was fighting

in such bad physical condition that it was tragic to watch him.
He knew that to lose out on a single season may put a bullfighter
in the discard so that he will have only two or three fights a
year and not be able to make a living, and all that season Zurito
was fighting; his face, that had been a healthy brown, now as
grey as weathered canvas; so short of breath that it was pitiful
to see him; yet attacking as straight, as close and with the same
classic style and the same bad luck. When the bull bumped
him off his feet or gave him one of those paletazos or strokes
with the flat of the horn that the bullfighters claim harm as
much as wounds, since they cause internal haemorrhages, he
would faint from weakness, be carried into the infirmary,
brought to, and come out again, weak as a convalescent, to kill
his other bull. Due to his style of killing he was bumped nearly
every time he killed. He fought twenty-one times, fainted dead
away in twelve of them, and killed all of his forty-two bulls. It
was not enough though, because his work with the cape and
muleta, never stylish, in the condition he was in was not even
competent and the public did not like to see him faint. There
was an editorial against it in the San Sebastian paper. That was
the town where he had been most successful, and they did not
contract him again since his fainting was very repugnant to
foreigners and the best people. So that season, in which he gave
the most harrowing display of courage I have ever seen, did
him no good. He married at the end of it. She wanted to marry
him, they said, before he died, and instead he got much better;
became rather fat, and loving his wife, did not go in quite so
straight on the bulls, and fought only fourteen times. The next
year he fought only seven times, in Spain and South America.
The next year he was going in as straight as ever, but he had
only two contracts in Spain for the whole year; not enough to
support his family. Of course his fainting that year was not
pleasant to see, but he only knew one way to kill and that was
perfectly, and if, in attempting it, the horn or the muzzle struck
him and he lost the consciousness of this world that was his

hard luck, and he always returned to fight as soon as he was conscious. The public did not like it. It became an old story so rapidly. I did not like it myself, but by Christ how I admired it. Too much honour destroys a man quicker than too much of any other fine quality, and with a little bad luck it ruined Zurito in one season.

Old Zurito, the father, brought up one son to be a matador and taught him honour, technique and classic style, and that boy is a failure in spite of great skill and integrity. He taught the other boy to be a picador, and he has a perfect style, great courage, is a splendid horseman, and would be the best picador in Spain but for one thing. He is too light to be able to punish the bulls. No matter how hard he pegs them he can barely draw blood. So he, with the most ability and style of any picador living, is pic-ing in novilladas at fifty to a hundred pesetas apiece, when with fifty pounds more weight he would be continuing the great tradition of the father. There is another son, too, who is a picador that I have not seen; but they tell me he too is too light. They are not a lucky family.

Martín Aguero, the third of the killers, was a boy from Bilbao who did not look like a bullfighter at all but more like a husky, well-built, professional ballplayer, a third baseman or shortstop. He had a full-lipped face, German–American looking in the sense that Nick Altrock's was, and was no artist with cape or muleta, although he managed a cape well enough; sometimes excellently; understood bullfighting; was not ignorant; and did what he did with the muleta well, although he was altogether without artistic imagination. Put him down as a capable and close worker with the cape and a competent but dull performer with the muleta. With the sword he was a secure and rapid killer. His estocadas always looked wonderful in photographs because the photograph does not give any sense of time, but when you watched him kill he went in so lightning fast that even though he killed more securely than Zurito, crossing magnificently, and nine times out of ten getting the sword in all the way to the hilt, yet one estocada of Zurito's was worth many of Aguero's to watch, since Zurito went in so slowly and directly, marking the time of the killing so completely that there was no element of taking the bull by surprise. Aguero killed like a butcher boy and Zurito like a priest at benediction.

Aguero was very brave and very efficient, and was one of the leading matadors in 1925, 1926, and 1927, fighting fifty and fifty-two times in those last two years and almost never being tossed. In 1928 he was gored severely twice, the second cornada coming as a result of his fighting before he was in good shape after the first, and the two of them breaking down his fine health and physique. A nerve in one of his legs was so badly injured that it atrophied and this led to gangrene of the toes of his right foot and an operation for their removal in 1931. The last I heard his foot had been so mutilated that it was considered impossible that he would ever fight again. He leaves two younger brothers as novilleros with the same looks, the same athletic physique and the beginnings of the same skill with the sword.

Diego Mazquiaran, 'Fortuna' of Bilbao, is another great killer of the butcher-boy type. Fortuna is curly-haired, big-wristed, husky, swaggering, married much money, fights just enough to have money of his own, is brave as the bull himself, and just a little less intelligent. He is the luckiest man that ever fought bulls. He knows only one way to work with a bull; he treats them as though they were all difficult and chops them and doubles them into position with the muleta no matter what sort of faena they require. If the bull happens to be difficult this is very satisfactory, but if he is asking for a grand faena it is not. Once he gets their two front feet together, Fortuna furls the muleta, profiles with the sword, looks over his shoulder at his friends, and says, 'See if we can kill him this way!' and goes in straight, strong, and well. He is so lucky that the sword may even cut the spinal marrow and drop the bull as though he were struck by lightning. If he is not lucky he will sweat and his hair will get more frizzy, he will explain to the spectators with gestures the difficulties of the animal; will call on them all to witness it is not his, Fortuna's, fault. The next day in his regular seat in tendido two (he is one of the few bullfighters who attend bullfights regularly), when a really difficult bull comes out for some other fighter to handle, he will tell all the rest of us, 'That's not a difficult bull. That bull is good. He ought to do something with that bull.' Fortuna is really brave though, brave and stupid. He has absolutely no nervousness about the fight. I have heard him say to a picador, 'Come on. Come on. Hurry it up. I'm bored in here. The whole thing bores me. Hurry it up.' Among the fragile artists, he stands out as a survival from a different time. But he will bore you blinder than he ever has been bored in the ring if you sit near him for a season.

Manolo Martínez of the barrio of Ruzafa in Valencia, slight, with his round eyes, his twisted-crooked face, his thin smile, looks as though he belonged around a race track or like one of the best of the tough citizens you knew around the pool-rooms when you were a boy. Many critics deny he is a great killer because he has never had any luck in Madrid and the editors of the French bullfight paper, Le Toril, a very good periodical, deny him all merit because he has sense enough to not risk his life when fighting in the south of France where any sword that disappears into the bull, no matter how placed, or how trickily inserted, is universally applauded. Martínez is as brave as Fortuna, and he is never bored. He loves to kill, and he is not conceited as Villalta is; when it comes out well he is pleased, seemingly as much for you as for himself. He has been greatly punished by the bulls, and I saw him get a terrible cornada one year in Valencia. His work with cape and muleta is unsound, but if the bull is a frank, fast charger, Martínez works as close as any man can pass bulls. This day he had a bull that hooked to the right and he seemingly did not notice the defect. The bull bumped him once in passing with the cape, and the next time Martínez passed him on the same side and did not give him room, he caught him with the horn and tossed him. He was un-wounded, the horn had slid along the skin without catching and had only torn his trousers, but he had come down on his head and was groggy and on his next turn with the cape he took the bull all the way out into the centre of the ring, and there, alone, tried to pass him closely on the right side again. Of course the bull caught him, his defect had been accentuated by his success at getting the man before, and this time the horn went in, and Martínez went into the air on the horn, the bull tossed him clear and as he lay still on the ground gored at him again and again before the other bullfighters running to the centre of the ring could attract the bull away. As Manolo rose to his feet he saw the blood pumping from his groin, and knowing the femoral artery was severed he put both hands over it to try to contain the haemorrhage, and ran as fast as he could for the infirmary. He knew his life was going out in that stream that spurted between his fingers and he could not wait to be carried. They tried to grab him, but he shook his head. Dr Serra came running down the passageway and Martínez shouted to him, 'Don Paco, I've got a big cornada!' and with Dr Serra pressing with his thumb to stop the artery they went into the infirmary together. The horn had passed almost completely through his thigh, his loss of blood was so tremendous, and he was so weak and prostrated no one believed he would live, and at one time being unable to get any pulse, they announced he was dead. The destruction in the muscle was so great no one thought he would be able to fight again if he lived, but being gored on the 31st of July he was well enough to fight in Mexico on the 18th of October, due to his constitution and the skill of Dr Paco Serra. Martínez has suffered terrible horn wounds, rarely when killing; but usually from his desire to work close to bulls that will not permit it and his fundamental unsoundness in handling the cape and muleta and desire to keep his feet absolutely to-gether when letting the bull pass; but his horn wounds only seem to refresh his valour. He is a local fighter. I have never seen

him really good except in Valencia, but in 1927 in a fair that was
built around Juan Belmonte and Marcial Lalanda, and for which
Martínez was not even contracted, when Belmonte and Marcial
were gored he came in to substitute and fought three fights in
which he was superb, doing everything with cape and muleta so
closely and dangerously and taking such chances you could not
believe it possible the bulls would not kill him, and then, when
it was time to kill, profiling closely, arrogantly, rocking a little
back on his heels to plant himself solidly, his left knee a little
bent, settling his weight on the other foot, then going in and
killing in a way no living man could better. In 1931 he was
dangerously gored in Madrid and was still unrecovered when
he fought in Valencia. The critics all say he is finished now, but
he has made his living, proving them wrong from the start, and
I believe as soon as his nerves and muscles will obey his heart
again he will be the same as ever until a bull destroys him.
With his unsoundness and inability to dominate a difficult bull,
coupled to his great bravery, that seems inevitable. His valour
is almost humorous. It is a sort of cockney bravery, while
Villalta's is conceited, Fortuna's is dumb and Zurito's is mystic.

The valour of Luis Freg – he has no art, except with the sword
– is the strangest that I know. It is as indestructible as the sea, but
there is no salt in it unless it is the salt of his own blood, and
human blood has a sweet and sickly taste in spite of its saline
quality. If Luis Freg had died in any of the four times that I remember him being given up as dead, I could write more freely
of his character. He is a Mexican Indian, heavy-set now, soft-
voiced, soft-handed, nose rather hooked, slant-eyed, full
mouth, very black hair, the only matador who still wears the
pigtail plaited on his head, and he has been a full matador in
Mexico since Johnson fought Jeffries at Reno, Nevada, in 1910,
and in Spain since the year after that fight. In the twenty-one
years he has fought as a matador the bulls have given him
seventy-two severe horn wounds. No bullfighter who ever
lived has been so punished by the bulls as he has. He has received

extreme unction five different times when he was believed certain to die. His legs are as gnarled and twisted by scars as the branches of an old oak tree, and his chest and his abdomen are covered with scars of wounds that should have killed him. Most of them have come from his heaviness on his feet and his inability to control the bulls with cape and muleta. He was a great killer though; slow, secure, and straight, and the few times, few in proportion to his other gorings, that he was wounded when killing were due to his lack of speed of foot to come out from between the horns and along the flank after he had the sword in rather than to any defects in his technique. His terrible gorings, his months in the hospitals, which used up all his money, had no effect on his valour at all. But it was a strange valour. It never fired you; it was not contagious. You saw it, appreciated it, and knew the man was brave, but somehow it was as though courage was a syrup rather than a wine or the taste of salt and ashes in your mouth. If qualities have odours, the odour of courage to me is the smell of smoked leather or the smell of a frozen road or the smell of the sea when the wind rips the top from a wave, but the valour of Luis Freg did not have that odour. It was clotted and heavy, and there was a thin part underneath that was unpleasant and oozy, and when he is dead I will tell you about him and it is a strange enough story.

The last time he was given up for dead at Barcelona, torn open terribly, the wound full of pus, delirious and dying, everyone believed, he said, 'I see death. I see it clearly. Ayee. Ayee. It is an ugly thing.' He saw death clearly, but it did not come. He is broke now and giving a final series of farewell performances. He was marked for death for twenty years and death never took him.

There you have portraits of five killers. If we can synthesize from studying good killers you might say that a great killer needs honour, courage, a good physique, a good style, a great left hand, and much luck. Then he needs a good press and plenty of contracts. The location, and the effect, of estocadas and the various manners of killing are described in the glossary.

If the people of Spain have one common trait it is pride, and if they have another it is common sense, and if they have a third it is impracticality. Because they have pride they do not mind killing, feeling that they are worthy to give this gift. As they have common sense they are interested in death and do not spend their lives avoiding the thought of it and hoping it does not exist only to discover it when they come to die. This common sense that they possess is as hard and dry as the plains and mesas of Castilla and it diminishes in hardness and dryness as it goes away from Castilla. At its best it is combined with a complete impracticality. In the south it becomes picturesque; along the littoral it becomes mannerless and Mediterranean; in the north in Navarra and Aragón there is such tradition of bravery that it becomes romantic, and along the Atlantic coast, as in all countries bounded by a cold sea, life is so practical there is no time for common sense. Death, to people who fish in the cold parts of the Atlantic ocean, is something that may come at any time, that comes often and is to be avoided as an industrial accident; so that they are not preoccupied with it and it has no fascination for them.

There are two things that are necessary for a country to love bullfights. One is that the bulls must be raised in that country, and the other that the people must have an interest in death. The English and the French live for life. The French have a cult of respect for the dead, but the enjoyment of the daily material things, family, security, position and money, are the things that are most important. The English live for this world, too, and death is not a thing to think of, to consider, to mention, to seek, or to risk except in the service of the country, or for sport, or for adequate reward. Otherwise it is an unpleasant subject to be avoided, or at best, moralized on, but never to be studied. Never discuss casualties, they say, and I have heard them say it very well. When the English kill they kill for sport and the French kill for the pot. It is a fine pot too, the loveliest in the world, and well worth killing for. However, any killing which is not for the pot, nor for sport, seems to the English and the French to be cruel. Like all general statements things are not as simple as I have written them, but I am seeking to state a principle and refrain from listing exceptions.

Now in Spain the bullfight is out of place in Galicia and in most of Catalonia. They do not raise bulls in those provinces. Galicia is beside the sea and because it is a poor country where the men emigrate or go to sea, death is not a mystery to be sought and meditated on, but rather a daily peril to be avoided, and the people are practical, cunning, often stupid, often avaricious, and their favourite amusement is choral singing. Catalonia is Spain, but the people are not Spanish, and although bullfighting flourishes in Barcelona it is on a fake basis, because the public that attends goes as to a circus for excitement and entertainment, and is as ignorant, almost, as the publics of Nîmes, Béziers, and Arles. The Catalans have a rich country, a great part of it at least; they are good farmers, good business men, good salesmen; they are the commercially elect of Spain. The richer the country the simpler the peasantry, and they combine a simple peasantry and a childish language with a highly developed commercial class. With them, as in Galicia, life is too practical for there to be much of the hardest kind of common sense nor much feeling about death.

In Castilla the peasant has nothing of the simple-mindedness, combined as always with cunning, of the Catalan or Gallego. He lives in a country with as severe a climate as any that is farmed, but it is a very healthy country; he has food, wine, his wife and children, or he has had them, but he has no comfort, nor much capital, and these possessions are not ends in themselves; they are only a part of life and life is something that comes before death. Someone with English blood has written: 'Life is real; life is earnest, and the grave is not its goal.' And where did they bury him? and what became of the reality and the earnestness? The people of Castilla have great common sense. They could not produce a poet who would write a line like that. They know death is the unescapable reality, the one thing any man may be sure of; the only security; that it transcends all modern comforts and that with it you do not need a bath-tub in every American home, nor, when you have it, do you need the radio. They think a great deal about death, and when they have a religion they have one which believes that life is much shorter than death. Having this feeling they take an intelligent interest in death, and when they can see it being given, avoided, refused, and accepted in the afternoon for a nominal price of admission they pay their money and go to the bull ring, continuing to go even when, for certain reasons that I have tried to show in this book, they are most often artistically disappointed and emotionally defrauded.

Most of the great bullfighters have come from Andalucia, where the best bulls are raised and where with the warm climate and the Moorish blood the men have a grace and indolence that is foreign to Castilla, although they have, mixed with the Moorish blood, the blood of the men of Castilla who drove out the Moors and occupied that pleasant country. Of the truly great fighters both Cayetano Sanchez and Frascuelo were from around Madrid (although Frascuelo was born to the south), as well as Vicente Pastor of the minor greats, and Marcial Lalanda, the best of the present fighters. There are fewer bullfights given all the time in Andalucia, due to the agrarian troubles, and fewer first-rate matadors produced. In 1931 out of the first ten matadors there were only three from Andalucia, Cagancho and the two Bienvenidas; and Manolo Bienvenida, although of Andalucian parentage, was born and raised in South America, while his brother, although born in Spain, was also raised out of the country. Chicuelo and Niño de la Palma representing Sevilla and Ronda are both finished, and Gitanillo de Triana, of Sevilla, was killed.

Marcial Lalanda is from near Madrid as are Antonio Már-

DEATH IN THE AFTERNOON

quez, who will be fighting again, and Domingo Ortega. Villalta is from Zaragoza, and Barrera from Valencia along with Manolo Martínez and Enrique Torres. Félix Rodríguez was born in Santander and raised in Valencia, and Armillita Chico, Solorzano, and Heriberto Garcia are all Mexicans. Nearly all the leading young novilleros are from Madrid or from around Madrid, the north, or Valencia. Since the death of Joselito and Maera, and the final retirement of Belmonte, the reign of Andalucia in modern bullfighting has been over. The centre of bullfighting in Spain now, both as to the production of fighters and the great enthusiasm for the fight itself, is Madrid and the country around Madrid. Valencia comes next. The most complete and masterly fighter in bullfighting today is unquestionably Marcial Lalanda, and the most complete young fighters in point of view of valour and technical equipment are being turned out in Mexico. The bullfight is undoubtedly losing ground in Sevilla, which was once, with Cordoba, its great centre, and it is undoubtedly gaining in Madrid where all spring and early summer in 1931, in bad financial times, in a time of much political unrest, and with only ordinary pro-grammes, the ring was filled to capacity two and sometimes three times a week.

Judging from the enthusiasm I saw shown for it under the Republic the modern bullfight will continue in Spain in spite of the great wish of her present European-minded politicians to see it abolished so that they will have no intellectual embarrass-ments at being different from their European colleagues that they meet at the League of Nations, and at the foreign embassies and courts. At present a violent campaign is being conducted against it by certain newspapers with govern-ment subsidies, but so many people derive their livings from the many ramifications of raising, shipping, fighting, feeding, and butchering of fighting cattle that I do not believe the government will abolish it even if they felt themselves strong enough.

An exhaustive study is being made of the actual and potential use of all lands used for the grazing of fighting-bull stock. In the agrarian readjustments that must come in Andalucia some of the biggest ranches are sure to be broken up, but since Spain is a grazing as well as an agricultural country and much of the grazing land is unfit for cultivation and none of the cattle produced are wasted, all being butchered and sold whether killed in the ring or the slaughter-house, much of the land now used for fighting-bull grazing in the south will certainly be retained. In a country where to give work to the agricultural labourers all machines for harvesting and sowing had to be banned in 1931, the government will go slowly about putting much new land under cultivation. There is no question of trying to cultivate the grazing land used for bulls around Colmenar and Salamanca. I look for a certain reduction of acreage in bull-raising land in Andalucia and the breaking up of a number of ranches, but believe there will be no great change in the industry under the present government, although many of its members would be proud to abolish the bullfight and doubtless will do all they can toward that end, and the quickest way to get at it is through the bulls, since bullfighters grow up, unencouraged, having a natural talent as acrobats or jockeys or even writers have, and none of them are irreplaceable; but fighting bulls are the products of many generations of careful breeding, as race horses are, and when you send that strain to the slaughter-house that strain is finished.

Chapter 20

If I could have made this enough of a book it would have had everything in it. The Prado, looking like some big American college building with sprinklers watering the grass early in the bright Madrid summer morning; the bare white mud hills looking across toward Carabanchel; days on the train in August with the blinds pulled down on the side against the sun and the wind blowing them; chaff blown against the car in the wind from the hard earthen threshing floors; the odour of grain and the stone windmills. It would have had the change when you leave the green country behind at Alsasua; it would have had Burgos far across the plain, and eating the cheese later up in the room; it would have had the boy taking wicker-bound jugs of wine on the train as samples; his first trip to Madrid, and opening them in enthusiasm, and they all got drunk including the pair of Guardia Civil, and I lost the tickets and we were taken through the wicket by the two Guardia Civil (who took us out as though prisoners because there were no tickets and then saluted as they put us in the cab); Hadley, with the bull's ear wrapped in a handkerchief, the ear was very stiff and dry and the hair all wore off it and the man who cut the ear is bald now too and slicks long strips of hair over the top of his head and he was beau then. He was, all right.

It should make clear the change in the country as you come down out of the mountains and into Valencia in the dusk on the train holding a rooster for a woman who was bringing it to her sister; and it should show the wooden ring at Alcira where they dragged the dead horses out in the field and you had to pick

255

your way over them; and the noise in the streets in Madrid after midnight, and the fair that goes on all night long, in June, and walking home on Sundays from the ring; or with Rafael in the cab. Que tal? Malo, hombre, malo; with that lift of the shoulders, or with Roberto, Don Roberto, Don Ernesto, so polite always, so gentle and such a good friend. Also the house where Rafael lived before being a republican became respectable with the mounted head of the bull Gitanillo had killed and the great oil jar and always presents, and the excellent cooking.

It should have the smell of burnt powder and the smoke and the flash and the noise of the traca going off through the green leaves of the trees, and it should have the taste of horchata, ice-cold horchata, and the new-washed streets in the sun, and the melons and beads of cool on the outside of the pitchers of beer; the storks on the houses in Barco de Avila and wheeling in the sky, and the red-mud colour of the ring; and at night dancing to the pipes, and the drum with lights through the green leaves and the portrait of Garibaldi framed in leaves. It should, if it were enough of a book, have the forced smile of Lagartijo; it was once a real smile, and the unsuccessful matadors swimming with the cheap whores out on the Manzanares along the Prado road; beggars can't be choosers, Luis said; playing ball on the grass by the stream where the fairy marquis came out in his car with the boxer; where we made the paellas, and walked home in the dark with the cars coming fast along the road; and with electric lights through the green leaves and the dew settling the dust, in the cool at night; cider in Bombilla and the road to Pontevedra from Santiago de Compostella with the high turn in the pines and blackberries beside the road; Algabeno the worst faker of them all; and Maera up in the room at Quintana's changing outfits with the priest the one year everyone drank so much and no one was nasty. There really was such a year, but this is not enough of a book.

Make all that come true again; throw grasshoppers to the trout in the Tambre on the bridge in the evening; have the serious brown face of Félix Merino at the old Aguilar; have the brave, awkward, wall-eyed Pedro Montes dressing away from home because he had promised his mother he had stopped fighting, after Mariano, his brother, was killed at Tetuan; and Litri, like a little rabbit, his eyes winking nervously as the bull came; he was very bow-legged and brave, and those three are all killed and never any mention made about the beer place on the cool side of the street underneath the Palace where he sat with his father, and how it is a Citroën showroom now; nor about them carrying Pedro Carreño, dead, through the streets with torches and finally into the church and putting him naked on the altar.

There is nothing in this book about Francisco Gomez, Aldeano, who worked in Ohio in a steel plant and came home to be a matador, and now is scarred and marked worse than anyone except Freg, his eye twisted so a tear runs down his nose. Nor Gavira dead at the very instant as the bull with the same cornada that killed El Espartero. Nor does it tell about Zaragoza; at night on the bridge watching the Ebro, and the parachute jumper the next day and Rafael's cigars; nor the jota contests in the old red plush theatre and the wonderful boy and girl pairs; nor when they killed the Noy de Sucre in Barcelona, nor about any of that; nor anything about Navarra; nor about the lousy town León is; nor about lying with a muscle torn in a hotel on the sunny side of the street in Palencia when it was hot and you do not know what hot is when you have not been there; nor on the road where dust is deeper than the hubs between Requena and Madrid; nor when it was one hundred and twenty in the shade in Aragón, and the car, with no carbon nor anything wrong, would boil the water out of the radiator in fifteen minutes on a level road.

If it were more of a book it would make the last night of feria when Maera fought Alfredo David in the Café Kutz; and it should show the bootblacks. My God, you could not get in all the bootblacks; nor all the fine girls passing; nor the whores;

nor all of us ourselves as we were then. Pamplona now is changed; they have built new apartment buildings out over all the sweep of plain that ran to the edge of the plateau; so now you cannot see the mountains. They tore down the old Gayarre and spoiled the square to cut a wide thoroughfare to the ring, and in the old days there was Chicuelo's uncle sitting drunk in the upstairs dining-room watching the dancing in the square; Chicuelo was in his room alone, and the cuadrilla in the café and around the town. I wrote a story about it called *A Lack of Passion*, but it was not good enough, although when they threw the dead cats at the train and afterwards the wheels clicking and Chicuelo in the berth, alone; able to do it alone – it was fair enough.

It should, if it had Spain in it, have the tall thin boy, eight feet six inches; he advertised the Empastre show before they came to town, and that night, at the feria de ganado, the whores wouldn't have anything to do with the dwarf – he was full size except that his legs were only six inches long – and he said, 'I'm a man like any man,' and the whore said, 'No you're not and that's the trouble.' There are many dwarfs in Spain and cripples that you wouldn't believe that follow all the fairs.

In the morning there we would have breakfast and then go out to swim in the Irati at Aoiz, the water clear as light, and varying in temperature as you sunk down, cool, deep cool, cold, and the shade from the trees on the bank when the sun was hot, the ripe wheat in the wind up on the other side and sloping to the mountain. There was an old castle at the head of the valley where the river came out between two rocks; and we lay naked on the short grass in the sun and later in the shade. The wine at Aoiz was no good, so then we brought our own, and neither was the ham, so the next time we brought a lunch from Quintana's. Quintana, the best aficionado and most loyal friend in Spain, and with a fine hotel with all the rooms, full. Que tal, Juanito? Que tal, hombre, que tal?

And why should it not have the cavalry crossing another

stream at a ford, the shadow of the leaves on the horses, if it is Spain, and why not have them marching out from the machine-gun school across the clay-white ground, very small so far away, and looking beyond from Quintanilla's window were the mountains. Or waking in the morning, the streets empty on Sunday, and the shouting far away, and then the firing. That happens many times if you live long enough and move around.

And if you ride and if your memory is good you may ride still through the forest of the Irati with trees like drawings in a child's fairy book. They cut those down. They ran logs down the river and they killed the fish, or in Galicia they bombed and poisoned them; results the same; so in the end it's just like home except for yellow gorse on the high meadows and the thin rain. Clouds come across the mountains from the sea, but when the wind is from the south, Navarra is all the colour of wheat except it does not grow on level plains but up and down the sides of hills and cut by roads with trees and many villages with bells, pelota courts, the smell of sheep manure and squares with standing horses.

If you could make the yellow flames of candles in the sun, that shines on steel of bayonets freshly oiled and yellow patent leather belts of those who guard the Host; or hunt in pairs through scrub oak in the mountains for the ones who fell into the trap at Deva (it was a bad, long way to come from the Café Rotonde to be garrotted in a draughty room with consolation of the church at order of the state, acquitted once and held until the captain general of Burgos reversed the finding of the court) and in the same town where Loyola got his wound that made him think, the bravest of those who were betrayed that year dived from the balcony on to the paving of the court, head first, because he had sworn they would not kill him (his mother tried to make him promise not to take his life because she worried most about his soul, but he dived well and cleanly with his hands tied while they walked with him praying); if I could make him; make a bishop; make Candido Tiebas and Toron;

make clouds come fast in shadows moving over wheat and the small, careful stepping horses; the smell of olive oil; the feel of leather; rope-soled shoes; the loops of twisted garlics; earthen pots; saddle bags carried across the shoulder; wine skins; the pitchforks made of natural wood (the tines were branches); the early morning smells; the cold mountain nights and long hot days of summer, with always trees and shade under the trees, then you would have a little of Navarra. But it's not in this book.

There ought to be Astorga, Lugo, Orense, Soria, Tarragona, and Calatayud, the chestnut woods on the high hills, the green country and the rivers, the red dust, the small shade beside the dry rivers and the white, baked clay hills; cool walking under palms in the old city on the cliff above the sea, cool in the evening with the breeze; mosquitoes at night, but in the morning the water clear and the sand white; then sitting in the heavy twilight at Miro's; vines as far as you can see, cut by the hedges and the road; the railroad and the sea with pebbly beach and tall papyrus grass. There were earthen jars for the different years of wine, twelve feet high, set side by side in a dark room; a tower on the house to climb to in the evening to see the vines, the villages and the mountains, and to listen and to hear how quiet it was. In front of the barn a woman held a duck whose throat she had cut and stroked her gently while a little girl held up a cup to catch the blood for making gravy. The duck seemed very contented, and when they put her down (the blood all in the cup) she waddled twice and found that she was dead. We ate her later, stuffed and roasted; and many other dishes, with the wine of that year and the year before, and the great year four years before that, and other years that I lost track of, while the long arms of a mechanical fly-chaser that wound by clockwork went round and round and we talked French. We all knew Spanish better.

That is Montroig, pronounced Montroych, one of many places in Spain, where there are also the streets of Santiago in the rain; seeing the town down in the cup of hills as you come home across the high country; and all the carts that roll, piled high, on smooth stone tracks along the road to Grau should be there with the temporary wooden ring in Noya, smelling of fresh cut boards; Chiquito with his girl's face, a great artist, fino muy fino, pero frio. Valencia II with his eye they sewed up wrong so that the inside of the lid showed and he could not be arrogant any more. Also the boy who missed the bull entirely when he went in to kill and missed him again the second time. If you could stay awake for the nocturnals you saw them funny.

In Madrid the comic bullfighter, beaten up twice by Rodalito, stabbing him in the belly because he thought there was another beating coming. Aguero eating with his whole family in the dining-room; they all looking alike in different ages. He looked like a shortstop or a quarterback, not like a matador. Cagancho eating in his room with his fingers because he could not use a fork. He could not learn it, so when he had enough money he never ate in public. Ortega engaged to Miss España the ugliest and the prettiest, and who was the wittiest? Derperdicios in *La Gaceta del Norte* was the wittiest; the wittiest I ever read.

And up in Sidney's rooms, the ones coming to ask for work when he was fighting, the ones to borrow money, the ones for an old shirt, a suit of clothes; all bullfighters, all well known somewhere at the hour of eating, all formally polite, all out of luck; the muletas folded and piled; the capes all folded flat; swords in the embossed leather cases; all in the armoire; muleta sticks are in the bottom drawer, suits hung in the trunk, cloth covered to protect the gold; my whisky in an earthen crock; Mercedes, bring the glasses; she says he had a fever all night long and only went out an hour ago. So then he comes in. How do you feel? Great. She says you had fever. But I feel great now. What do you say, Doctor, why not eat here? She can get something and make a salad. Mercedes, oh Mercedes.

Then you could walk across the town and to the café where

they say you get your education learning who owed who money and who chiselled this from who and why he told him he could kiss his what and who had children by who and who married who before and after what and how long it took for this and that and what the doctor said. Who was so pleased because the bulls were delayed, being unloaded only the day of the fight, naturally weak in the legs, just two passes, poom, and it is all over, he said, and then it rained and the fight postponed a week and that was when he got it. Who wouldn't fight with who and when and why, and does she, of course she does, you fool you didn't know she does? Absolutely and that's all and in no other fashion, she gobbles them alive, and all such valuable news you learn in cafés. In cafés where the boys are never wrong; in cafés where they are all brave; in cafés where the saucers pile and drinks are figured in pencil on the marble table tops among the shucked shrimps; of seasons lost and feeling good because there are no other triumphs so secure and every man a success by eight o'clock if somebody can pay the score in cafés.

What else should it contain about a country you love very much? Rafael says things are very changed and he won't go to Pamplona any more. *La Libertad* I find is getting like *Le Temps*. It is no longer the paper where you could put a notice and know the pickpocket would see it now that Republicans are all respectable and Pamplona is changed, of course, but not as much as we are older. I found that if you took a drink that it got very much the same as it was always. I know things change now and I do not care. It's all been changed for me. Let it all change. We'll all be gone before it's changed too much and if no deluge comes when we are gone it still will rain in summer in the north and hawks will nest in the Cathedral at Santiago and in La Granja, where we practised with the cape on the long gravelled paths between the shadows; it makes no difference if the fountains play or not. We never will ride back from Toledo in the dark, washing the dust out with Fundador, nor will there be that week of what happened in the night in that July in Madrid. We've seen it all go and we'll watch it go again. The great thing is to last and get your work done and see and hear and learn and understand; and write when there is something that you know; and not before; and not too damned much after. Let those who want to save the world if you can get to see it clear and as a whole. Then any part you make will represent the whole if it's made truly. The thing to do is work and learn to make it. No. It is not enough of a book, but still there were a few things to be said. There were a few practical things to be said.

An Explanatory Glossary

A

Abanico: spread like a fan.

Abano: a bull which comes out in a cowardly way, refusing to charge, but may improve under punishment.

Abierto de cuerna: wide horned.

Abrir el Toro: to take the bull out into the ring away from the barrera.

Aburrimiento: boredom, the predominant sensation at a bad bullfight. Can be alleviated slightly by cold beer. Unless beer is very cold the aburrimiento increases.

Acero: the steel. A common word for the sword.

Acometida: the charge of the bull.

Acornear: goring with the horn.

Acosar: part of the testing of young bulls on the ranch. The horseman cuts the young bull or calf out of the herd, pursues him until he turns at bay and charges.

Acoson: when the bullfighter is closely pursued by the bull.

Acostarse: a tendency in the bull to come closer to the bullfighter on one side or the other when charging. If the bull cuts in close on one side the bullfighter must give him room on that side or he will be caught.

Achuchón: the bull bumping the man in passing.

Adentro: the part of the ring between the bull and the barrera.

Adorno: any useless or flowery theatricality performed by the bullfighter to show his domination over the bull. It may be in good or

265

bad taste varying from kneeling with the back toward the animal to hanging the straw hat of a spectator on the bull's horn. The worst adorno I ever saw performed was by Antonio Márquez who bit the bull's horn. The finest was by Rafael El Gallo who placed four pairs of banderillas in the bull and later, very delicately, in the pauses he gave the bull to refresh him while working with the muleta, extracted the banderillas one at a time.

Afición: love of bullfights. It also means the entire bull-ring public, but is usually used in this generic sense to denote the most intelligent part of the public.

Aficionado: one who understands bullfights in general and in detail and still cares for them.

Afueras: the part of the ring between the bull and the centre of the ring.

Aguantar: a method of killing the bull with sword and muleta in which, if the bull charges unexpectedly while the matador is profiled and is furling his muleta, the matador awaits him as he stands, guides him past with the muleta held low in the left hand while with his right hand he puts in the sword. Nine out of ten of the killings in this form that I have seen turn out badly since the matador will not wait for the bull to get close enough to place the sword properly, but lets the blade slip into the neck which can be reached by the man practically without exposition.

Aguja: agujas or needles are one of the names for the bull's horns. It also means the top forward ribs beside the shoulder blades.

Ahondar el estoque: to push the sword farther in after it has been already placed. This is often attempted by the sword handler when the bull is close to the barrera if the matador is showing himself unable to kill the bull. It is sometimes accomplished by the banderilleros throwing a cape over the sword and pulling down on it.

Ahormar la cabeza: getting the bull's head in correct position for killing. The matador should accomplish this by his work with the muleta. He brings it down with low passes and up with high, but sometimes a few high passes will bring down a head held too high by making the bull stretch his neck so high that he tires it. If the matador cannot bring the bull's head up a banderillero will usually raise it with a few upward flops of a cape. Whether the matador will have much or little regulating to do depends on the manner in which the bull has been treated by the picadors and how the banderillas have been placed.

Aire: the wind; worst enemy of the bullfighter. Capes and muletas are wet and scuffed into the sand to make them more manageable in wind. They cannot be made much heavier than the cloth is naturally or they will deaden the bull-fighter's wrist and if there is enough wind the man could not hold them. The cape or muleta may at any time be blown clear of the man so that he will have the bull on top of him. In each fight there is some part of the ring where the wind is least strong and the bullfighter should find that lee and do all his fancy work with cape and muleta there if possible, if the bull can be worked with in that section of the ring.

Al Alimón: a very silly pass in which two men each hold one end of the cape and the bull passes under the cape between them. There is no danger in this pass and you will only see it used in France or where the public is very naïve.

Alegrar al Toro: to rouse the bull's attention when he has become dull.

Alegría: lightheartedness, in bullfighting; a graceful, picturesque Sevillian style as opposed to the classical tragic manner of the Ronda school.

Alguacil: a mounted bailiff under the orders of the president who rides at the head of the bullfighters in the entry or Paseo wearing a costume of the reign of Philip II, receives the key of the toril from the president, and during the bullfight transmits any orders of the president to those engaged in the bullfight. These orders are usually given by a speaking tube which connects the president's box with the runway between the ring and the seats. There are ordinarily two alguacils at each bullfight.

Alternativa: is the formal envesture of an apprentice matador or matador de novillos as a full matador de toros. It consists in the senior matador of the fight giving up his right to kill the first bull and signifying it by presenting muleta and sword to the bullfighter who is alternating for the first time in the killing of bulls with full matadors de toros. The ceremony takes place when the trumpet sounds for the death of the first bull. The man who is being initiated as a matador goes out with a fighting cape over his arm to meet the senior matador who gives him the sword and muletta, and receives the cape. They shake hands and the new matador kills the first bull. On the second bull he returns sword and muleta to his sponsor who then kills that animal. After that they alternate in the usual manner, the fourth bull being killed by the senior, the fifth by the next in seniority and the new matador killing the last one. Once he has taken the alternativa in Spain his ranking as a formal matador is valid in all bull rings in the Peninsula except Madrid. On his first presentation in Madrid after a provincial alternativa the ceremony must be repeated. Alternativas given in Mexico or South America are not recognized in Spain until confirmed in the provinces and Madrid.

Alto: a *pase por alto* is a pass in which the bull passes under the muleta.

Alto (en todo lo): a sword thrust or estocada placed properly high up between the shoulder blades.

Ambos: both; *ambos manos,* both hands.

Amor propio: amour-propre, self-respect, a rare thing in modern bull-fighters especially after their first successful season or when they have fifty or sixty engagements ahead of them.

Anda: go on! You will hear this frequently shouted at picadors who are reluctant to approach the bull.

Andanada: the high cheap seats on the sunny side of the ring which correspond in position to the boxes on the shady side.

Anillo: the bull ring. Also the ring at the base of the horn by which the bull's age can be told. The first ring means three years. There is a ring thereafter for each year.

Anojo: a yearling bull.

Apartado: the sorting of the bulls, usually at noon before the fight, separating them and putting them in the pens in the order in which it has been decided they are to be fought.

Aplomado: the heavy or leaden state the bull is often in toward the end of the fight.

Apoderado: bullfighter's representative or manager. Unlike the managers of boxers they rarely get more than five per cent for each fight they sign for their matador.

Apodo: the professional nickname of a bullfighter.

Aprovechar: to take advantage of and profit by the good bull a matador has drawn. The worst a matador can do is not to make the most of an easy and noble bull in order to perform brilliantly. He will get many more difficult bulls than good ones and if he does not *aprovechar* good bulls to do his utmost, the crowd is much more severe than if he had been really poor with a difficult bull.

Apurado: a bull worn out and empty of force through being badly fought.

Arena: the sand which covers the ring.

Arenero: a bull-ring servant who flattens out the sand after each bull has been killed and drawn out.

Armarse: when the matador furls the muleta, and sights along the sword, which should form a continuous line with his face and arm preparatory to killing.

Arrancada: another name for the bull's charge.

Arrastre: the dragging out by a trio of mules or horses of the dead horses and the body of the bull after each bull has been killed. The horses are taken out first. If the bull has been exceptionally brave the crowd applauds him very much. He is sometimes given a tour of the ring as he is dragged out.

Arreglar los pies: to make the bull put his front feet together before going in to kill. If one foot is in front of the other one shoulder blade will be farther forward than the other, closing the opening between the shoulder blades into which the sword must go or greatly reducing its opening.

Arrimar: to work close to the bull. If the matadors *arriman al toro* it will be a good bullfight. The boredom comes when they see how far away they can work from the bull's horns.

Asiento: seat.

Astas: bayonets – another synonym for the horn.

Astifino: a bull with thin sharp horns.

Astillado: a bull with the ends of one or both of his horns splintered, usually from battering against his cage or charging in the corral when unloaded. Such horns make the worst wounds.

Atrás: to the rear; backwards.

Atravesada: crosswise – a sword thrust that goes in on the bias so that the point of the sword comes out through the skin of the bull's flank. Such a thrust, unless the bull obviously deviated in his charge shows that the man did not go in straight at the moment of killing.

Atronar: a stroke with the point of the puntilla or dagger between the cervical vertebrae given from behind when the bull is on the ground mortally wounded which severs the spinal marrow and kills the animal instantly. This *coup de grâce* is given by the puntillero, one of the banderilleros, who pulls an oilcloth sleeve over his right arm to save his clothes from blood before he approaches the bull. When the bull is on his feet and this same thrust is given from in front by the matador, either armed with a special sword with a straight, stiff point, or with the *puntilla*, it is called a descabello.

Avíos de matar: the tools for killing, i.e. sword and muleta.

Aviso: a warning given by a bugle at the signal of the president to a matador whose bull is still alive ten minutes after the man has gone out to kill with sword and muleta. The second aviso comes three minutes after the first and the third and final aviso is given two minutes later. At the third aviso the matador is compelled to retire to the barrera, and the steers, which are held in readiness after the first warning, come into the ring and take the bull out alive. There is a large clock displayed in all of the more important rings in order that the spectators may keep track of the time the matador takes for his work.

Ayudada: pass in which the point of the sword is pricked into the cloth of the muleta to spread the serge; the muleta thus being referred to as being aided by the sword.

Ayuntamiento: the city hall or municipal government in Spanish towns. A box is reserved for the *ayuntamiento* in Spanish bull rings.

B

Bajo: low. A low pic is one which is placed on the side of the neck near the shoulder blades. A sword thrust into the right side anywhere below the top of the shoulder blades and forward on the neck is also called bajo.

Bajonazo: is usually a deliberate sword thrust into the neck or lower part of the shoulder by a matador who seeks to kill the bull without exposing himself. In a bajonazo the matador seeks to cut arteries or veins in the neck or to reach the lungs with the sword. By such a thrust he assassinates the bull without having gone in and passed the horn with his body.

Banderilla: a rounded dowel, seventy centimetres long, wrapped in coloured paper, with a harpoon-shaped steel point, placed in pairs in the withers of the bull in the second act of the bullfight; the prong of the harpoon catching under the skin. They should be placed high on the very top of the withers and close together.

Banderillas cortas: short banderillas only twenty-five centimetres long. Seldom used now.

Banderillas de fuego: banderillas with firecrackers along their shafts which are placed in bulls which have not charged the picadors in order that the explosion of the powder may make the bull jump, toss his head, and tire his neck muscles; the object sought in the encounter with the picador which the bull has refused.

Banderillas de lujos: heavily ornamented banderillas used in benefit performances. Hard to place because of their weight and awkwardness.

Banderillero: bullfighter under the orders of the matador and paid by him, who helps run the bull with the cape and places banderillas. Each matador employs four banderilleros who are sometimes called *peones.* They were once called *chulos,* but that term is no longer used. Banderilleros make from 150 to 250 pesetas a fight. They take turns placing the banderillas, two of them placing them on one bull and the other two on the next. When travelling their expenses, except wine, coffee, and tobacco, are paid by the matador, who, in turn, collects them from the promoter.

Barbas – El Barbas: fighters' slang term for the big mature bulls, which at four and a half years old will dress out three hundred and twenty kilos of meat with horns, head, hooves and hide gone, know how to use their horns when alive, and make the bullfighters earn their money.

Barrenar: pushing on the sword by the matador after he has gone in to kill and is coming along the flank after having passed the bull's horn. Once he is past the horn he may push on the sword without danger.

Barrera: the red painted wooden fence around the sanded ring in which the bull is fought. The first row of seats are also called barreras.

Basto: heavy on the feet, lacking in grace, art, and agility.

Batacazo: a heavy fall by a picador.

Becerrada: benefit performance by amateurs or apprentice bullfighters in which bulls too young to be dangerous are used.

Becerro: a calf.

Bicho: bug or insect. A slang name for the bull.

Billetes: tickets to the bullfight. NO HAY BILLETES – a sign at the ticket window meaning all tickets sold; the promoter's dream. But the waiter at the café can nearly always get you one if you will pay scalper's prices.

Bisco: a bull with one horn lower than the other.

Blando: a bull which cannot stand punishment.

Blandos: meat without bone. An estocada is said to be in the blandos when the sword went in easily in the proper place without hitting bone.

Bota: individual wine skin, called gourd by the English. These are thrown into the ring by their exalted owners in the north of Spain as an ovation to a bullfighter who is making a tour of the ring. The triumphant fighter is supposed to take a drink and throw the wine skin back. The bullfighters dislike this practice very much as the wine is liable, if any spills, to spot their expensive frilled shirt fronts.

Botella: a bottle, these are thrown into the ring by savages, drunks, and exalted spectators to express their disapproval.

Botellazo: a stroke on the head with a bottle; avoided by not arguing with drunks.

Boyante: an easy bull to work with and one which follows the cloth well and charges bravely and frankly.

Bravo – toros bravos: brave and savage bulls.

Bravucón: a bull who bluffs and is not really brave.

Brazuelo: the upper part of the foreleg. The bull can be lamed and ruined for the fight by the picadors wounding him in the tendons of the brazuelo.

Brega: the routine work that must be accomplished with each bull fought up to and including the killing.

Brindis: the formal salute or dedication of the bull to the president or to any individual made by the matador before going out to kill. The salute to the president is obligatory in the first bull each matador kills in an afternoon. After saluting the president he may dedicate the bull to any high governmental authority present at the corrida, any distinguished spectator, or a friend. When the matador dedicates or toasts a bull to an individual he throws up his hat at the conclusion of the toast and the person honoured keeps the hat until the bull has been killed. After the bull is dead the matador comes back for the hat, which is thrown down with the card of the man who has held it, or some gift in it if the man has come prepared to be dedicated to. The gift is obligatory by etiquette unless the dedication is between friends in the same profession.

Brío: brilliance and vivacity.

Bronca: a noisy protest of disapproval.

Bronco: a bull that is savage, nervous, uncertain, and difficult.

Buey: steer or ox; or a bull which is heavy and oxlike in his actions.

Bulto: bundle; the man rather than the cloth. A bull that makes for the bundle is one that pays no attention to the cape or muleta no matter how well managed, but goes after the man instead. A bull that does this nearly always has been fought before either on the ranch as a calf or, contrary to the regulations, has appeared in some village ring without being killed.

Burladero: a shelter of planks set close together and a little out from the corral or barrera behind which the bullfighters and herders can dodge if pursued.

Burriciegos: (bulls) with defective vision. Either far-sighted, near-sighted or simply hazy visioned. Near-sighted bulls can be fought well by a bullfighter who is not afraid to get close and by turning with the bull keep him from losing sight of the lure when he turns. Far-sighted bulls are very dangerous since they will charge suddenly and with great speed from an abnormal distance at the largest object that attracts their attention. Hazy-visioned bulls, often caused by their eyes becoming congested during the fight, when the bull is over-weight and the day is hot, or from driving into and scattering the visceral content of a horse over them, are almost impossible to do any brilliant work with.

C

Caballero en Plaza: a Portuguese or Spanish mounted bullfighter riding trained, blooded horses, who, aided by one or more men on foot with capes who help place the bull for him, puts in banderillas with either one or both hands and kills the bull with a javelin from on horseback. These riders are also called *rejoneadores* from the rejón or javelin they use. These are razor-sharp, narrow, dagger-shaped lance points which are on a shaft which has been partially cut through to weaken it so that the point can be driven in by a straight thrust and the long shaft then broken off in order that the point will remain in the wound, sinking deeper as the bull tosses his head, and often killing him from what seems a slight thrust. The equestrian ability required for this form of bullfighting is very great and the manoeuvres are complicated and difficult, but after you have seen it a few times, it lacks the appeal of the ordinary bullfight, since the man undergoes no danger. It is the horse that takes the risks, not the rider, since the horse is in motion whenever he approaches the bull and any wound he may receive through his rider's lack of judgement or skill will not be of a sort to bring him to the ground and expose the rider. The bull, too, is bled and rapidly exhausted by the deep lance wounds which are often made in the forbidden territory of the neck. Also, since the horse, after the first twenty yards, can always outdistance the bull, it becomes a chase of an animal of superior speed by one less fast, in the course of which the pursuing animal is stabbed from horseback. This is altogether opposed to the theory of the bullfight on foot in which the bullfighter is supposed to stand his ground while the bull attacks him and deceive the animal by a movement of a cloth held in his arms. In bullfighting on horseback the man uses the horse as a lure to draw the bull's charge, often approaching the bull from the rear, but the lure is always in motion and I find the business, the more I see of it, very dull. The horsemanship is always admirable, and the degree of training of the horses amazing, but the whole thing is closer to the circus than it is to formal bullfighting.

Caballo: horse. Picadors' horses are also called *pencos* or more literally *rocinantes* and a variety of names which correspond to our calling poor race horses, skins, skates, dogs, etc.

Cabestros: the trained steers used in handling fighting bulls. The older and more experienced these are the greater their value and usefulness.

Cabeza: head.

Cabeza á rabo: a pass in which the bull passes his entire length under the muleta from head to tail.

Cabezada: a toss of the head.

Cachete: another name for the despatching of the bull with the puntilla once he has gone to the ground.

Cachetero: one who gives the *coup de grâce* with the *puntilla.*

Caída: fall of a picador when his horse is knocked over by the bull. Sword thrusts which are placed lower toward the neck than they should be without being intentionally bajonazos are also called caídas.

Calle: street; the worst bullfighters are usually the ones seen most constantly on the street. It is implied in Spain that someone seen always on the street has no better place to go or, if he has, is unwelcome there.

Callejon: the passageway between the wooden fence or barrera which surrounds the ring and the first row of seats.

Cambio: change. A pase with the cape or muleta in which the bullfighter, after taking the bull's charge into the cloth, changes the animal's direction with a movement of the cloth so that when the animal would have passed to one side of the man he is made to pass on the other side. The muleta may also be changed from one hand to the other in a cambio, doubling the bull on himself to fix him in place. Sometimes the man will change the muleta from hand to hand behind his back. This is merely ornamental and without effect on the bull. The cambio in banderillas is a feint made by the body to change the bull's direction; it has been fully described in the text.

Camelo: fake; a bullfighter who by tricks tries to appear to work close to the bull while in reality never taking any chances.

Campo: the country. *Faenas del campo* are all the operations in the breeding, branding, testing, herding, selecting, caging, and shipping of the bulls from the ranches.

Capa or *capote:* the cape used in bullfighting. Shaped like the capes commonly worn in Spain in the winter, it is usually made of raw silk on one side and percale on the other, heavy, stiff, and reinforced in the collar, cerise-coloured on the outside and yellow on the inner side. A good fighting cape costs 250 pesetas. They are heavy to hold and at the lower extremities small corks have been stitched into the cloth of the capes the matadors use. These the matador holds in his hands when he lifts the lower ends of the cape and gathers them together for handholds when swinging the cape with both hands.

Caparacón: the mattresslike covering for the chest and belly of a picador's horse.

Capea: informal bullfights or bull baitings in village squares in which amateurs and aspirant bullfighters take part. Also a parody of the formal bullfight given in parts of France or where the killing of

11

the bull is prohibited in which no picadors are used and the killing of the bull is simulated.

Capilla: the chapel in the bull ring where the bullfighters may pray before entering the ring.

Capote de brega: the fighting cape as above described.

Capote de paseo: the luxurious cape the bullfighter wears into the ring. These are heavily brocaded with gold or silver and cost from fifteen hundred to five thousand pesetas.

Cargar la suerte: the first movement of the arms made by the matador when the bull reaches the cloth to move the lure ahead of the bull and send him away from the man.

Carpintero: bull-ring carpenter who waits in the callejón ready to repair any damage to the barrera or gates of the ring.

Carril: a rut, furrow or railway track; a carril in bullfighting is a bull that charges perfectly straight as though coming down a groove or mounted on rails, permitting the utmost in brilliance to the matador.

Cartel: the composed programme for a bullfight. May also mean the amount of popularity a bullfighter has in any determined locality. For instance, you ask a friend in the business, 'What cartel have you in Málaga?' 'Wonderful; in Málaga no one has more cartel than me. My cartel is unmeasurable.' As a matter of record on his last appearance in Málaga he may have been chased out of the city by angry and disappointed customers.

Carteles: the posters announcing a bullfight.

Castigaderas: the long poles used from above in herding and sorting the bulls into the various runways and passages of the corrals when placing them in their compartments before the fight.

Castoreños: or beavers: the wide hats with pompoms at the side worn by the picadors.

Cazar: to kill the bull deceitfully and treacherously with the sword without the man allowing his body to come close to the horn.

Ceñido: close to the bull.

Ceñirse: to close in on. Applied to the bull it means those which pass as close to the man as he will permit, gaining a little ground each attack. The man is said to ciñe when he works very close to the animal.

Cerca: close; as in close to the horns.

Cerrar: to shut in. *Cerrar el toto:* to bring the bull close into the barrera; the opposite of *Abrir*. The bullfighter is called *encerrado en Tablas* when he has provoked the charge of the bull close to the barrera so that the bull cuts off his retreat on one side and the barrera cuts it on the other.

Cerveza: beer; there is good draught beer almost anywhere in Madrid, but the best is found at the Cervecería Alvarez in the calle Victoria. Draught beer is served in pint glasses which are called *dobles* or in half-pint glasses called *cañas*, *cañitas* or *medias*. The Madrid breweries were founded by Germans and the beer is the best anywhere on the Continent outside of Germany and Czechoslovakia. The best bottled beer in Madrid is the *Aguilar*. In the provinces good beer is brewed in Santander, the *Cruz Blanca*, and in San Sebastian. In the latter town the best beer I have drunk has been at the Café de Madrid, Café de la Marina, and Café Kutz. In Valencia the best draught beer I have ever drunk has been at the Hotel Valencia where it is served ice-cold in large glass pitchers. The food at this hotel, which has only very modest accommodation as to rooms, is superb. In Pamplona the finest beer is at the Café Kutz and the Café Iruña. The beer at the other cafés cannot be recommended. I have drunk excellent draught beer in Palencia, Vigo, and La Coruña, but have never encountered good draught beer in any very small Spanish town.

Cerviguillo: the high part of the bull's neck where the hump of muscle forms the so-called morillo or erective muscular crest of the neck.

Chato: snub-nosed.

Chico: small; also means youngster. The younger brothers of bullfighters are usually referred to by the family name or professional name with Chico appended, as: Armillita Chico, Amoros Chico, etc.

Chicuelinas: a pass with the cape invented by Manuel Jiminez, 'Chicuelo'. The man offers the cape to the bull and when the bull has charged and is past, the man, while the bull turns, makes a pirouette in which the cape wraps itself around him. At the conclusion of the pirouette he is facing the bull ready to make another pass.

Chiquero: the closed stalls in which the bulls await their entrance into the ring.

Choto: a calf which is still nursing; a term of contempt to describe under-aged and undersized bulls.

Citar: challenging the bull's attention to provoke a charge.

Clarínes: the trumpets that give the signals at the president's orders to announce the different changes in the fight.

Claro: a bull that is simple and easy to work with.

Cobarde: a cowardly bull or bullfighter.

Cobrar: to collect; *el mano de cobrar* is the right hand.

Cogida: the tossing of a man by the bull; means literally the catching; if the bull catches he tosses.

Cojo: lame; a bull which comes into the ring lame may be retired. The spectators will commence to shout '*Cojo*' as soon as they perceive the lameness.

Cojones: testicles; a valorous bullfighter is said to be plentifully equipped with these. In a cowardly bullfighter they are said to be absent. Those of the bull are called *criadillas* and prepared in any of the ways sweetbreads are usually cooked they are a great delicacy. During the killing of the fifth bull the criadillas of the first bull were sometimes served in the royal box. Primo de Rivera was so fond of interlarding his discourse with reference to manly virtues that he was said to have eaten so many criadillas that they had gone to his brain.

Cola: the bull's tail; usually called *rabo*. Cola may also mean the line in front of a ticket window.

Colada: the instant in which the bullfighter finds his position untenable when through mismanagement of the cloth or through the bull paying no attention to it or abandoning it to seek the man, the man must save himself from the charge as best he can.

Coleando: hanging on to the bull's tail, twisting it toward his head. This gives great pain to the bull and often damages his spinal column. It is only permissible when the bull is goring, or trying to gore, a man on the ground.

Coleta: the short, tightly braided, curved pigtail worn at the back of the head by the bullfighter to attach the *mona*, a black sort of hollow, dull, silk-covered button about twice the size of a silver dollar which supports the hat. Bullfighters formerly all wore this tress of hair pinned forward on their head out of sight when not fighting. Now they have found that they can attach both mona and a made-up coleta at the same time by a clasp to the hair at the back of their heads when dressing for the ring. You only see the pigtail now, once the caste mark of all bullfighters, on the heads of young aspirant fighters in the provinces.

Colocar: to place, a man is bien colocado when he places himself correctly in the ring for all the different parts of the bullfight. It is also used when speaking of the placing of the sword, the pic, and the banderillas in the bull. A bullfighter is also said to be bien colocado when he has finally arrived at a recognized position in his profession.

Compuesto: composed; holding his figure straight while the bull charges.

Confianza: self-confidence; *peón de confianza:* confidential banderillero who represents and may even advise the matador.

Confiar: to become confident and sure of himself with a bull.

Conocedor: a professional overseer of the fighting bulls on a breeder's estates.

Consentirse: to get very close to the bull with the body or lure in order to force a charge and then keep close and keep the bull charging.

Contrabarrera: a second row of seats at the bull ring.

Contratas: contracts signed by bullfighters.

Contratista de Caballos: horse contractor; furnishes horses for a fight for a fixed sum.

Cornada: a horn wound; a real wound as distinct from a *varetazo* or bruising scratch. A cornada de cabello is a huge cornada, the same sort of wound in a man that the bull usually makes in the chest of a horse.

Cornalón: bull with exceptionally large horns.

Corniabierto: exceptionally wide horned.

Corniavacado: cowhorned. Bull in which the horns turn up and back.

Cornicorto: shorthorned.

Cornigacho: bull with low horns coming quite straight forward.

Corniveleto: high straight horns.

Corral: enclosure adjoining the ring in which the bulls are kept immediately before they are to be fought. Provided with feed-boxes, salt, and fresh water.

Correr: to run; used to denote the running of the bull by the banderillero when the animal first enters the ring.

Corrida or *Corrida de Toros:* the Spanish bullfight.

Corrida de Novillos Toros: fight in which young or big but defective bulls are used.

Corta: short; an estocada in which the sword goes in a little more than half-way.

Cortar: to cut; bullfighters often sustain slight cuts on the hands with the sword when managing sword and muleta. *Cortar la oreja:* to cut the bull's ear. *Cortar la coleta:* to cut the pigtail or retire.

Cortar terreno: the bull is said to cut in on the terrain of the bull-fighter when after the man has provoked a charge and is running toward and across the line of the bull's charge to place the banderillas, say, at the point where their two courses will meet, the bull changes his direction while charging in order to cut in toward the man, gaining ground by running sideways.

Corto (torero corto): matador with a limited repertoire.

Corto – vestido de corto: wearing the short jacket of the Andalucian bull herders. Bullfighters formerly dressed in their costume when not in the ring.

Crecer: to increase; a bull that increases in bravery under punishment.

Cruz: the cross. Where the line of the top of the bull's shoulder blades would cross the spine. The place the sword should go in if the matador kills perfectly. The cruz is also the crossing of the sword arm over the arm that holds the lowered muleta as the matador goes in to kill. He is said to cross well when his left hand manages the cloth so that it moves low and well out, accentuating the cross made with the other arm, thus getting well rid of the bull as the man follows the sword in. Fernando Gomez, father of the Gallos, is supposed first to have remarked that the bullfighter who does not cross in this way belongs to the devil at once. Another saying is that the first time you do not cross is your first trip to the hospital.

Cuadrar: squaring the bull for killing; both front and hind feet together and the head neither too high nor too low. In banderillas: the moment when the bull lowers his head to hook and the man puts his feet together, his hands together, and sinks the shafts into the bull.

Cuadrilla: the troupe of bullfighters under the orders of a matador, including picadors and banderilleros, one of whom acts as puntillero.

Cuarteo: the most common form of placing banderillas, described in the text; a feint with the body or dodging motion used to avoid going in straight toward the bull when killing.

Cuidado: watch out! when it is an ejaculation. When applied to the bull as a descriptive term means one who has learned in the course of the fight and become dangerous.

Cuidando la linea: looking after the line; taking care that his movements shall be aesthetically graceful while working with the bull.

Cumbre: summit; *torero cumbre:* the very best possible; *faena cumbre:* the absolute top in work with the muleta.

Cuna: the cradle formed on the bull's head between the bull's horns. The one temporary refuge of a man whose position has become hopelessly compromised.

D

Defenderse: to defend; a bull is said to defend himself when he refuses to charge but pays close attention to everything and gores at anything that comes close to him.

Dehesa: pasture land.

Déjalo: leave him alone! Let him be! Shouted by the bullfighter to his peones when they have the bull correctly placed or when the matador wishes the bull left alone and not tired any more by the capes.

Delantal: a pass with the cape invented by Chicuelo in which the cape is swung in front of the man so that it billows out like an apron on a pregnant woman in a breeze.

Delantera de tendido: third row of seats at the ringside behind contra-barrera and barrera; *delantera de grada:* first row of seats in gallery.

Delantero: a pair of banderillas or estocadas placed too far forward.

Derecho: straight; *mano derecha:* the right hand.

Derramar la vista: scattering the vision; a bull which fixes his sight rapidly on a number of different objects before suddenly fixing on one and charging.

Derrame: haemorrhage, from the mouth usually; always, if the blood is bright or frothy, a sign that the sword has been badly placed and has entered the lungs. A bull may bleed from the mouth when he has been struck properly, but it is very rare.

Derribar: to knock over; the riding after young bulls on the ranch by a man armed with a long pole with which, while both bull and horse are galloping, the man upsets the bull by placing the point of the pole near the root of the tail and throwing the animal off balance so that it falls to the ground.

Derrote: high-chopping motion of the bull's horns.

Desarmar: to disarm the matador by loss of his muleta either through the horn catching in it and the bull tossing it away or through the bull deliberately chopping upward with his horns as the man comes in to kill.

Desarrollador: where the bulls are dressed out and the meat butchered after the fight.

Descabellar: to descabello or kill the bull from in front after he has been mortally wounded through an estocada by driving the point of the sword between the base of the skull and the first vertebra so that the spinal cord is severed. This is a *coup de grâce* administered by the matador while the bull is still on his feet. If the bull is nearly dead and carries his head low, the stroke is not difficult, since with the head nearly to the ground the space between the vertebra and the skull will be open. However, many matadors not caring to risk going in and passing the horn again if they have administered one estocada, whether mortal or not, try to descabello while the bull is in no sense nearly dead and, since the animal must then be tricked into lowering his head and may chop up with it as he sees or feels the sword, the descabello then becomes difficult and dangerous. It is dangerous both for spectators and matador, since the bull with an upward chop of his head will often send the sword thirty or more feet into the air. Swords tossed in this way by bulls have frequently killed spectators in Spanish rings. A Cuban visitor at Biarritz was killed a few years ago in the bull ring at Bayonne, France, by a sword with which Antonio Márquez was attempting to descabello. Márquez was tried for manslaughter, but was acquitted. In 1930 a spectator was killed by a tossed sword in Tolosa, Spain, the matador engaged in descabelloing being Manolo Martinez. The sword, entering the man's back, pierced his body completely, and was withdrawn with difficulty by two men, both of whom cut their hands badly on the blade. The practice of attempting to descabello on a bull, which is still strong and requires another estocada to kill or wound him mortally, is one of the worst and most shameful practices of modern bullfighting. Most of the scandalous and shameful disasters suffered by bullfighters subject to attacks of cowardice such as Cagancho, Niño de la Palma and Chicuelo have been due to their trying to descabellar a bull which was in a state to defend itself against this stroke. In the proper way of descabelloing the muleta is held low on the ground to force the bull to lower his muzzle. The matador may prick the bull's muzzle either with the point of the muleta or with the sword to force him to lower it. When the point of the sword used in this thrust, the blade of which is straight and stiff rather than curved down in the usual way, is properly placed, it strikes and severs the spinal marrow and the bull falls as suddenly as light goes off when a button is turned to extinguish an electric light.

Descansar: to rest; the descanso is the intermission between the third and fourth bulls which occurs in some bull rings while the ring is being sprinkled and smoothed. A man may also rest the bull a moment between two series of passes while passing him with the muleta if he finds the bull is winded.

Descompuesto: gone to pieces nervously.

Desconfiado: worried or lacking in confidence.

Descordando: an estocada or sword thrust which accidentally going between two vertebrae cuts the spinal cord and brings the bull down instantly. This is not to be confused with the descabello or the puntilla stroke which cuts the spinal marrow deliberately.

Descubrirse: to uncover; in the bull to lower the head well so that the part where the sword is to enter is easily reached. In the man, to leave himself uncovered by the cloth when working with the bull.

Desgarradura: a torn rip in the hide of the bull made by an unskilful or conscienceless picador.

Desigual: a bullfighter whose performances are not consistent; brilliant one day and boring the next.

Despedida: the farewell performance of a bullfighter; not to be taken any more seriously than that of a singer. The actual final performances of bullfighters are usually very poor affairs, since the man usually has some incapabilities which force him to retire or else he is retiring to live on his money and will be very careful to take no chances in the last time bulls will have a chance to kill him.

Despedir: when the man with cape or muleta sends the bull out and away from him at the end of a pass. The pushing away of the bull by the picador at the end of a charge as the picador turns his horse.

Despejo: clearing of the public from the ring before the fight commences. The spectators are no longer allowed to parade in the Madrid ring before the fight commences.

Desplante: any theatrical gesture by a bullfighter.

Destronque: the damage suffered by a bull through too sudden twisting of his spinal column by turning him too shortly with cape or muleta.

Diestro: skilful; generic term for the matador.

Divisa: the colours of the bull breeder which are attached to a small harpoon-shaped iron and placed in the bull's morrillo as he enters the ring.

División de Plaza: dividing the ring into two parts by running a barrera across the centre and giving two bullfights at once. Never seen now since the bullfight has become formalized except very occasionally in nocturnal fights, when it is done, for lack of other attractions, as a curiosity and relic of old days.

Doblar: to turn; a bull that turns after a charge and recharges; *doblando con el:* a bullfighter who turns with the bull, keeping the cape or muleta in front of the bull to hold his attention when he has a tendency to leave after each charge.

Doctorado: slang for alternativa; taking the doctor's degree in Tauromachia.

Dominio: the ability to dominate the bull.

Duro: hard, tough, and resistant. Also slang for the bony structure which the sword may strike in killing; also a silver five-peseta piece.

E

Embestir: to charge; *embestir bien:* to follow the cloth well; to charge freshly and frankly.

Embolado: a bull, steer or cow whose horns have been covered with a leather sheath thickened at the ends in order to blunt the points.

Embroque: space between the bull's horns; to be between the horns.

Emendar: to correct or improve the position he has taken the bull in, to change from a place or a pass in which he is compromised to another that is successful.

Empapar: to centre the bull's head well into the cloth of either cape or muleta when receiving a charge so that the animal can see nothing beyond the folds of the lure as it is moved ahead of him.

Emplazarse: for the bull to take a position well out in the centre of the ring and refuse to leave it.

Empresa: organization in charge of promoting bullfights in any given ring.

Encajonamiento: the putting of bulls into their individual travelling boxes or cages for shipment from ranch to ring.

Encierro: the driving of fighting bulls on foot, surrounded by steers, from one corral to the corral of the ring. In Pamplona the running of the bulls through the streets with the crowd running ahead of them from the corral at the edge of the town into and through the bull ring into the corral of the ring. The bulls to be fought in the afternoon are run through the streets at seven o'clock in the morning of the day they are to be fought.

Encorvado: bent over; bullfighter who works leaning forward in order to hold the lure so that the bull will pass as far as possible from his body. The straighter the man stands the closer the bull will come to his body.

Enfermería: operating-room attached to all bull rings.

Enganchar: to hook into anything with the horn and raise it into the air.

Engaño: anything used to deceive the bull or the spectator. In the first case the cape and muleta, in the second any tricks to simulate a danger not really experienced.

Entablerarse: for the bull to take up a position which he refuses to leave along the planks of the barrera.

Entero: complete, a bull which has arrived at the stage of the killing without having been slowed or weakened by his encounters with the picadors and bandcrilleros.

Entrar á matar: to go in to kill.

Eral: two-year-old bull.

Erguido: erect and straight; bullfighter who holds himself very straight when working with the animal.

Espada: synonym for the sword; also used to refer to the matador himself.

Espalda: the shoulders or back of the man. A man who is said to work from the back is a sodomite.

Estocada: sword thrust or estocade in which the matador goes in from the front to attempt to place the sword high up between the bull's shoulder blades.

Estoque: the sword used in bullfighting. It has a lead-weighted, chamois-covered pommel, a straight cross-guard five centimeters from the pommel and the hilt and cross-guard are wrapped in red flannel. It is not *jewel hilted* as we read in *Virgin Spain*. The blade is about seventy-five centimetres long and is curved downward at the tip in order that it may penetrate better and take a deeper direction between the ribs, vertebrae, shoulder blades, and other bony structure which it may encounter. Modern swords are made with one, two or three grooves or canals along the back of the blade, the purpose of these being to allow air to be introduced into the wound caused by the sword, otherwise the blade of the sword serves as a plug to the wound it makes. The best swords are made in Valencia and their prices vary according to the number of canals and the quality of steel used. The usual equipment for a matador is four ordinary killing swords and one straight-tipped sword with slightly widened point for the descabello. The blades of all these swords except that used for the descabello are ground razor-sharp half-way up their length from the tip. They are kept in soft leather sheaths and the complete outfit is carried in a large, usually embossed, leather sword-case.

Estribo: metal stirrup of the picador; also the ridge of wood about eighteen inches above the ground which runs around the inside of the barrera which aids the bullfighters in vaulting the wooden fence.

Extraño: sudden movement to one side or the other made by either bull or man.

F

Facultades: physical abilities or assets in the man; in the bull preserving his facultades is called keeping his qualities intact in spite of punishment.

Facultativo – Parte Facultativo: official diagnosis to be sent to the president of the fights of a bullfighter's wounds or wounds dictated by the surgeon in charge in the infirmary after he has treated or operated on the man.

Faena: the sum of the work done by the matador with the muleta in the final third of the bullfight; it also means any work carried out; a *faena de campo* being any of the operations of bull raising.

Faja: sash worn around the waist as a belt.

Falsa: false, incorrect, phoney. *Salidas en falsa* are attempts to place the banderillas in which the man passes the bull's head without deciding to place the sticks, either because the bull has not charged, in which case the man's action is correct, or because the man simply had made an error in lack of decision. They are sometimes made, very gracefully, simply to show the matador's judgement of distance.

Farol: pass with the cape which commences as a veronica with the cape held in both hands, but as the bull passes the man the cape is swung around the man's head and behind his back as he turns with the bull following the swing of the cape.

Farpa: long, heavy banderilla used by Portuguese bullfighters who place them on horseback.

Fenómeno: a phenomenon; originally used to designate a young matador who showed exceptional aptitude for his profession, it now is principally used as a sarcasm to describe a bullfighter who is advanced by publicity faster than his experience and aptitudes warrant.

Fiera: wild beast; slang for the bull. Also slang for loose women, as we would say bitch.

Fiesta: holiday time or time of enjoyment; *Fiesta de los toros:* the bullfight. *Fiesta nacional:* bullfight; used in a sneering way by writers opposed to the corrida as a symbol of Spain's backwardness as a European nation.

Fijar: to cut short the bull's running and fix him in a certain place.

Filigranas: fancy business done with the bull; or artistic refinements of any pass or act in bullfighting.

Flaco: – *Toro flaco:* bull that is lean, flaccid or hollow. Not well filled in.

Flogo: weak, so-so, unconvincing, spiritless.

Franco: noble bull easy to work with.

Frenar: to put on the brakes; bull which slows suddenly when passing the man to stop and gore instead of pursuing his normal course; one of the most dangerous bulls to work with as he appears to be going to pass and gives no previous indication of his intention of braking.

Frente par detrás: pass with the cape in which the man's back is turned toward the bull but his body covered with the cape which is extended to one side by both arms. It is really a form of the veronica performed with the back toward the bull.

Fresco: calmly, shamelessly, cynical.

Fuera: Get away! Get out! Get the hell out! Depending on the degree of vehemence with which it is shouted.

G

Gachís: tarts about town.

Gacho: horns that point down.

Galleando: the man with the cape on his back as though he were wearing it looks back over his shoulder toward the bull and moving in a series of zig-zags, feints and dodgings, causes the bull to follow the turns and swings of the lower part of the cape.

Gallo: fighting cock; the professional name of the great Gomez family of gipsy bullfighters.

Ganadería: ranch where fighting bulls are raised; all the bulls, cows, calves, and steers on such a ranch.

Ganadero: breeder of fighting bulls.

Ganar terreno: bull which forces the man to give ground each time he charges, thus gaining it for himself.

Garrocha: synonym for the pike or pic used by the picador; a vaulting-pole used for leaping over the bull in old-time fights.

Gente: people; *gente coletudo* or the pigtailed citizenry refers to the bullfighters.

Ginete: horseman, picador; *buen ginete:* a good rider.

Golletazo: sword thrust in the side of the neck of the bull which goes into the lung causing death almost at once from choking haemorrhage; used to assassinate bulls by panic-stricken matadors who are afraid to approach the horns; this estocada is only justified on bulls that have received one or more proper estocadas or attempts and which defend themselves so well, refusing to uncover the space where they should be killed between the shoulders, tossing the muleta out of the man's hand as he comes in and refusing to charge, that the man has no other choice than to attempt a golletazo.

Gótico: gothic; *un niño gótico* in bullfighting is a conceited boy fond of striking gothic architectural attitudes.

Gracia: grace and elegance of manner while undergoing danger; *gracia gitana:* gipsy grace.

Grado: the balcony or covered seats in a bull ring above the open seats or tendidos and the covered boxes or palcos.

Grotesca: grotesque; the opposite of graceful.

Guardia: municipal policeman; not taken seriously even by himself. *Guardia Civil:* national police, are taken very seriously; armed with sabres and seven-mm. calibre mauser carbines, they are, or were, a model of ruthless, disciplined constabulary.

H

Hachazo: chopping stroke of the bull's horns.

Herida: wound.

Herradera: branding of calves on the ranch.

Herradura: horseshoe; *cortar la herradura:* to cut the horseshoe, an estocada well placed, fairly high up but in which the blade, once in, takes an oblique, downward direction into the bull's chest, cutting the pleura, and causing immediate death without any external haemorrhage.

Hierro: branding iron; brand of a bull breeder of fighting bulls.

Hombre: man, as an ejaculation expresses surprise, pleasure, shock, disapproval, or delight, according to tone used. *Muy Hombre:* very much of a man, i.e. plentifully supplied with *huevos, cojones,* etc.

Hondo: deep; *estocada honda:* sword in up to the hilt.

Hueso: bone; in slang means a tough one.

Huevos: eggs; slang for testicles, as we say balls.

Huir: to run away; shameful both in bull and matador.

Hule: oilcloth; slang for the operating-table.

Humillar: lower the head.

I

Ida: estocada in which the blade takes a pronounced downward direction without being perpendicular. Such an estocada although well placed may cause haemorrhage from the mouth through the blade going so nearly straight down that it touches the lungs.

Ida y Vuelta — allez et retour: round trip; a bull which turns by himself at the end of a charge and comes again on a straight line. Ideal for the bullfighter who can look after his aesthetic effects without having to bring the bull around at the end of the charge with cape or muleta.

Igualar: get the bull's front feet together.

Inquieto: nervous

Izquierda: left; *mano izquierda:* the left hand, called *zurda* in bull-ring dialect.

J

Jaca: riding horse, mare or pony; *Jaca torera:* a mare so well trained by the Portuguese bullfighter, Simao Da Veiga, that he was able, when he was mounted on her, to place banderillas with both hands, not touching the bridle, the horse being guided by spur and pressure of the knees alone.

Jalear: to applaud.

Jaulones: the individual boxes or cages in which bulls are shipped from the ranch to the ring. These are owned by each breeder, marked with his brand, name and address, and returned after the fight.

Jornalero: day labourer; bullfighter who barely makes his living through his profession.

Jugar: to play; *jugando con el toro:* when one or more matadors unarmed with a cape but carrying the banderillas held together in one hand play with the bull by half provoking a series of charges; running in zig-zags or seeing how close they can approach the bull while playing without provoking a charge. To do this attractively much grace and knowledge of the bull's mental processes is necessary.

Jurisdicción: the moment in which the bull while charging arrives within reach of where the man is standing and lowers his head to hook; more technically speaking, when the bull leaves his terrain and enters the terrain of the bullfighter, arriving at the place the man wishes to receive him with the cloth.

K

Kilos: a kilo equals two and one-fifth pounds. Bulls are weighed in kilos sometimes after they are killed and before being dressed out and always after they are dressed, drawn, skinned, heads and hoofs and all parts of the meat that have been damaged cut away. This latter state is called *en canal,* and for many years the weight of bulls has been judged when they are in this state. A four-and-a-half-year-old fighting bull should weigh from 295 to 340 kilos *en canal*, depending on his size and type; the present legal minimum that they may weigh is 285 kilos. The dressed-out or *en canal* weight of a bull is estimated as 52½ per cent of his live weight. Just as in money, where the legal unit is the peseta, yet sums are never mentioned in conversation in pesetas, but rather in *reales* or 25 centimos, a fourth of a peseta, or in duros, five pesetas; in the weight of bulls for conversational purpose the *arroba* or weight unit of twenty-five pounds is the measuring unit. A bull is measured or estimated in the number of arrobas of meat he will dress out when butchered. A bull of 26 arrobas will dress out a fraction over 291 kilos. That is as small as bulls should be fought if the animal is to be imposing enough to give real emotion to the corrida. From 26 to 30 arrobas is the ideal weight for fighting bulls that have not been fattened on grain. Each arroba between 24 and 30 means as definite a difference in the hitting power, size and destructiveness as there is between the different classes in boxing. To make a comparison we may say that in point of strength and destructive power bulls under 24 arrobas are the fly-weights, bantam-weights, and feather-weights. Bulls from 24 to 25 arrobas are light-weights and welter-weights. Bulls of 26 arrobas are middle-weights and light-heavy-weights; 27 to 30 arrobas are heavy-weights, and all above 30 arrobas approach the Primo Carnera class. A cornada or horn wound from a bull that weighs only 24 arrobas will, if it is properly placed, be as fatal as one from a much larger animal. It is a dagger stroke with ordinary force, while the bull of 30 arrobas gives the same dagger stroke with the force of a pile-driver. It is a fact, however, that a bull of 24 arrobas is generally immature, little over three years old; and bulls of that age do not know how to use their horns skilfully, either offensively or defensively. The ideal bull therefore to provide a sufficiently dangerous enemy for the bullfighters so that the corrida will retain its emotion should be at least four and a half years old in order to be mature, and weigh, when dressed out, an absolute minimum of 25 arrobas. The more arrobas it weighs from 25 up, without losing speed and not simply gaining weight by being fattened, the greater the emotion will be and the more meritorious will be any work accomplished by the man with the animal. To follow bullfights intelligently or understand them thoroughly you must learn to think in arrobas, just as in boxing you must class the men in the various formal classifications by weight. At present the bullfight is being killed by unscrupulous bull breeders who sell under-aged, under-weight and under-bred bulls, not testing them sufficiently for bravery, and thus abusing and forfeiting the tolerance that had been extended to their undersized products as long as they were brave and liable to provide a brilliant if unemotional corrida.

L

Ladeada: to one side; especially refers to an estocada.

Lances: any formalized passes made by the cape.

Largas: a pass to draw the bull toward and then send him away from the man made with the cape fully extended and held at extremity by one hand.

Lazar: to lasso; or use the lariat or riata of the American west to catch cattle or the lazo with a weight on one end used in South America.

Levantado: first stage of the bull on entering the ring when he tries to sweep everything out of the ring without concentrating his charges.

Liar: to furl with a twist of the left wrist the cloth of the muleta over the stick which supports it before profiling on going in to kill with the sword.

Librar: to free; *librar la acometida:* to free himself from the un-suspected charge either by foot-work or by an improvised pass with muleta or cape.

Libre de cacho: anything performed with the bull out of range of his horns; either from a distance or after the horn has passed; means literally free from the possibility of being caught.

Lidia: the fight; *toro de lidia:* fighting bull. Also the name of the most famous and oldest bullfight weekly.

Lidiador: one who fights bulls.

Ligereza: agility, one of the three qualities necessary to be a matador according to the great Francisco Montés; the three being agility or lightness on the feet, valour, and a perfect knowledge of his profession.

Llegar: to arrive; the bull is said to llegar when he actually reaches the horse with his horn in spite of the picador's opposition.

Lleno: a full house or sell-out; every seat in the ring occupied.

M

Macheteo: chopping as with a cane-knife or machete; *macheteo por la cara* is a series of chopping strokes from side to side with the muleta, with the man retreating by foot-work if the bull charges, designed to tire the bull's neck muscles and prepare him for killing. It is the simplest and safest way to tire a bull with the muleta and employed by bull-fighters who do not desire to take any risks or to attempt anything difficult.

Macho: male, masculine, abundantly endowed with male reproductive organs; *torero macho:* bullfighter whose work is on a basis of courage rather than perfected technique and style, although the style may come later.

Maestro: a master at anything; as a matador might be addressed by his peones. Has come to be used sarcastically, in Madrid especially. You address any one as maestro to whom you wish to show the minimum of respect.

Maldito or *Maldita:* damned; cursed, as in speaking to a bull, 'Damned be the cow that dropped you!'

Maleante: crook or cheap criminal; the type of maleante encountered most often going to or leaving the bullfight is the pickpocket or carterista; literally pocket-booker. These citizens are numerous, tolerated, in the sense that the police in Madrid have lists of them all and if you were robbed and saw the pickpocket they will have several hundred of them called in off the streets or from their homes and paraded for you; and extremely skilful. The way to avoid them is never to ride on a street car or the subway, for that is where they work most easily. They have one good quality – they do not destroy your personal papers or passports or keep them as other pickpockets would do, but after taking the money, drop the pocket-book with the papers it contains into a mail-box either in a tobacco store or in one of those ambulatory boxes attached to tramways. The pocket-book will then be obtainable at the general post office. From my own and my friends' experiences at being pickpocketed in Spain I should say that in their own walk of life these gentry combine the same qualities that Montés listed as indispensable to a bullfighter – lightness, valour and a perfect knowledge of their profession.

Maleta: literally valise; is slang for a bad or cheap bullfighter.

Malo: bad, imperfect, defective, unhealthy, vicious, disagreeable, obnoxious, lousy, rotten, filthy, stinking, putrid, crooked, etc., depending on the circumstances. *Toro malo:* bull having these attributes and other inherent defects such as a tendency to jump the barrera into the crowd; to run at the sight of a cape, etc.

Mamarracho: insult shouted at deficient bullfighter; American would be awkward bum, stumble-bum, flat-footed tramp or yellow bastard.

Mancornar: bull-dogging or throwing a calf by twisting the horns by hand, at the same time throwing the weight of the man's body on them.

Mandar: to command or order; in bullfighting to make the bull obey the cloth; to dominate him with it.

Manejable: manageable; bull possible to work with.

Mano: hand; *mano bajo:* with the hand low; the proper way to move the cape in the veronica. *Manos* also refers to the feet of the bull.

Mansedumbre: slow, oxlike peacefulness in a bull.

Manso: tame, mild and unwarlike; a bull which does not have the fighting blood is *manso,* as are also the steers called *cabestros* when they are trained.

Manzanilla: natural light dry sherry wine which has not been fortified by adding more than its natural alcohol. Much drunk in Andalucia and by all connected with bullfights. It is ordered in *chatos* or short glasses and is usually served with a *tapa* or bit of food of some sort such as an olive and anchovy, a sardine, piece of tuna fish, and red sweet pepper, or a slice of smoked ham. One *chato* lightens the spirits, three or four make you rather feel good, but if you eat the tapas as you drink, a dozen of them will not make you drunk. Manzanilla also means camomile, but if you remember to ask for a *chato* of manzanilla there is no danger that you will be served camomile tea.

Marear: to make seasick; to make the bull dizzy by turning him from side to side by flopping a cape on each side of his head or turn him round and round. This is done to get him to his knees after he has received an inconclusive estocada, and is ugly to watch and dishonourable to perform.

Maricón: a sodomite, nance, queen, fairy, fag, etc. They have these in Spain, too, but I only know of two of them among the forty-some matadors de toros. This is no guarantee that those interested parties who are continually proving that Leonardo da Vinci, Shakespeare, etc., were fags would not be able to find more. Of the two, one is almost pathologically miserly, is lacking in valour, but is very skilful and delicate with the cape, a sort of exterior decorator of bullfighting, and the other has a reputation for great valour and awkwardness and has been unable to save a peseta. In bullfighting circles the word is used as a term of opprobrium or ridicule or as an insult. There are many very, very funny Spanish fairy stories.

Mariposa: butterfly; series of passes with cape over the man's shoulders and the man facing the bull, zig-zagging slowly backwards, drawing the bull on, with a wave of first one side of the cape, then the other, supposedly imitating the flight of a butterfly. Invented by Marcial Lalanda, this *quite* requires great knowledge of bulls to execute properly.

Mariscos: shellfish eaten in the cafés while drinking beer before or after bullfights; the best of these are *percebes*, a sort of goose barnacle with a tasty stem of a very delicate and delicious flavour; *langostinos:* large, plump, over-sized Mediterranean prawns; *cigalas:* a pink-and-white, long, narrow-clawed member of the lobster family whose claws and tail you crack with a nut-cracker or a hammer; *cangrejos del rio:* écrevisse or fresh-water crayfish, cooked with whole black pepper seeds in their tails, and *gambas* or common shrimps served in their shells to be shucked and eaten by hand. *Percebes*, which grow along the rocks of the Atlantic coast of Spain, are not obtainable in Madrid after April until September due to the closed season. Eaten while drinking beer or absinthe they are very good, the stems of the barnacles having a taste more delicate and attractive than any oysters, clam or shellfish I have ever eaten.

Marronazo: the picador missing the bull when he charges and the point of the pic slipping over the bull's hide without tearing it.

Matadero: slaughter-house. Training place for the use of puntilla and sword.

Matador: a formal killer of bulls, as a Mata Toros is only a bull butcher.

Mayoral: overseer on a bull-raising ranch; also those *vaqueros* or herders who accompany the caged bulls from the ranch to the ring, sleeping with the cages on the freight cars, seeing the bulls are fed and watered, and assisting in their unloading and sorting before the fight.

Media-estocada: an estocada in which only half of the blade goes into the bull. If properly placed on a medium-sized bull a media-estocada will kill as quickly as one that goes in the full length. If the bull is very large, however, half a blade may not be long enough to reach the aorta or other large blood vessels, the cutting of which produces death quickly.

Media-luna: sickle-shaped blade attached to a long pole used in the early days of bullfighting to hamstring bulls which the matador had been unable to kill. For a long time after it passed out of use and the bull which a matador had failed to kill was removed by steers, the *media-luna* was still exhibited to shame the matador and order the entry of the steers into the ring. It is no longer exhibited.

Medias: long stockings such as are worn by bullfighters.

Media veronica: a recorte, or cutting short of the bull's charge, which ends a series of passes with the cape known as veronicas (see explanation). The media veronica is accomplished by the man holding the cape in both hands, as for the veronica, and as the bull passes the man, moving from left to right, the man brings his left hand close to his hip and gathers the cape toward his hip with his right hand, shortening the swing of the veronica and making the cape swing half full, turning the bull on himself and fixing him in place so that the man may walk away with his back toward the animal. This fixing in place is accomplished by the swirl of the cape cutting the bull's normal course through making him attempt to turn in a shorter distance than his own length. Juan Belmonte was the perfecter of this lance with the cape, and it is now the obligatory ending for any series of veronicas. The half-passes made by the matador when holding the cape in both hands and running backward swaying the cape from side to side to take the bull from one part of the ring to another were once called *media veronicas*, but the real media veronica at present is the one described above.

Media-vuelta: method of placing banderillas on bulls that do not charge well in which the man takes his position at the rear of the bull and runs in toward the bull's head as the latter turns to come toward him. Bulls which are impossible to kill from the front are also stuck with the sword by the man going in to kill by a media-vuelta.

Medios: central part of the ring which is divided into three terrains for the purpose of executing different suertes with the bull; the centre or medios; the next third or tercios and the ground next to the barrera called tablas.

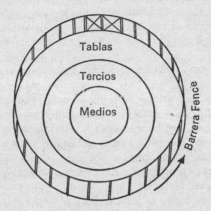

Mejorar: to improve; *mejorando su estilo:* improving his style; *mejorar el terreno* is when a bullfighter finds himself too close to the barrera to be able to accomplish the pass which he is preparing without being caught and using cape or muleta to aid him change to a better or safer position.

Meter el pie: to incite the bull to charge by bending forward the knee and then straightening up, profiled toward the bull, when awaiting him in order to kill in the manner known as recibiendo (see text).

Metisacas: put and pulled; estocadas in which the matador through lack of decision puts the sword in a little way and then pulls it out.

Mogón: bull with one horn broken off or crumpled, sometimes leaving a rounded protuberance; such bulls are used in *novilladas.*

Mojiganga: masquerade; in the old days bulls would be let into the ring at *novilladas* while a procession was in progress or a play being acted. They were called mojigangas; the last survival of this are the various bands imitating the bull-fighting band, *El Empastre,* founded by Rafael Dutrus, in which a young bull is released into the ring while the band is playing and is fought and killed by some of the musicians while the rest continue to play their instruments.

Molinete: pass with the muleta in which the man turns a complete circle on himself, letting the muleta wind itself round his body. Is of greatest effect when done between the bull's horns or just beside them, in this case the bull being turned completely on himself while following the loose end of the cloth.

Mona: silk-covered button worn at the base of the bullfighter's pigtail.

Monerías: monkey business; childish extravagances committed with the bull.

Monosabios: red-shirted bull-ring servants who aid the picadors when they fall, help them to mount, lead horses toward the bull, kill horses that have been wounded, unsaddle them, spread canvas over them, etc. They were first so nicknamed when a troupe of performing monkeys uniformed in the same colours were presented in Madrid in 1847 shortly after the direction of the ring had put the servants into red blouses.

Morrillo: the hump of muscle rising from the neck of a fighting bull which erects when the bull is angry. In the top part of this hump, nearest the shoulders, is where the picador should place his pic and the banderilleros their sticks.

Morucho: half-bred bull, sometimes brave, vicious, and dangerous, but without the type or caste of the thoroughbred. In many parts of Spain bulls are raised which have a strain of wild fighting blood by breeders who do not belong to any of the associations of thoroughbred fighting-bull raisers, and these bulls are sold to be fought in novilladas in the small rings and in capeas. Their lack of good blood can be most easily seen in the thickness of their tails, the size of their horns and hoofs, and the lack of morrillo when they otherwise have the appearance of real fighting bulls.

Movido: moving; *toreo movido:* using too much foot-work when working with the bull.

Mozo de estoques: personal servant and sword handler for the matador. In the ring he prepares the muletas and hands his master the swords as he needs them, wiping off the used swords with a sponge and drying them before putting them away. While the matador is killing he must follow him around in the passageway to be always opposite him ready to hand him a new sword or muleta over the barrera as he needs it. When it is windy he dampens capes and muletas from a water jug he carries and also looks after all personal wants of the matador. Outside the ring, before the fight, he takes around the envelopes containing the matador's card and a certain sum of money to the different bullfight critics, aids the matador to dress, and sees that all the equipment is transported to the ring. After the fight he sends the telefonemas – messages sent by the telephone company and written and delivered as telegrams are in the United States – or the more rare verbal messages to the matador's family, friends, the press, and any clubs of bullfight enthusiasts that may be organized in the matador's name.

Mucha: much; *de muchas piernas:* with plenty of legs; very strong in the legs; *muchas arrobas:* very heavy. *De mucho cuidado:* very suspicious, that is, a bull very difficult to work with.

Muchacho: boy; youth.

Muerte: death; also the place where the sword should enter to kill the bull properly. Bullfighters say the bull uncovers the *muerte* when he lowers his head well. *Pase de la muerte:* pass with the muleta explained in the text.

Muleta: heart-shaped scarlet cloth of serge or flannel folded and doubled over a tapered wooden stick equipped with a sharp steel point at the narrow end and a grooved handle at the widened extremity; the sharp point is pricked through the cloth where it is folded to a point and the loose end is fastened to the handle with a thumbscrew so that the wood supports the folds of the cloth. The muleta is used to defend the man; to tire the bull and regulate the position of his head and feet; to perform a series of passes of more or less aesthetic value with the bull; and to aid the man in the killing.

Muletazo: a pass performed with the muleta.

Multa: fine assessed by the presiding officer of the corrida or by the civil-governor against a bullfighter, bull raiser, or the management of the ring itself. Fines assessed against bullfighters are a farce, since all matadors' contracts contain a clause which stipulates that any fines assessed against them must be paid by the promoters. This clause dates from over thirty-five years and was first inserted to prevent promoters from contracting a matador at his own figure and then having the president fine him the difference between the figure he asked in order to fight and the figure the promoter was willing to pay. At present with the matadors, picadors and banderilleros organized as they are and able to place a boycott on any ring whose promoter does not pay his debts and maintain that boycott until the debt is paid, not permitting fights to be held even under another promoter until their claims have been satisfied, there is no need to maintain the clause about fines to protect the bullfighters. Its only effect at present is to let unscrupulous fighters know that any fines they may be assessed, no matter how justly, for deficient or dishonest work will not come out of their own pockets. This is one of the abuses that should be corrected the next time a new government ordinance for regulation of the bullfight is drawn up.

N

Nalgas: buttocks, or rump; location of many horn wounds caused by the matador turning his back on the bull without having fixed him properly to avoid a charge. Prominent buttocks destroy the line that the bullfighter seeks to make in working with the bull and prevent him being taken seriously as a stylist, hence a tendency to carry weight there is a source of much worry to a matador in modern bullfighting.

Natural: pass made with the muleta held low in the left hand, the man citing the bull from in front; with his right leg toward the bull, the muleta held by the centre of the stick in the left hand, left arm extended and the cloth in front of the man, it is swung slightly toward the bull to start him, this swing being almost imperceptible to the spectator; as the bull charges and arrives at the muleta the man turns with him, his arms fully extended and moving the muleta slowly ahead of the bull, making him turn in a quarter of a circle around the man; giving a swinging flip imparted with a lift of the wrist at the conclusion of the pass to hold the bull in position for another pass. This pass is fully described in the text. It is the fundamental pass of bullfighting, the simplest, capable of greatest purity of line and the most dangerous to make.

Navarra: province in North of Spain; name of pass with the cape, no longer used, in which the matador first swings the cape as in the veronica, then, as the bull is about to leave the cape, the man makes a complete turn in the opposite direction from which he has been swinging the cape, swinging the cape low in front of and below the bull's muzzle.

Nervio: energy and vigour of the bull.

Niño: child or young boy; lately there has been a plague of *niños* as *noms de guerre* in bullfighting. Following on the success of *El Niño de la Palma* there have been over three hundred bullfighters who have dubbed themselves the Niño of this or that, from the Niño of the slaughter-house to the Niño of the Sierra Nevada. In earlier times there were pairs or trios of child bullfighters called after the towns they came from, such as the Niños Sevillanos, Niños Cordobeses, etc. The bullfighters who graduated from these juvenile associations did not continue to call themselves Niños, however, but were called Gallito, Machaquito, and so on; making their names famous, and abandoning the childish designation when they ceased to be children, even though they kept the affectionate diminutive of their fighting name.

Noble: bull that is frank in its charges, brave, simple, and easily deceived.

No Hay Derecho: you have no right; common phrase of protest against any violation of the rules or the rights of the individual.

Noticiero: notice; El Noticiero de Lunes is the official sheet giving government news and a short report of the Sunday bullfights issued in Spanish cities on Monday morning in the absence of any newspapers on Sunday night and Monday morning, due to the no-work-on-Sunday law put through by the workers on Spanish newspapers several years ago.

Novedad: novelty; new fighter who attracts by his novelty.

Novillada: at the present time a novillada is a bullfight in which bulls which are under-aged, or over-aged, for a formal bullfight, that is, under four years and over five, or defective in vision or horn, are fought by bullfighters who have either never taken or renounced the title of matador de toros. In every way except the quality of the bulls and the inexperience or admitted failure of the bullfighters, a novillada or corrida de *novillos-toros* is the same as a regular bullfight. In former times a novillada was any form of bull entertainment other than the formal corrida, but the present-day novillada has come about through the desire to present a regular bullfight at less than formal prices due to the bulls being bargains, and the men, due to a desire to present themselves and make a name, or to the fact that they have failed as formal matadors, are less exigent in their demands for money than the full matadors. The season for novilladas in Madrid is from early March until Easter and from July until the middle of September. In the provinces they go on during the entire bullfight season, being given by all small towns which cannot afford a formal corrida. The admission to a novillada is usually about half that of an ordinary corrida. Bulls fought are often larger and more dangerous than those used in *corridas de toros*; the *novilleros* being forced to accept bulls refused by the stars of their profession. It is in the novilladas that the majority of the bullfighters who die in the ring are killed each year since men with little experience fight exceedingly dangerous bulls in small towns where the ring often has only rudimentary operating equipment and no surgeon skilled in the very special technique of horn wounds.

Novillero: a matador of novillos-toros, the bulls described above. He may either be an aspirant or a matador who has failed to make a living in the class above and renounced his alternativa in search of contracts. The most a novillero makes in Madrid is 5000 pesetas a fight, and he may, if a débutant, fight for as low as a thousand pesetas. If out of this latter sum he must pay the rent of a suit, wages to two picadors, two banderilleros and his sword handler, and send envelopes containing fifty or a hundred pesetas around to the critics of the press, he will owe money after the fight is over. Novilleros who are protected by the management of the bull ring may only have to fight young bulls and may be very successful with these and fail completely when they become full matadors, due to the difference in danger, strength and speed between the immature and mature bulls. It is never safe to judge a bullfighter on his performance with immature animals, for no matter how perfect his technique and training he may completely lack the heart necessary for working with the real bull.

Novillo: bull used in novilladas.

Nuevo: new; *Nuevo en esta Plaza* after a bullfighter's name on a programme means that this is his presentation in that ring.

Nulidad: a complete nobody; bullfighter who is a drawback rather than an attraction on a programme.

O

Ojo: eye, a matador who wishes to give the crowd the information, either true or false, that the bull does not see well, as an excuse for his own lack of brilliance, will point to his own eye. *Buen-ojo:* means a good eye or good judgement.

Olivo: olive tree; *tomar el olivo:* to take to the olive tree, phrase used to describe the action of the matador when seized by panic or through having let the bull put him in an impossible terrain he scrambles head first over the barrera. The matador should never run with his back toward the bull; let alone run and flop over the barrera.

Oreja: ear; when the matador has been excellent with the bull both with muleta and sword, killing him promptly and well after a good faena with the muleta, or if the work with the muleta has not been brilliant, making up for it by killing superbly, the crowd will wave handkerchiefs to request that the president concede the ear of the bull as a token of honour to the matador. If the president agrees and believes the demands to be justified, he will wave his own handkerchief, after which a banderillero may cut the ear and present it to the matador. In reality several matadors who are anxious to have a long list of ears for the publicity value it gives them, have a banderillero who is instructed to cut the ear at the first sign of a display of any handkerchiefs. If the public shows any signs of demanding the ear this peón cuts it off and runs with it to the matador, who shows it, raising it in his hand toward the president and smiling, and the president confronted with an accomplished fact, is most liable to agree to the concession of the ear and bring out his own handkerchief. This way of falsifying the concession of the ear, which was formerly a great honour, has taken all value away from it, and now if a bullfighter puts up a decent performance and has any luck killing he will probably cut the ear of his bull. These professional ear-cutting peónes have established an even worse custom; that, if the president actually gives the signal to cut the ear without the matador first begging it from him, of cutting both ears and the tail, which they rush over and present to the matador on the excuse of the most moderate enthusiasm. The matadors, I am thinking of two especially, one a short, eagle-nosed, black-haired conceited Valencian, and the other a conceited, brave, simple-minded, long-necked, telephone pole from Aragon, then make a tour of the ring carrying an ear in one hand, another ear and a dung-covered tail in the other, smirking and believing they have triumphed in an absolute apotheosis, while in reality they have only performed conscientiously and employed a skilful trimmer of the visible parts of the bull to flatter them. Originally the cutting of the ear signified the bull became the property of the matador to dispose of as beef to his own advantage. This significance has long been obsolete.

P

Padrear: to breed.

Padrino: godfather or sponsor; in bullfighting the older matador who cedes sword and muleta to the younger matador who is alternating for the first time as killer in a formal corrida de toros.

Pala: shovel, bat, or oar blade; in bullfighting the flat of the horn on the outside; blows received by a bullfighter from the flat of the horn are called paletazos or varetazos and are often very serious, causing severe internal haemorrhage and other internal injuries without there being anything more visible than a bruise.

Palitroques: twigs; another name for banderillas.

Palmas: handclappings, applause.

Palos: sticks; slang for the banderillas.

Pañuelo: handkerchief; a white handkerchief exhibited by the president signals the termination or the commencement of the acts of pic-ing, banderillas, and sword; a green one that the bull should be taken out; a red one that explosive banderillas should be placed. The signal for each warning or aviso to the matador, denoting the lapse of time in killing, is given by the president showing a white handkerchief.

Par: pair of banderillas.

Parado: slowed or fixed without being exhausted; the second state of the bull during the course of the fight and the one in which the bullfighter should be able to get the most out of him. To *torear parado* is to work with the bull with the minimum of movement of the feet. It is the only way worthy of applause to fight a brave bull that is without faults of hooking to one side or the other.

Parar: to stand still and calmly watch the bull come; *parar los pies:* to keep the feet still while the bull charges. *Parar:* to keep the feet quiet; *templar:* to move the cloth slowly; and *mandar:* to dominate and control the animal by the cloth, are the three major commandments of bullfighting.

Parear: to place a pair of banderillas.

Parón: modern term to designate a pass made by the bullfighter with either cape or muleta in which he keeps his feet close together and does not move them from the time the bull charges until the pass is finished. These passes in which the man stands like a statue are brilliant additions to a bullfighter's repertoire, but they cannot be made with a bull that moves other than in a perfectly straight line when he charges; otherwise the man will go up in the air. Also they break one of the commandments for bullfighting; they parar, they templar; but they do not mandar, since the man with his feet together cannot swing the cloth far enough to keep the bull dominated by its folds, and so unless the bull is so perfect that he turns automatically each time to recharge, the man will be unable to hold him in the folds of the muleta enough to turn him so that he may link up a series of passes. With an ideal bull, however, the parones are highly emotional and impressive, and all bullfighters should be able to do them when they draw such an animal, but should not neglect the real art of dominating bulls, making them deviate from their line of attack by moving the lure, while they wait for a bull who will make the entire faena himself while the man plays the statue. The gyratory passes made by Villalta and his imitators, in which the man spins on the tips of his toes in half-circles with the bull, are also called parones.

Pase: pass made with either cape or muleta; movements of the lure to draw a charge by the animal in which his horns pass the man's body.

Paseo: entry of the bullfighters into the ring and their passage across it.

Paso atrás: step to the rear taken by the matador after profiling to kill in order to lengthen his distance from the bull, while giving the impression he is profiled very close, and give him more time to dodge as he goes in to kill in case the bull should not lower his head well to the muleta.

Paso de banderillas: going in to kill not straight, but moving on a quarter of a circle past the bull's horns, as a banderillero goes in. Permissible on bulls that can be killed in no other way.

Pecho: chest; the pase de pecho is a pass made with the muleta in the left hand at the finish of a natural in which the bull, having turned at the end of the natural, recharges and the man brings him by his chest and sends him out with a forward sweep of the muleta. The pase de pecho should be the ending of any series of naturales. It is also of great merit when it is used by the bullfighter to liberate himself from an unexpected charge or sudden return of the bull. In this case it is called a *forzado de pecho* or a forced pass. It is called preparado, or prepared, when it is given as a separate pass without having been preceded by a natural. The same pass may be done with the right hand, but it is not then a true pase de pecho, since the real *natural* the real *de pecho* are done only with the left hand. When either of these passes is done with the right hand the sword, which must always be held in the right hand, spreads the cloth and makes a much bigger lure, thus enabling the matador to keep the bull a greater distance away from him and send him farther away after each charge. Work done with the muleta held in the right hand and spread by the sword is often very brilliant and meritorious, but it lacks the difficulty, danger and sincerity of work done with the muleta in the left hand and the sword in the right.

Pelea: fight, the fight put up by the bull.

Peón: banderillero; torero who works on foot under the orders of the matador.

Pequeño: small, little.

Perder el sitio: bullfighter who through illness, lack of confidence, cowardice or nervousness has lost his style and even his sense of where and how things should be done.

Perder terreno: to lose ground while working with the bull; to have to use foot-work rather than control the bull with the cloth; also to lose ground in your profession.

Perfilar: to profile before going in to kill with sword in right hand, right fore-arm straight along the chest, muleta in left hand, left shoulder toward the bull, eyes following the line of the sword.

Periódicos: newspapers; those Madrid papers having the most accurate and disinterested accounts of bullfights in Madrid and the provinces are *La Libertad* among the daily papers and *El Eco Taurino* among the bullfight papers. *La Fiesta Brava* of Barcelona, while its accounts of fights are far from impartial, has excellent articles and features.

Periodistas: those who write for the papers; journalists.

Perros: bulldogs used in the old days before explosive banderillas were employed to worry a bull that would not charge the picadors, making him toss his head and tire his neck muscles, thus replacing the effect of the pics.

Pesado: heavy; dull; tiresome.

Peso: weight.

Pesuña: hoof of bull. Fighting bulls are ruined by *glosopeda*, or hoof-and-mouth disease, which leaves the feet tender and the hooves liable to crack loose and even break off entirely.

Peto: mattress covering worn over chest, right flank, and belly of picador's horse. Introduced during the late Primo de Rivera's dictatorship at the instigation of the English-born ex-Queen of Spain.

Pica: the pic or pike pole used in bullfighting. It is composed of a wooden shaft 2 metres and between 55 and 70 centimeters long, made of ash, has a triangular steel point 29 millimeters long. Below the steel point the head of the shaft is wrapped with cord and it is equipped with a round metal guard to prevent its entering more than 108 millimeters into the bull at the very most. The present model of pic is very hard on the bull, and bulls which really charge and insist under punishment can rarely accept more than four pics without losing most of their force. This is especially true since the picadors, handicapped by the peto, often place their pics well behind the morrillo, the place they are supposed to pic, and where the hump of muscle can support the punishment and, pic-ing directly over the unprotected spine, injure the bull severely and destroy most of his force. A wound by the present pic too low down at the side so that it goes between the ribs is also liable to reach the lungs or at least the pleura. Part of this bad pic-ing is intentional, at the orders of the matador, who wishes the bull to be deprived of all force, but much of it is not since the picador is so handicapped by the peto or protective mattress that he must strike the bull well out as he comes in, at a distance where the aim cannot be sure; instead of being able to pic carefully he pics where and how he can. The reason for this is that if the picador waits for the bull to get close enough so he can place the pic properly, the bull, if he is of any size, will strike the solid wall of the mattress and topple man and horse over with a crash before the pic can take hold. There is nothing for the bull to hook and lift and to have his head and neck muscles pushed on by the pic while lifting. For this reason picadors, when a bull, disillusioned by the mattress, has refused to charge it heavily more than once, have made a custom of turning the horse as they push the bull away so that the bull may gore the horse in his unprotected hindquarters and tire his neck with that lifting. Since these wounds are almost never fatal and very little apparent unless you look for them, you will see the same horse brought back again and again, the wound being sewn up and washed off between bulls, where, in the days before the peto, the bull would have been allowed to reach the horse, to gore and lift him, in order to tire the bull's neck muscles, but the horse would have been killed. Now with the peto few horses are killed in the ring, but nearly all are wounded in the hindquarters or between the legs in the manner described. The frank admission of the necessity for killing horses to have a bullfight has been replaced by a hypocritical semblance of protection which causes the horses much more suffering but, once implanted, will be maintained as long as possible, because it saves the horse-contractor money, enabling the promoters to save money and allowing the authorities to feel that they have civilized the bullfight. Technically, not morally, the point to remember is that the slowing of the bull without depriving him of his force or his wish to attack, which is accomplished by his charge arriving at its destination, lifting with his neck, pushing with all four feet, resisting the pic pressing on his hump of neck muscle, overthrowing, and killing, puts him into the next two stages of the fight in a desirable condition for the consummation of the bullfight which cannot be produced by the picador simply punishing him severely in a way to injure him and make him lose strength, blood, and all desire to attack. This is what happens to the bull when he is pic-ed in the shoulder blades, centre of the spine or in the ribsand instead of arriving at the next two stages ready to make a bullfight, once he has suffered the damage the present pic can inflict, there is no bull left to fight.

Picador: man who pics bulls from on horseback under the orders of the matador. Is paid from one hundred to two hundred and fifty pesetas a fight, has his right leg and foot armoured under chamois-skin breeches, wears short jacket and a shirt and tie like any other bullfighter, and a wide low-crowned hat with a pompom on the side. Picadors are seldom gored by the bull since the matadors must protect them with their capes when they fall toward the bull. If they fall away from the bull they are protected by the horse. Picadors suffer broken arms, jaws, legs, and ribs frequently, and fractured skulls occasionally. Few are killed in the ring in proportion to matadors, but many suffer permanently from concussion of the brain. Of all ill-paid professions in civil life I believe it is the roughest and the most constantly exposed to danger of death, which, fortunately, is nearly always removed by the matador's cape.

Picar arriba: to place the pic well up on the morrillo of the bull.

Picar atrás: to pic too far back behind the morrillo.

Picar corta: to pic holding well down on the wood of the shaft close to the steel point. Exposes the man more since he may fall forward between horse and bull, but makes his shot at the bull much more secure.

Picar delante: to pic too far forward on the neck.

Piernas: legs; *Tiene muchas piernas* of either bull or man means very strong in the legs.

Pinchazo: puncture, a pinchazo is an estocada that has only gone in a very little way. *Pinchar en el duro:* is to go in a little way and hit bone. A pinchazo in which the matador goes in well, puts the sword in the proper place but hits bone is not to his discredit, since the point of the sword striking or not striking a rib or part of a vertebra is altogether a matter of luck. If the man has gone in straight, directed the sword properly, he should be applauded even though the sword hits bone and refuses to go in. On the other hand cowardly matadors will give a series of pinchazos, never attempting to follow the sword in and drive it to the hilt, avoiding all chance of coming close to the horn in the hope of bleeding the bull with these punctures and then trying to do away with him by a descabello. The merit or lack of merit of a pinchazo should be judged by the way the man goes in and his evident intention.

Pisar: to tread; *pisar terreno del toro:* to work so close to the bull that you are in his terrain.

Pisotear: to trample on – bull stepping on man on the ground while trying to gore him.

Pitillo: a cigarette.

Pitón: points of a bull's horns; or, sometimes, the entire horn. *Pases de pitón á pitón* are the chopping strokes with the muleta from one horn to the other to tire the bull's neck muscles. Pitónes are the two horns.

Pitos: whistlings; expressions of disapproval. Sometimes when a matador is fighting who is known to be cowardly or is in a bad epoch in his career or unpopular in that particular town, spectators go to the ring armed with police or dog whistles in order to demonstrate more loudly. One of these armed whistlers immediately behind you can deafen you temporarily. There is nothing to do about it but put your fingers in your ears. These whistles are commonly used in Valencia where the deafening of anyone is regarded as a great joke.

Plaza: public place; *Plaza de toros:* bull ring.

Poder á poder: force to force; method of placing banderillas described in text.

Pollo: chicken – also young man about town. Young bullfighter who fancies himself as a man of the world.

Polvo: dust, raised in the ring by the wind and laid by sprinkling. When the wind raises dust in a ring spectators will shout '¡Agua! Agua!' until a sprinkling-cart is brought in or the dust laid with a hose.

Pomo: pommel of a sword.

Presidencia: authority in charge of the conduct of the bullfight.

Prueba: test, trial or proof; *Prueba de caballos* is the testing of the horses by the picadors. Prueba is also the name of one of the bullfights given each year at Pamplona in which four local bulls were formerly used, and the fight given at popular prices was supposed to be a test of local breeds. It is now a fight in which six matadors take part, each killing one bull.

Punta de Capote: point of the cape; running the bull after the cape which is held by one end so that it stretches out its full length; proper way to run bulls when they first enter the ring.

Puntazo: slight horn wound, as a cornada is a big wound.

Puntilla: dagger used to kill bull or horse after he has been mortally wounded. (See cachete.)

Puntillero: man who kills bull with the puntilla. (See cachetero.)

Puro: Havana cigar; puros are smoked by most people engaged in the bullfight business who can afford them.

Puta: a whore, harlot, jade, broad, chippy, tart or prostitute; *hijo de puta:* son of any of the above; common insult shouted at bullfighter. In Spanish they insult most fully when speaking or wishing ill of the parents rather than of the person directly.

Puya: another name for the pic – also refers to the triangular steel point.

Puyazo: pic placed in the bull.

Q

Quedar: to remain or to stay in a place; *Quedar sin toro:* for a bullfighter to be without any enemy due to the bull's force and spirit having been destroyed by a wound or series of wounds by a picador.

¡Qué lástima! : what a shame! Expression uttered when you have heard that a friend has been badly gored, or has contracted a venereal disease, or has married a whore, or has had something happen to his wife or children, or when a good bull comes out for a poor bullfighter or a poor bull comes out for a good bullfighter.

Querencia: part of the ring that the bull prefers to be in where he feels at home.

Querer: to want; *no quiere:* in bullfighting means the matador doesn't want to try anything, content to get through with the afternoon as easily as possible; of a bull it means he does not want to charge the horse or the cloth.

¡Qué se vaya! : meaning that he should get the hell out of here and not return. Shouted at bullfighters.

Quiebro: any inclination of the body, especially the waist, to one side or the other to avoid the horn of the bull; any dodging or feinting movement of the body done close to the bull to avoid being caught.

Quiebro de muleta: inclining and swinging the muleta with the left wrist low and to the right to guide the bull out and away from the man as he puts the sword in; it is because of the left hand guiding and getting rid of the bull while the right pushes in the sword that bullfighters say you kill more with the left hand than with the right.

Quinto: fifth; *No hay quinto malo:* the fifth one can't be bad; old belief that the fifth bull would always be good. Probably originated in the days when the bull breeders decided the order in which their bulls should be fought, before they were drawn by the matadors by lot as they are now, and so knowing the value of the bulls would place the best in fifth position. Today the fifth is as liable to be bad as any other.

Quite: from *quitar* – to take away – is the taking away of the bull from any one who has been placed in immediate danger by him. It especially refers to the taking away of the bull from the horse and man after he has charged the picadors, by the matadors armed with capes and taking their turns in rotation, each one taking the bull after a charge. The matador who is to kill the bull makes the first *quite* and the others follow in order. From going in close with the cape, bringing the bull out and away from fallen horse and man and placing him in position before the next picador the quite has changed now so that a series of lances with the cape after taking the bull out is obligatory on a matador each time he makes a quite; they supposedly rivalling to see how close and artistically they can pass the bull. *Quites* made to take the bull away from a man he is goring, or who is on the ground with the bull over him, are participated in by all the bullfighters, and it is at this time that you can judge their valour, knowledge of bulls and degree of abnegation, since a quite in these circumstances is highly dangerous and very difficult to make, as the men must get so close to the bull in order to make him leave the object he is trying to gore that their retreat, taking him out with the cape when he charges, is very compromised.

R

Rabioso: raging – matador is said to be *rabioso* when he has lashed himself, mentally, into a rage of bravery as contrasted with the cold, consistent valour of a truly brave man; a bullfighter who is coldly brave will only be *rabioso* when he has been made furious either by the taunts of the crowd or by the bull bumping and tossing him.

Rabo: tail of bull.

Racha: a run of luck; *mala racha:* streak of bad luck; bullfighter drawing a series of poor bulls; succession of bullfights turning out badly.

Ración: a portion; as in the café you will order *un ración* of shrimps, prawns, *percebes* or whatever it is. *A ración* of shellfish usually consists of a hundred grams, a little under a quarter of a pound. It is for this reason that you may get two huge prawns one time and at another four smaller ones and still be charged the same, since they are served by weight.

Rebolera: decorative pass with the cape in which it is held by one extremity and swung so that it describes a circle around the man.

Rebotado: to come out after killing bumped by the bull's head; to be bounced or jostled without falling.

Rebrincar: to make a sidewise jump; occasionally made by bulls when the cape is first offered them.

Recargar: bull recharging under the punishment of being held off by the pic.

Receloso: bull which is reluctant to charge, not through being worn out by punishment, but through lack of combative temperament and yet, if challenged repeatedly, will charge.

Recibir: to kill the bull from in front, awaiting his charge with sword without moving the feet once the charge has started; with the muleta low in the left hand and the sword in the right hand, right forearm across the chest pointing toward the bull, and as he comes in and takes the muleta, putting the sword in with the right hand and swinging him out with the muleta in the left as in a pase de pecho, not moving the feet until the sword has gone in. Most difficult, dangerous and emotional way to kill bulls; rarely seen in modern times. I have seen it executed completely three times in almost three hundred bullfights.

Recoger: to regore; for the bull to toss something into the air from the ground; or having tossed a man in the air, to catch him again on the other horn.

Recorte: any pass with the cape in which it is snatched away from the bull or turned sharply from him; or quick movement by the man which cuts the bull's charge; turning the bull on himself sharply with the consequent twist on his legs and spinal column.

Recursos: resources; a bullfighter with many *recursos* is one who has tricks in reserve and knows how to cope with difficulties as they may arise.

Redondel: synonym for the ring where the bull is fought.

Redondo: En redondo – are several passes in succession such as naturals in which the man and the bull finally execute a complete circle; any pass which tends to make a circle.

Regalo: gift or keepsake given to the matador who has dedicated a bull to a spectator by the person who has received the dedication. Used sarcastically to refer to a difficult bull.

Reglamento: government ordinance covering the giving of bull-fights in Spain. It was originally intended to publish a translation of the present government regulation as an appendix to this book but since the reglamento in force dates from the era of Primo de Rivera it was decided to await the publication of a newer ruling for inclusion in translation in subsequent editions of this book if there should be such editions.

Regular: normal, ordinary or so-so when applied to a matador's work or the result of a corrida.

Rehiletes: darts; synonym for banderillas.

Rehilitero: banderillero.

Rejón: javelin used to kill bulls from on horseback.

Rejoneador: man who attempts to kill bulls from on horseback with a rejón.

Relance: al relance – to place a pair of banderillas by surprise in a bull which is still charging after the placing of a previous pair.

Reloj: clock; placed by law in all bull rings in order that the spectators may keep track of the time employed by the matador in killing.

Rematar: to finish; to make the last pass of any series of passes with the cape; to perform some act that will provide an emotional or artistic climax. In regard to the bull he is said to *rematar en tablas* or finish on the planks when he chases a man over the fence and then drives his horns against the wood.

Remojar: to wet the capes and muletas heavily for use on a windy day.

Remos: fore and hind legs of either bull or horse.

Rendido: worn out; surrendered to the will of the man.

Renovador: reformer, renewer of the art, etc. Many of these are announced in bullfighting, almost one each year, but the only real one in modern bullfighting was Juan Belmonte.

Renunciar: to renounce or give up; a bullfighter renounces his alternativa when he abandons his position as a full *matador de toros* to accept any contracts he may obtain as a novillero.

Reparado de vista: bull with defective vision in one eye though not completely blind. Defects of vision are often caused by a straw or a thistle injuring the eye when the bull is feeding.

Res: wild animal; any head of cattle on fighting-bull-breeding ranch with fighting blood.

Resabio: viciousness; *toro de resabio:* vicious bull.

Retirada: retirement; bullfighters sometimes retire when they are short of contracts or very much in love with their wives and return to fight again in a few years, hoping in the first case that the novelty of their re-appearance will bring contracts and in the second simply returning because they need money or because the intensity of their domestic relations has relaxed.

Revistas: magazines or revues; revistas de toros are bullfight periodicals. Most of them at present are propaganda sheets in which photographs and coloured accounts of the performances of bull-fighters who pay a certain sum to the editors appear. Bullfighters who owe money for unpaid propaganda or others who have refused to accept propositions made to them for propaganda, usually in the form of paying for a cover featuring a photograph of themselves or, cheaper, an inside picture, are attacked more or less scurrilously in the cheaper sheets. *Le Toril*, published in Toulouse, France, is an impartial bullfight revue sustained by subscription and accepting no propaganda or advertising either hidden in the text or open. Its sincerity and impartiality are handicapped in writing good criticism by the small number of corridas its editors can afford to see each year and by the fact that they do not see the first and second subscription season in Madrid, and so see each fight as an individual action rather than as a part of a bullfighter's season or campaign. *El Echo Taurino*, published in Madrid, contains the most complete and accurate accounts of bullfights in Spain and Mexico. *La Fiesta Brava* of Barcelona, while it is a propaganda weekly, has excellent photographs, and a certain amount of news and fact. None of the others is serious, although some, such as *Toreros y Toros*, are interesting papers. *El Clarín* of Valencia is well gotten out with excellent photographs, but is only a propaganda sheet. *Torerías* is always interesting and is the most scur-rilous of the blackmail sheets. In the old days *La Lidia, Sol y Sombra*,

315

and for a short time *Zig-Zag*, were real bullfight revues in whose bound volumes you can read the bullfight history of their epoch, although none of them appears ever to have been free of the financial influence, manifested in one way or another, of certain matadors.

Revistero: bullfight critic or reviewer.

Revolcón: tossed by the bull without being wounded due to the horn catching in the clothing, lifting between the legs, or under an arm.

Revoltoso: bull which turns rapidly, excessively rapidly, to recharge after the man has passed the bull with cape or muleta.

Rodillas: the knees.

Rodillazos: passes made with the bullfighter on one or both knees. Vary in merit according to the terrain they are performed in and whether the matador goes to his knees before or after the horn has passed.

Rondeño: Escuela Rondeña: Ronda school or the Ronda style of bullfighting, sober, limited in repertoire, simple, classic and tragic as against the more varied, playful and gracious style of Sevilla. Belmonte, for example, although an innovator, was essentially of the Ronda school, although born and bred in Sevilla. Joselito was an example of the so-called Sevillian school. As in most talk of schools in art or literature the separating of people into schools is artificial and arbitrary with the critic; in bullfighting more than anywhere else the style is made up of the habits in action, attitude toward the fight and physical capabilities. If a bullfighter is very serious in temperament, sober rather than cheerful in the ring and with a limited repertoire due to lack of imagination, faulty apprenticeship or physical defects that prevent him, for instance, from putting in banderillas, they class him as belonging to the Ronda school, although he may not have any allegiance or belief that the sober way of fighting is better than the gay. He simply happens to be sober. On the other hand many bullfighters who are far from gay or cheerful in the ring, simply because they are from Sevilla and trained there, employ all the Sevillian tricks, light-hearted airs and graces, smiling forcedly and being very flowery and gracious when they have nothing but cold fear in their hearts. The Sevillian and Ronda schools of bullfighting as real schools of thought and opposing views on the subject did exist in the early days of professional bullfighting when there was great rivalry between the great matadors of the two towns and their disciples in their ways of fighting, but now Ronda means sober and tragic in the Plaza with a limited repertoire and Sevillano means light-hearted or imitation light-hearted with flowery style and a lengthy repertoire.

Rozandole los alamares: when the bull's horns graze the ornaments on the bullfighter's jacket.

Rubios: blonds in men; in bulls the place between the top of the shoulder blades where the sword should enter. Rubias are blondes in women.

S

Sacar: to bring out; *Sacar el estoque:* to pull out a sword in order that the wound may bleed more freely and the bull go down; or simply to remove it because badly placed. Usually accomplished by a banderillero running forward from behind the bull and tossing the length of a cape across the sword so that the weight of the cape pulled forward on the sword will bring it out. If the bull is nearly dead the matador may pull the sword out himself by hand or with a banderilla, sometimes using the same sword to descabellar with. *Sacar el toro* is to bring the bull out into the ring when he has taken up a position close to the barrera.

Sacar el corcho: to pull out the cork from a bottle. A *Sacacorchos* is a corkscrew. In bullfighting it is the anti-aesthetic, twisting style of working with the cape made by citing the bull too far on the bias when taking him to make veronicas.

Salida en hombros: for a matador to be carried out in triumph on the shoulders of members of the crowd. May mean much or little depending on whether his representative has prepared it beforehand by distribution of free tickets and instructions, or whether it is spontaneous.

Salidas: exits; in bullfighting to *da Salida* is to send the bull away from the man with the cloth at the finish of a pass. The *salida* in each pass is the place at which the bull should leave the man's territory in cases where the bull passes the man. The respective exits of both man and bull from the juncture they make in the putting in of the banderillas and the killing are called their *salidas*.

DEATH IN THE AFTERNOON

Salir por piés: is to run at full speed at the conclusion of any manoeuvre attempted with the bull in order to escape being caught.

Salsa torera: literally salsa means sauce, but salsa is the indefinable quality which being lacking in a bullfighter makes his work dull no matter how perfect.

Saltos: in the old days were jumps made over the bull either unaided or vaulted with the aid of a pole. The only jumps made now are those of the bullfighters who are forced to jump the barrera.

Sangre torera: bullfighting blood – as in coming from a family of professional fighters.

Sano: healthy; bulls must be passed by a veterinary as in good health before being fought. Weakness of the hooves caused by the after effects of hoof-and-mouth disease called glosopeda is not easily detected since it is often only in the fight that this weakness will appear.

Santo: a saint; *El santo de espaldas:* is said of a bullfighter who has had a bad day; the saint turned his back on him. Bullfighters take their patrons from the local Virgin of their town, village or district, but the *Virgen de la Soledad* is the patron of all bullfighters and it is her portrait and image which are in the chapel of the bull ring at Madrid.

Seco: dry, harsh; *torero seco* is one who works in a jerky, sharp rather than suave manner. *Valor seco:* is natural unadorned courage; *golpe seco:* is the sharp hard chop the bull sometimes gives with his head to try to dislodge the pic. It is this sort of chop that given by a bull to horse or man makes the worst horn wounds. *Vino Seco:* is wine that is not sweet.

Sencillo: a bull that is frank in his charges, noble and easily deceived.

Sentido: understanding; bull which pays little attention to the cloth but makes for the man, having in the course of the fight learned more rapidly than the men have fought him through their defective actions with cape and banderillas. If a bullfighter runs and works at a distance rather than skilfully deceiving the bull by being so close the bull can only concentrate on the cloth, the animal, seeing the man apart from the lure, learns to distinguish them apart very rapidly. Thus a bull is made difficult by the men, through fear, working far away from him, and failing to get the banderillas in promptly, while he is made easy and dominated by the man working so close that the bull sees nothing but the cloth and by putting in the banderillas promptly before the bull has time to figure out how to catch the man.

Señorito: young gentleman; *Señoritos:* in bullfighting are bull-fighters who give themselves the airs of young men about town or sometimes sons of well-off parents who take up bullfighting.

Sesgo: bias; *al sesgo:* form of placing banderillas explained in the text.

Sevillano: escuela sevillana: Sevillian school or style of bullfighting, gay, varied, and flowery as opposed to the sober, limited, and classic Ronda school. A Sevillano is a five-peseta piece minted in the south, at one time containing the same amount of silver as the ordinary coin of that denomination, but refused in the north in trade because not legal tender for certain debts. Do not take any five-peseta coins stamped with the head of the late King as a small boy and you will keep out of trouble. They will give you other coins if you ask for them.

Silla: chair; banderillas were sometimes placed with the man seated in a chair; waiting the charge seated; rising as the bull came close; feinting to one side to draw the bull's charge, swaying back to the other to free himself; then placing the sticks and, after the bull has passed, reseating himself in the chair.

Simulacro: simulation; bullfights given where the killing of the bull is forbidden in Portugal and France in which the act of killing is simulated by the placing of a rosette or banderilla by the matador at the moment of going in with what would be the sword in a real bullfight.

Sobaquillo: armpit, frequent site of horn wounds when the man, in going in to kill, has not lowered the bull's head properly with the muleta.

Sobreros: substitutes, bulls in reserve in case any of those to be fought are refused in the ring by the public.

Sobresaliente: when two matadors fight six bulls between them a novillero or aspirant matador makes the entry with them as sobre-saliente or substitute and is charged with killing the bulls in case both matadors should be wounded and unable to continue. A sobresaliente is usually paid only two or three hundred pesetas and is expected to aid with his cape in the routine work of the placing of the banderillas. He is usually allowed by the matadors to make one or two quites toward the end of the fight.

Sol y sombra: sun and shade; seats in the bull ring which are in the sun as the fight commences, but will be in the shade as it progresses. Midway in price between the seats in the shade and those in the sun, they afford a considerable saving to anyone who must watch expenditure closely.

Sorteo: making up the lots and drawing of the bulls before the fight to determine which bulls shall be killed by which matadors. Also the drawings of the Spanish lottery.

Suertes: all predetermined manoeuvres in a bullfight; any move in a bullfight which has rules for the manner of its execution. Suerte in the singular also means luck.

Sustos: scares, frights, shocks.

T

Tablas: planks; the barrera which surrounds the ring in which the bull is fought. *Entablada* is said of a bull that takes up a position close to this plank fence and is reluctant to leave it.

Tabloncillo: highest row of open seats in bull ring below the covered galleries.

Tacónes: heels; *tacónes de goma* are rubber heels; these are sold by ambulatory vendors who will come up to you while you are seated in the café, cut the heel off your shoe with a sort of instant-acting leather-cutting pincers they carry, in order to force you to put on a rubber heel. The rubber heels they attach are of a low, worthless grade. Their excuse when you protest against the heel rape is that they understood you wanted heels. It is a racket. If any rubber-heel attacker ever cuts a heel of your shoe without your having first definitely ordered a pair of rubber heels, kick him in the belly or under the jaw and get the heels put on by someone else. I believe the law will sustain you, but if they take you to jail they will not fine you much more than the price of the rubber heels. There is one sinister-faced Catalan high-pressured heel ripper whom you can identify at all the ferias by a scar on his right cheek. I gave him that, but he is more of a dodger by now and you might have difficulty landing on him. The best thing when you see this particular heel-selling bastard (*hijo de puta* will do) approaching is to take off your shoes and put them inside your shirt. If he then attempts to attach rubber heels to your bare feet, send for the American or British Consul.

Tal: such, similar, so, etc. But *¿Que tal?* is all you have to know to be able to ask, How are you? How was it? What's new? How are things going? What do you say, old timer? What do you think? How is everything since I saw you last? And if you add to Qué tal the words *la familia* you inquire about a man's family, a necessary politeness; *¿la madre?* his mother; *su señora,* his wife; *el negocio,* his business (usually *fatal*); *los toros,* the bulls (usually *muy malo*); *el movimiento,* the movement, anarchistic, revolutionary, catholic or monarchial (usually going badly); or *las cosas,* which includes all of these and much besides. Las cosas are usually going not too badly, there usually existing this personal optimism through pride no matter how detailed and generic the pessimism.

Taleguilla: bullfighter's breeches.

Tantear: to calculate; *lances de tanteo* are the first passes made by the matador with the cape without the man getting close to the bull in order to see how he charges before taking a chance and passing him really close.

Tapar: to veil; *Tapando la cara con la muleta* (veiling the face with the muleta) is to go in to kill and by covering the bull's whole face with the cloth, blind him, and then lean over the head to kill; a way of cheating in killing used often by tall matadors whose height enables them to trick in this way with ease (instead of lowering the muleta, making the bull follow it and swinging him away from the man).

Taparse: to cover; is when the bull by lifting his head covers the place where the sword or banderillas should go in; or when he lifts his head so that he covers the place between the neck vertebrae where the matador should descabellar. A bull with quick reflexes who is on the defensive will sometimes raise his head in this way each time he feels the steel of the sword, making it impossible for the matador to get it in.

Tapas: or covers, so called since they were originally placed across the top of the glass instead of being served on small saucers as now, are the appetizers of smoked salmon, tuna and sweet red-peppers, sardines, anchovies, smoked Sierra ham, sausage, sea foods, toasted almonds, olives stuffed with anchovies which are served free with Manzanilla wine or vermouth, in cafés, bars, or *bodegas.*

Tarascadas: sudden rushes or attacks by the bull.

Tarde: afternoon, also late; *muy tarde:* very late.

DEATH IN THE AFTERNOON

Tardo: slow; *toro tardo:* a bull that is slow to charge.

Taurino: anything to do with the bullfight.

Tauromachia: art of fighting bulls on foot and on horseback. Most famous of many books of rules for old-time bullfighting are the Tauromachias of José Delgado (Pepé Hillo), Francisco Montés, and more recently Rafael Guerra (Guerrita). The Pepé Hillo book and that of Guerrita were written for them. Montés is said to have written his own. Certainly it is the cleverest and simplest.

Tela: cloth or stuff; *Más tela* in a bullfight account means the bull was given another dose of flopping capes; tela is used always in a deprecatory sense; *largando tela:* means spreading the cape too wide; stretching out cloth to keep the man as far from the bull as possible; spreading the awning.

Temoroso: cowardly bull which shakes his head and retreats from an object, sometimes giving a sudden jump and turning away, or backing away slowly while tossing his head instead of charging.

Templador: small four-sided wooden enclosure erected in centre of some bull rings in South America with entrance at each corner as place of refuge to afford additional protection to their local bullfighters.

Templar: to move cape or muleta slowly, suavely, and calmly, thus prolonging the moment of the pass and the danger and giving a rhythm to the action of the man and bull and cape, or man, bull and muleta.

Temple: the quality of slowness, suavity, and rhythm in a bullfighter's work.

Temporada: a bullfight season; in Spain from Easter until the first of November. In Mexico from the first of November until the end of February.

Tendido: rows of open seats in a bull ring which rise from the barrera to the covered gallery or grada. These rows of seats are divided into as many as ten different sections, each with its own entrance, and numbered Tendido 1, Tendido 2, etc.

Tercio: third; the bullfight is divided into three parts, the *tercio de varas*, that of the pic, *tercio de banderillas*, and *tercio del muerte* or third of death. In the division of the terrain of the ring itself for fighting purposes, the tercios is the second third of the ring if its diameter is divided into three parts – the tercios extending from between the third of terrain called *tablas* which is nearest the barrera and the centre third called the *medios*.

Terreno: terrain; in the broadest technical sense the terrain of the bull is called that ground between the point where he is standing and the centre of the ring; that of the bullfighter is the ground between where he is standing and the barrera. It is assumed that the bull at the conclusion of a pass will make for the centre of the ring where he has most space and freedom. This is not always true, since a tired bull or a cowardly bull will usually make for the barrera. In such cases the terrains may be reversed, the man taking as his terrain the outside and leaving the bull the inside. The idea is to leave the bull his natural exit clear at the end of any meeting between man and bull or any series of passes. The terrain is also the third of ground chosen by the bullfighter for the execution of any manoeuvre or series of passes, whether the centre of the ring, the middle third or the third next to the planks. A bullfighter's terrain is also said to be the amount of ground he needs to execute successfully a pass or series of passes in. In killing in the ordinary natural way, with the bull in his terrain and the bullfighter in his, the bull will have his right flank toward the barrera and his left flank toward the centre of the ring, so that as the matador goes in to kill, the bull, after the man has passed, will go toward the centre and the man toward the fence. In the case of bulls who have shown that their natural exit is toward the fence rather than toward the centre of the ring the matador will reverse this natural position when going in to kill and will take the bull with the *terrenos cambiados* or the terrains changed, placing him so that his left flank is toward the barrera and his right toward the centre of the ring. In this position the man will go toward the centre after he has passed and the bull's exit will be left free toward the fence. The most certain way for a bullfighter to be caught is not to understand the terrains or directions of natural exits or the particular directions of exit observed in the individual bulls, so that he finds himself in the bull's way at the end of a suerte instead of sending the bull on his preferred way. A *querencia* or special place the bull has taken a fondness to is always his natural exit at the end of a pass.

Tiempo – estocadas á un tiempo: are those in which the bull charges at the same instant as the man goes in to kill. To be well placed they need much coolness in the matador.

Tienta: the testing of calves for bravery on a bull-breeding ranch.

Tijerillas: scissors; pass with the cape made with the arms crossed; rarely seen, although there is a tendency to revive its use at present.

Tirónes: passes with the muleta, the lower end flopped close under the bull's muzzle and then withdrawn, the muleta swinging to one side, to draw the bull after it from one place in the ring to another.

Tomar: to take; the bull is said to take the muleta well when he charges the cloth avidly; a man is said to take the bull *de corto* when he provokes the charge from close to the animal and *de largo* when he provokes it from a distance.

Tonterías: nonsense; ornamental foolishness done with the bull, such as hanging hats on his horns, etc.

Toreador: Frenchification of the word torero. Not used in Spanish except to refer slightingly to a French bullfighter.

Torear: to fight bulls in an enclosed place either on foot or on horseback.

Toreo: the art of fighting bulls. *Toreo de salón:* practising cape and muleta work for form and style without any bull being present; necessary part of a matador's training.

Torerazo: great bullfighter.

Torerito: a small bullfighter.

Torero: professional bullfighter. Matadors, banderilleros, picadors are all toreros. *Torera* means having to do with bullfighting.

Torete: little bull.

Toril: enclosure from which bulls come into the ring to be fought.

Toro: fighting bull. *Todo es toro: It's all bull:* sarcasm applied to banderillero who has placed the sticks in some ridiculous place on the animal. *Los toros dan y los toros quitan: the bulls give and the bulls take away*; they give you money and they can take away your life.

Toro de paja: bull of straw; inoffensive bull; simple to the point of being without danger. *Toro de lidia:* fighting bull. *Toro bravo:* brave bull. *Toro de bandera:* super-grade of bravery in bull. *Torazo:* enormous bull. *Torito:* little bull. *Toro de fuego:* life-size papier-mâché bull mounted on wheels and loaded with fireworks, pulled through the streets at night in celebrating fiestas in the North of Spain; also called in Basque – *Zezenzuzko. Toro de Aguardiente:* bull with a rope attached to his horns held by a number of people and let run in a village street for the amusement of the populace.

Traje de luces: bullfighting suit.

Trampas: tricks, frauds; ways of simulating danger without experiencing it.

Trapío: general condition in a fighting bull. *Buen trapío:* uniting all the desired qualities of type, condition, and size in bulls of fighting strain.

Trapo: the rag; the muleta.

Trasera: estocada placed too far back.

Trastear: to work with the muleta.

Trastos: the tools, in bullfighting the sword and muleta.

Trinchera: trench; *de trinchera:* pass with the muleta given with the man safely out of reach of the bull; going into the refuge of the neck beside the horn as the bull turns.

Trucos: tricks.

Tuerto: one-eyed; bulls blind in one eye are fought in the novilladas. Tuertos or one-eyed people are considered very bad luck. One-eyed bulls are not exceptionally difficult to fight but are almost impossible to do any brilliant work with.

Tumbos: falls or spills; the falls taken by picadors.

Turno: in turn; in regular order of seniority as in the action of matadors; everything is done in turn in bullfighting so that the bullfight may be run off rapidly and without disputes.

U

Último: the last; *último tercio:* the last third of the bullfight in which the bull is killed with sword and muleta.

Uretritis: gonorrhoea; common ailment in the Peninsula. Referring to this there is a Spanish proverb: *Más cornadas dan las mujeres:* the women gore more often than the bulls.

Urinario: comfort station.

Utrero: three-year-old bull. Utrera is a cow of the same age. Many bulls now sold to be fought in Spanish rings are little more than utreros. Bulls in which the crosses of different strains made in breeding have not turned out well are often very brave as calves and utreros, but steadily lose bravery after they are mature at four years. This is especially true of bulls raised in the province of Salamanca. Consequently their breeders try to pass as many utreros as they can as bulls; fattening them on grain to make the required weight. It is these bulls sold to be fought before they are mature which eliminate all emotion and seriousness from the bullfight and by depriving it of its fundamental necessity, the bull, do more than any other agency to discredit it.

V

Vaca: cow.

Vacuna: having to do with cattle.

Valiente: courageous, brave.

Valla: wall or wooden fence or barrera.

Valour: courage, bravery, coolness. First quality a bullfighter must have.

Vaquero: caretaker or herder of fighting bulls on the ranch; cowboy, cowpuncher.

Vaquilla: small cow.

Vara: shaft, pic used in bullfighting.

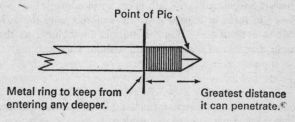

Point of Pic

Metal ring to keep from entering any deeper.

Greatest distance it can penetrate.

Varetazo: blow by the flat of the bull's horn; any horn stroke which does not wound. May be a serious bruise with internal haemorrhage or merely a scratch.

Ver llegar: to watch them come; the ability to watch the bull come as he charges with no thought except to calmly see what he is doing and make the moves necessary to the manoeuvre you have in mind. To calmly watch the bull come is the most necessary and primarily difficult thing in bullfighting.

Vergüenza: shame or honour; a sinvergüenza is a bullfighter without honour or shame – ¡ Qué vergüenza! means what a shame or what a disgrace.

Veronica: pass with the cape so called because the cape was originally grasped in the two hands in the manner in which Saint Veronica is shown in religious paintings to have held the napkin with which she wiped the face of Christ. It has nothing to do with the man wiping the face of the bull, as one writer on Spain has suggested. In making the veronica the matador stands either facing or profiled toward the bull with left leg slightly advanced and offers the cape which he holds with both hands, having grasped the lower front corners of the cape where the corks are attached and raised them, bunching up the material so that he has a good hand-hold with each hand, the fingers pointing down, the thumb up. As the bull charges, the man awaits him until his horns lower to hook the cape, at which instant the man moves the cape ahead of the bull's charge with a suave movement of the arms, his arms held low, passing the bull's head and his body past the man's waist. He passes the bull out with the cape, pivoting slightly on his toes or the balls of his feet as he does so, and at the end of the pass, as the bull turns, the man is in position to repeat the pass, his right leg slightly advanced this time, drawing cape ahead of the bull so that he passes by in the other direction. The veronica is tricked by the man making a sidestep as the bull charges to take him farther away from the horns, by the man putting his feet together once the horn has passed and by the man leaning or stepping toward the bull once the horn has passed to make it look as though he had passed the horn close. A matador who is not faking the veronica will sometimes pass the bull so close that the horns will pick off the gold rosettes that ornament his jacket. Matadors, too, will sometimes cite the bull with both feet together and make a series of veronicas in this way with the feet as still as though the man were nailed to the ground. This can only be done with a bull that turns and recharges of his own accord and in a perfectly straight line. The feet must be slightly apart in making a bull pass and repass if the bull needs to be made to follow the swing of the cape at the end of the pass in order to turn. In any case the merit in the veronica is not determined by whether the feet are together or apart, but by whether they remain immobile from the moment of the charge until the bull has been passed and the closeness with which the man passes the horn by his body. The slower, suaver and lower the man swings the cape with his arms the better the veronica.

Viaje: voyage; the direction followed by the bull's charge or by the man as he goes in to place banderillas or to kill.

Viento or *aire:* wind, the worst enemy of the bullfighter.

Vientre: belly; frequent site of horn wounds when the man is gored going in to kill through not being able to shrug his belly over the horn as he must in a really good estocada. Wounds here, and in the chest, are the most often fatal in bullfighting, not alone through the wound, but through the traumatic shock of the force of the blow received from head and horn. The most usual place for a horn wound is in the thigh, since it is there that the point, lowered as the bull charges, will first catch when it is raised to gore.

Vino: wine; *Vino corriente* is *vin ordinaire* or table wine; *vino del pais* is the local wine, always good to ask for; *vino Rioja* is wine of the Rioja region in the north of Spain; both red and white wines. The best are those of the *Bodegas Bilbainos, Marqués de Murrieta, Marqués de Riscal. Rioja Clarete* or *Rioja Alta* are the lightest and pleasantest of the red wines. *Diamante* is a good white wine with fish. *Valdepeñas* is fuller bodied than Rioja, but is excellent in both white and rosé. The Spanish vintners produce *Chablis* and *Burgundies* that I cannot recommend. The *Clarete Valdepeñas* is a very good wine. The table wines around Valencia are very good; those of Tarragona are better, but do not travel well. Galicia has good local table wine. In Asturias they drink cider. The local wines of Navarra are very good. For anyone who comes to Spain thinking only in terms of Sherry and Málaga, the splendid, light, dry, red wines will be a revelation. The *vin ordinaire* in Spain is consistently superior to that of France, since it is never tricked or adulterated, and is only about a third as expensive. I believe it to be the best in Europe by far. They have no *Grands Vins* to compare with those of France.

Vista: clear perception; *de mucha vista:* having a great perception and knowledge of bullfighting.

Vividores: livers off of; chisellers; those parasites of bullfighting who make their living out of it without contributing anything to it. The Spanish chiseller will make a living where his American or Greek brother would barely exist, and where the good American chiseller would starve the Spanish chiseller will gain enough to retire.

Volapié: flying while running; method of killing bulls invented by Joaquín Rodriguez (Costillares) at the time of the American Declaration of Independence from England to deal with those bulls which, because they were too worn out, could not be depended on to charge in order that they might be killed *recibiendo*, that is, by the man awaiting the charge and taking the bull on his sword. In the volapié the man places the bull with his four feet squared; profiles at a short distance, the muleta held low in his left hand; sights along the sword which makes a prolongation of his forearm held across his chest, and goes in on the bull his left shoulder forward, putting in the sword with his right hand between the bull's shoulders; gives the bull his exit with the muleta in the left hand and sucking in his belly to avoid the right horn, exits from the encounter along the bull's flank. Except that present-day matadors rarely go in close, at the moment of putting in the sword, and almost never arm themselves with the sword on a level with their chests, but instead sight along it anywhere from the level of their chins to above their noses, the volapié as described above and invented by Costillares is still the method of killing bulls used in modern times.

Volcar: to overturn or tumble; *volcando sobre el morrillo:* is said of a matador who has gone in to kill so hard and sincerely that he has almost literally fallen forward on to the bull's shoulders after the sword.

Voluntad: desire or good will; a matador is said to have shown *buena voluntad* when he has tried his best, and if the result has been bad it has been because of the defectiveness of the bull or else the man's incapacity rather than lack of intention.

Vuelta al ruedo: tour of the ring made by the matador at the insistence of the spectators to receive applause. He goes accompanied by his banderilleros who pick up and pocket cigars and pick up and throw back hats or other articles of clothing thrown down into the ring.

Z

Zapatillas: heel-less pumps worn by bullfighters in the ring.

Some Reactions of a few individuals to the Integral Spanish Bullfight

AGES GIVEN ARE THOSE AT WHICH THEY FIRST SAW FIGHTS

P. H. – Four years old; American; male. Taken by his nurse to a Spanish bullfight at Bordeaux without his parents' knowledge or permission, he called out on first seeing the bull charge the picadors, 'Il faut pas faire tomber le horsy!' A short time later he called out, 'Assis! Assis! Je ne peux pas voir le taureau!' Asked by his parents his impression of the bullfight, he said, 'J'aime ça!' Taken to a Spanish bullfight at Bayonne three months later he seemed very interested, but did not comment during the fight. After it he said, 'Quand j'étais jeune la course de taureaux n'était pas comme ça.'

J. H. – Nine years old; American; male; education, French Lycée; one year kindergarten in U.S. Ridden horses two years; allowed to go to bullfights with his father as reward for work in school and because his younger brother having without parents' intention seen one with no bad results, he felt it unjust that the smaller child should have seen the spectacle he was not to have been allowed to attend until twelve years old. Followed action with great interest and without comment. When cushions commenced to be thrown at cowardly matador, whispered, 'Can I throw mine, Papa?' Thought blood on horse's right front leg was paint and asked if horses were so painted so bull would charge them. Was greatly impressed by bulls, but thought work matadors did looked easy. Admired vulgar bravery of Saturio Torón. Said Torón was his favourite. The others were all frightened. Held firm belief that no bullfighter, no matter what he did, was doing his best. Took dislike for Villalta. Said 'I hate Villalta!'

First time he had ever employed this word in regard to a human being. Asked why, answered, 'I hate the way he looks and the way he acts.' Declared he did not believe there were any fighters as good as his friend Sidney, and that he did not want to see any more fights unless Sidney was going to fight. Said he did not like to see the horses injured, but laughed at the time and afterwards at only funny incident in regard to horses. On discovering matadors were killed decided he would rather be a guide in Wyoming or a trapper. Maybe a guide in summer and a trapper in the winter.

X. Y. – Twenty-seven years old; American; male; college education; ridden horses on farm as boy. Took flask of brandy to his first bullfight; took several drinks at ring; when bull charged picador and hit horse X. Y. gave sudden screeching intake of breath; took drink of brandy; repeated this on each encounter between bull and horse. Seemed to be in search of strong sensations. Doubted genuineness of my enthusiasm for bullfights. Declared it was a pose. He felt no enthusiasm and declared no one else could. Still convinced fondness for bullfights in others is a pose. Does not care for sport of any sort. Does not care for games of chance. Amusement and occupation – drinking, night life and gossip. Writes, travels about.

Capt. D. S. – Twenty-six years old; soldier; British; of Irish and English extraction; education, Public Schools and Sandhurst; went out to Mons in 1914 as infantry officer; wounded 27th August 1914; 1914–1918, brilliant record as infantry officer. Rides to hounds and in regimental point-to-points. Recreations, hunting, ski-ing, mountaineering; is widely read and has intelligent appreciation of modern writing and painting. Does not care for gaming or betting. Suffered sincerely and deeply at what happened to horses at first bullfight – said it was most hateful thing he had ever seen. Continued to attend them, he said, in order to understand mentality of people who would tolerate such a thing. At the end of his sixth fight understood them so well that he became embroiled in a dispute through defending the conduct of a matador, John Anllo, Nacional II, during the fight when a spectator insulted him. Went in the ring in the amateur fights in the mornings. Wrote two articles on bullfighting, one of them an apology for it, in the regimental gazette.

Mrs A. B. – Twenty-eight years old; American; not a horse-woman; finishing-school education; studied to sing in opera; does not care for games, or gaming. Does not wager. Attended bullfights – was moderately horrified. Did not like them. Did not go again.

Mrs E. R. – Thirty years old; American school and college education; ridden horses and owned pony as a child; musician; favourite author, Henry James; favourite sport, tennis; never seen either boxing or bullfighting until after her marriage. Enjoyed good prizefights. Did not want her to see horses in bullfight, but believed she would enjoy rest of corrida. Had her look away when the bull charged horse. Told her when not to look. Did not want to shock or horrify her. Found she was not shocked nor horrified by horses and enjoyed it as a part of bullfight, which she enjoyed greatly first time and became great admirer and partisan of. Developed almost unerring judgement for telling a matador's class, sincerity and possibilities as soon as she saw him work once. Was very much moved at one time by a certain matador. Matador was certainly much moved by her. Was fortunate enough to be away from the fights during this matador's moral débâcle.

Mrs S. T. – Thirty years old; English; private school and convent education; ridden horses; alcoholic nymphomaniac. Done some painting. Spent money much too fast to be able to gamble with it – gambled occasionally with borrowed money. Loved drinking more than excitement; rather shocked by horses, but so excited by bull-fighters and general strong emotion that she became a partisan of the spectacle. Drank herself out of any remembrance of it shortly after.

W. G. – Twenty-seven years old; American; male; college education; excellent baseball player; very good sportsman, keen intelligence and good aesthetic appreciation; only experience with horses on farm; recently recovered from maniac depression which followed nervous breakdown; shocked and horrified by horses. Unable to see anything else in fight. Put everything on moral basis. Suffered sincerely and truly at pain being inflicted. Took violent dislike to picadors. Felt they were to blame personally. After he was away from Spain, horror died out and he remembered parts of fight he liked, but he truly and sincerely disliked bullfighting.

333

R. S. – Twenty-eight years old; American; male; successful writer without private means; college education; enjoyed bullfights greatly; fond of music of fashionable composers, but not a musician; little aesthetic appreciation other than music; no horseman; was not at all distressed by horses; went into amateur fights in the morning and was a great crowd pleaser; came to Pamplona two years. Seemed very fond of the fights, but has not followed them since his marriage, although he often says he would like to. May possibly go to them again sometimes. Seemed genuinely fond of them, but has no time now for non-social or non-money-making manisfestations. Is genuinely fond of golf. Does very little gambling, but makes a few bets on questions of veracity, opinion, college loyalty, etc.

P. M. – Twenty-eight years old; American; convent and college graduate; not a musician; no musical ability or appreciation; intelligent appreciation of painting and letters; rode horses and owned pony as child. Saw first fight in Madrid in which three men were gored. Did not like it, and left before end. Saw fairly good fight second time and liked it. Completely unaffected by the horses. Came to understand fights and enjoyed them more than any other spectacle. Has attended them steadily. Does not care for boxing or football – enjoys bicycle-racing. Likes shooting, fishing. Does not like to gamble.

V. R. – Twenty-five years old; American; convent and college education; good horsewoman; liked fights tremendously from start; completely unaffected by horses; has attended fights whenever possible, ever since seeing her first one. Enjoys boxing very much; enjoys horse-racing; does not care for bicycle-racing; likes to gamble.

A. U. – Thirty-two years old; American; college education; poet; great sensitivity; all-round athlete; keen aesthetic appreciation of music, painting, letters; rode horses in the army; not a horseman. Does not care for gambling. Deeply affected by seeing bulls charge horses in first fight, but this did not prevent his enjoyment of bullfight. Appreciated matadors' work intensely, and was ready to row with spectators who were hooting them. Has not been where he could see bullfights since that fall.

S. A. – Internationally famous novelist writing in Yiddish. Had luck to see excellent bullfight his first time in Madrid; declared there was no emotion comparable in intensity except first sexual intercourse.

Mrs M. W. – Forty years old; American; education, private schools; not good at sports; has ridden horses; keen aesthetic appreciation of music, painting, writing; generous, intelligent, loyal, attractive; very good mother. Did not look at horses – kept her eyes away; enjoyed rest of bullfight, but would not care to see many. Very fond of having a good time and very intelligent about knowing what it consists in.

W. A. – Twenty-nine years old; American; male, successful journalist; college education; no horseman; very civilized appreciation of food and drink; well read and wide experience; was disappointed in first fight, but not at all shocked by horses; in fact enjoyed horse part, but tended to be bored by the rest of fight; became rather interested in fights finally and brought wife to Spain, but she disliked them, and the next year W. A. no longer followed them. Had bad luck nearly always to see bad fights. Was close follower of boxing for a time, but no longer goes to fights. Does little gambling. Loves food, drink, and good conversation. Extremely intelligent.

In these few reactions of individuals I have tried to be completely accurate as to their first and ultimate impressions of the bullfight. The only conclusion I draw from these reactions is that some people will like the fights and others will not. Because I had never seen her before I could not chronicle the history of an Englishwoman, who looked to be about thirty-five, I saw once at San Sebastian who was attending the bullfight with her husband, and was so overcome by the horses being charged by the bulls that she cried as though they were her own horses or her own children who were being gored. She left the ring crying, but urging her husband to stay. She had not meant to make a demonstration; it had only been too horrible for her to stand. She looked a very fine and pleasant woman and I felt very sorry for her. Nor have I described the reactions of a Spanish girl who attended a fight at La Coruña with either her young husband or fiancé and who cried very much and suffered all through the corrida but remained in her seat. These are, speaking absolutely truthfully, the only women I have seen cry at over three hundred bullfights. It is to be understood, of course, that at these fights I could only observe my very immediate neighbours.

A Short Estimate of the American,
Sidney Franklin, as a Matador

Most Spaniards do not go to bullfights, only a small proportion do, and of these who attend, the competent aficionados are limited in number. Yet many times I have heard people say that they asked a Spaniard, an actual Spaniard, mind you, what sort of bullfighter Sidney Franklin was, and the Spaniard said he was very brave but very awkward, and did not know what it was all about. If you asked that Spaniard if he had seen Franklin fight he would say no; what has happened is that he has told the way, from national pride, the Spaniards hope he would fight. He does not fight that way at all.

Franklin is brave with a cold, serene, and intelligent valour, but instead of being awkward and ignorant he is one of the most skilful, graceful, and slow manipulators of a cape fighting today. His repertoire with the cape is enormous but he does not attempt by a varied repertoire to escape from the performance of the veronica as the base of his cape work and his veronicas are classical, very emotional, and beautifully timed and executed. You will find no Spaniard who ever saw him fight who will deny his artistry and excellence with the cape.

He does not place banderillas, never having studied or practised this properly, and this is a serious omission since, with his physique, judgement of distance, and coolness, he could have been a very good banderillero.

Franklin manages the muleta well with his right hand but uses his left hand far too little. He kills easily and well. He does not give the importance to killing that it merits, since it is easy for him and because he ignores the danger. Profiling with more style, his kills would gain greatly in emotion.

He is a better, more scientific, more intelligent, and more finished matador than all but about six of the full matadors in Spain today, and the bullfighters know it and have the utmost respect for him.

It is too late for him to become a good banderillero, but he understands his other faults and is constantly correcting them. With the cape he has no improvement to make; he is a professor, a Doctor of Tauromachia, and not only a classic artist, but an inventor and innovator as well.

He was formed and taught by Rodolfo Gaona, the Mexican, the only matador who ever competed on equal terms with Joselito and Belmonte, and who himself was formed and taught by a banderillero of the great Frascuelo, who gave him the most complete training in the classic fundamentals of bullfighting which are ignored by most young matadors who have much courage, a little grace and youth, and posture, and hope for the best; and it was the art and soundness of Franklin's fighting which he learned in the best school possible which so amazed and enthused the Spaniards.

He had great and legitimate artistic triumphs in Sevilla, Madrid, and San Sebastian before the élite of the aficionados, as well as triumphs in Cadiz, Ceuta, and other towns in the provinces. He filled the Madrid ring so there was not a ticket to be had three times running, the first time as an American and a novelty everyone was curious to see after his great success in Sevilla, but the next two on his merits as a bullfighter. That was in 1929, and that year he could have taken the alternativa as a formal matador de toros at any one of half a dozen cities, and I would then have written of him in the body of this book with the other matadors de toros, but he wisely wanted another year as a novillero; he was fighting as often as he wished and getting more as a novillero than many matadors de toros, and another year as a novillero would give him that much more time to perfect his work with the muleta and his experience and knowledge of the Spanish bulls, which are quite different from the Mexican. He ran into bad luck on his second fight early in March of 1930, when he was gored by a bull he had turned his back to after having put the sword in and received a tremendous wound that perforated the rectum, sphincter muscle and large intestine, and when he was able to start filling his contracts his wound was still open and he fought through the season in bad physical shape. During the winter of 1930–1931 he fought in Mexico, and alternating with Marcial Lalanda in Nuevo Laredo, he received an unimportant horn wound in the calf of the leg which would have caused him no inconvenience (he fought the following Sunday) except that the surgeon who attended him insisted on administering anti-tetanus and anti-gangrene vaccine. These injections coming too soon after the usual injections of the same serums he had received when he was wounded in Madrid caused a breaking out in a sort of boil on his left arm, which swelled and made the arm nearly useless, and spoiled his 1931 season in Spain. Then, too, he came to Spain from Mexico with plenty of money from his winter campaign and more desire to enjoy life than to start in fighting at once. He had made the Madrid ring pay him the very top price when he was in such demand the year before, and as soon as he decided that he was ready to fight, the management took their revenge by the typically Spanish method of putting him off on one pretext or another until they had all their dates contracted for.

He has the ability in languages, the cold courage and the ability to command of the typical soldier of fortune; he is a charming companion, one of the best story-tellers I have ever heard; has enormous and omnivorous curiosity about everything, but gets his information through the eye and ear and reads only the *Saturday Evening Post*, which he goes through from cover to cover each week, usually finishing it in about three days and then having four bad days of waiting for the next number. He is a very hard master to those who work for him, yet commands amazing loyalty. He speaks Spanish not only perfectly, but with the accent of whatever place he may be in; he does all his own business and is very proud of his business judgement, which is terrible. He believes in himself as confidently as an opera singer does, but he is not conceited.

I have purposely written nothing about his life, since having led it at great peril and in an utterly fantastic manner he would seem to be entitled to whatever profits the story of it might bring. At one time and another I have heard the whole story from the beginning, through the fall of 1931, and I have been present while certain chapters of it were happening, and it is better than any picturesque novel you ever read. Any man's life, told truly, is a novel, but the bull-fighter's life has an order in the tragedy of its progression which tends to formalize the story into a groove. Sidney's life has escaped this and he has truly lived three lives – one Mexican, one Spanish, and one American – in a way that is unbelievable. The story of those lives belongs to him, and I will not tell it to you. But I can tell you truly, all question of race and nationality aside, that with the cape he is a great and fine artist and no history of bullfighting that is ever written can be complete unless it gives him the space he is entitled to.

Dates on which Bullfights will ordinarily be held in Spain, France, Mexico, and Central and South America

JANUARY

Bullfights every Sunday in Mexico City, Lima, Peru, and Caracas, Venezuela.

On 1st January there is always a fight at San Luis de Potosi in Mexico.

In the states of Tampico, Vera Cruz, Torreón, Puebla, León, Zacatecas, Ciudad Juárez, and Monterey occasional fights will be given on Sundays.

In Casablanca in Spanish Morocco one or more bullfights are given on Sundays in January.

Valencia, Maracay, and Maracaibo in Venezuela give occasional fights on Sundays.

Cartagena de Indias in Colombia also usually has fights in January.

FEBRUARY

Bullfights every Sunday in Mexico City, Lima, and Caracas, and occasionally a benefit fight announced for a weekday in Mexico City.

Formal fights or novilladas on Sundays in San Luis de Potosi, Ciudad Juárez, Puebla, Torreón, Monterey, Aguas Calientes, Tampico, León, Zacatecas in Mexico, and fights in Bogota, Baranquilla, and Panama in Central America.

Novilladas start in Madrid and Barcelona if the weather is favourable on Sundays and usually in Valencia.

MARCH

Bullfights every Sunday in Mexico City and Caracas (Venezuela). Occasionally fights will be given in Málaga, Barcelona, and Valencia in March and there is always a fight at Castellón de la Plana for the fiestas of the Magdalena, which you may look up in any religious calendar.

Novilladas are usually given, weather permitting, every Sunday in Madrid, Barcelona, Valencia, Zaragoza, and on one or two Sundays in Bilbao.

APRIL

Bullfights on Easter Sunday at Madrid, Barcelona, Sevilla, Zaragoza, Málaga, Murcia, Granada.

On the Monday after Easter the first subscription fight starts in Madrid.

The feria at Sevilla starts within a week after Easter and has three fights on successive days.

Twenty-fifth, feria at Lorca.

Twenty-ninth, feria at Jerez de la Frontera.

Bullfights each Sunday after Easter in Madrid, Barcelona, Valencia, and novilladas on Sundays in Zaragoza, Bilbao, and usually at the minor rings of Vista Alegre and Tetuán de las Victorias in Madrid. If you go to either one be careful not to have your pocket picked.

MAY

If Easter is early and Corpus Christi comes in May there will be bullfights on that day in Madrid, Sevilla, Granada, Málaga, Toledo, and Bilbao, possibly also at Zaragoza.

Fixed Dates for Fights

May 2 – Bilbao, Lucena.
May 3 – Bilbao, Figueras, Santa Cruz de Tenerife.
May 4 – Puertollano, Jerez de los Caballeros.
Between May 8 and 10 – Ecija and Caravaca.
Between May 13 and 15 – Osuna and Badajoz.
May 15 – Madrid.
May 16 – Madrid and Talavera de la Reina.

May 17 – Madrid. These three fights are for the feria of San Isidro, patron of Madrid. There is no longer much of a feria, but the fights remain.

May 18–19–20 – Ronda, Olivenza, Baeza.

May 21–22 – Zaragoza.

May 25–26 – Cordoba.

May 30 – Aranjuez and Cáceres (novillada in Madrid).

May 31 – Cáceres, Teruel, and Antequera.

On the last Sunday in May there is usually a bullfight in the Roman arena in Béziers, France.

In May the season of the summer novilladas starts in Mexico.

JUNE

Bullfights every Thursday and Sunday in Madrid and every Sunday in Barcelona.

June 2–4 – Trujillo.

June 9 – Plasencia.

June 9–11 – Big fair at Algeciras – usually three fights.

June 13–17 – Feria at Granada – usually three fights.

June 22 – Avila.

June 24 – Tolosa, Medina del Rio Seco, Cabra, Barcelona, Zafra, Badajoz – Feria at Badajoz with two fights.

June 25 – Tolosa, Badajoz.

June 27–29 – Feria at Segovia – usually two fights.

June 29 – Alicante.

June 29–30 – Feria at Burgos – usually two fights.

JULY

First Sunday in July – Fights at Palma de Mallorca.

July 6–12 – Feria of San Fermin at Pamplona, with five fights on successive days, starting 7th July. Amateur fights each morning at seven o'clock. Bulls run through the street the mornings of all bullfights. Better be at the ring by 6 a.m. to buy seats in the boxes. Other seats are free and filled. Tickets may usually be bought the night before between six and seven at the booths on the square.

July 14 – Bullfights at Bordeaux and Bayonne.

Between the 15th and 18th, fights at La Linea, near Gibraltar.

July 23 – Alcira. Usually a good fight.

July 25 – Big fight at San Sebastian and Santander. First fight of feria at Valencia, where there will be seven to nine fights on successive days until and through 2nd August.

The first Sunday of July there is a fight at Nîmes, France.

All through July there will be novilladas on every Thursday or Sunday on which formal fights are not given in Madrid or Barcelona. The big ferias, not to be missed, are Pamplona and Valencia.

AUGUST

On 2nd August there is a feria at Vitoria, with three fights on successive days, and another at La Coruña, also with three fights. Vitoria is easily reached by motor in three hours from the French frontier at Hendaye. In case of a Sunday coming opportunely these fights will sometimes start as late as the 4th or 5th.

Between 2nd and 5th August there are fights at Santander, San Sebastian, Cartagena, and Tomelloso.

Between the 8th and 10th there is a feria at Pontevedra in Galicia, usually with only one fight.

August 10 – Manzanares.

August 15, 16, and 17 is the Grande Semaine at San Sebastian, with three successive fights on those days. In case of Sunday coming earlier or later the fights may be on the 14th, 15th, and 16th, promoters always trying to bring one of the series of fights in a feria on a Sunday.

On 15th and 16th August there are also ferias at Gijón, Badajoz, and Almendralejo, with two fights each and single fights on those days at Puerto de Santa María (15th), Palma de Mallorca (15th), Jaén, Tafalla, and Játiba (15th). Tafalla can be reached from Biarritz in four and a half hours by car.

August 16 – Orihuela, Burgode, Osma, and Jumilla.

August 17–20 – Ciudad Real, Sanlúcar, Toledo, Málaga, Antequera, and, sometimes, Guadalajara.

August 21 – The summer fair at Bilbao starts with usually five successive fights. During this week there are fights on Sunday at San Sebastian, Oviedo, Almagro – two fights, Astorga, two fights (24th and 25th), Almería, two fights, usually the 26th and 27th, Tarazona de la Mancha (24th), Alcalá de Henares (25th).

August 28 – Tarazona de Aragon and Toro. San Sebastian if it is a Sunday.

August 28–30 – Málaga, Puerto de Santa María, Linares, Colmenar Viejo (sometimes two fights).

August 29 – Málaga (second fight of feria).

August 30 – Linares (second fight of feria).

August 31 – Calahorra, Requena, Constantina.

All of August there will be novilladas in Madrid and Barcelona and usually Zaragoza and Valencia every Sunday and usually every Thursday. The big fairs from a bullfighting standpoint in August are those of Bilbao and San Sebastian. If you want to see country go to Colmenar Viejo, Astorga or Toro.

SEPTEMBER

The great feria month.

Second and third – Palencia – usually good fights – intelligent public. Nice Castilian town, with good beer and excellent quail shooting.

Third and fourth – Mérida, Villarobledo, and Priego. Usually two fights at Mérida, one at each of the others.

The first Sunday of September there is a fight at San Sebastian, and if Sunday comes after the 4th, at Aranjuez.

Fifth and sixth – Feria at Cuenca, with usually two fights and a novillada. Wonderful town, terrible road there. Same dates, feria at Castellar, with two fights. Between 4th and 6th either fights or novilladas at Segovia, Huelva, Requena, Jerez de los Caballeros.

Feria starts at Murcia either 7th or 8th. Usually two fights.

Seventh or eighth – Utrera, Palma de Mallorca, Cabra, Belmez, Tortoza, Ayamonte, Cáceres, Barbastro, Santoña, Benavente, and occasionally Valdepeñas and Lorca.

September 9 – A two-fight feria starts at Calatayud, and on the 10th Albacete commences a feria with three successive fights, although sometimes as many as five are given. Either of these is good.

Ninth, also San Martín de Valdeiglesias, on the road from Madrid to the Sierra de Gredos, Villanueva del Arzobispo, Barcarrota, and Andújar.

Tenth or eleventh – Usually two-fight feria starts at Zamora, and on the 11th there will usually be fights at Haro, Utiel, and Cehegin.

345

September 12 – The feria starts at Salamanca, with three fights on successive days.

There are also fights at San Sebastian the second Sunday in September, this usually a cheap fight though sometimes good, and at Utiel, Melilla, and Barcelona.

The third Sunday in September the fall subscription season usually starts in Madrid, with fights each Sunday until the middle of October.

September 14 or 15 – There will usually be fights or novilladas at Jerez de la Frontera, Aranda de Duero, Castuera, and Aracena.

On the 15th or 16th there will usually be fights at San Clemente, Mora, Trujillo, and Tomelloso.

On either the 18th, 19th, or 20th, depending on where the Sunday comes in the month, three days of successive fights start for the feria of Valladolid. The town is easy to reach by rail or road. These are often good fights and the public is intelligent. On one of these three days fights are usually given for the ferias of Oviedo, Olivenza, and Zalamea la Real.

On the 21st of September a three-day bullfight feria starts at Logroño. This is the easiest of the September ferias to reach from the French frontier via Hendaye and Irún. The fights are usually of a high standard.

On the 21st, 22nd, and 23rd there will ordinarily be one fight at Talavera de la Reina, Fregenal de la Sierra, Soria, and Requena.

On the third Sunday in September, if the weather has been good in the north and visitors plenty, there will sometimes be a fight in San Sebastian. There will nearly always be a fight at Tarragona, Zaragoza, Barcelona, Malaga, Bilbao, and Cordoba. These were usually formerly held on the Feast of the Blessed Virgin.

Between 25th and 28th September there will usually be one fight at Quintanar de la Orden, Torrijos, Hellín, and Béjar.

On 28th September is the first fight of the two-fight feria of San Miguel in Sevilla. These two fights are usually much better than the spring feria corridas.

Fights may be given on the last three days of September in Caravaca, Úbeda, Jaén, Almendralejo, and Belmonte.

The most important ferias in September are those of Salamanca, Calatayud, Albacete, Valladolid, Logroño, and Sevilla. All of these are worth going to.

OCTOBER

On the first, second, and usually third Sundays in October there will be fights at Madrid and Barcelona, and usually Valencia.

October 1 and 2 – Úbeda, feria.

October 3 – Soria, feria.

Between October 2 and 4 – Zafra, feria.

Usually there will be a fight during the first week in October at Aranjuez.

On either the 12th or 13th of October commences the feria of Pilar in Zaragoza, consisting of four to five fights. This is the last important feria of the season.

Between the 15th and 20th there will be a feria at Guadalajara, with one fight, and on the 18th and 19th another at Jaén, with two. On either the 18th or 19th there will sometimes be fights at Gandía and Játiba.

The last Sunday in October there will be fights at Barcelona and Valencia, if the weather has been good, and occasionally a fight on the last day of October at Gerona.

The great feria of the month is that of Pilar at Zaragoza.

Toward the middle of October the formal bullfight season starts in Mexico City and throughout the country.

NOVEMBER

In case of good weather bullfights may be be given the first week of November in Barcelona or Valencia. They will be given each Sunday in Mexico City and in various Mexican cities, bullfighters contracted for Mexico usually leaving immediately after the feria of Pilar at Zaragoza.

The last fight in Spain is usually at Ondara, in the province of Alicante, between the 16th and 20th of November.

DECEMBER

The second big month of the Mexican season, with fights every Sunday in Mexico City and frequently in various other Mexican cities.

In Lima (Peru), Caracas (Venezuela), and Bogotá (Colombia) the bullfight season commences around the middle of December, usually with Spanish matadors in addition to whatever local phenomena are in fashion. In Venezuela there are occasional fights in Valencia and Maracaibo, as well as more or less serious occasional bullfights in Panamá and Guatemala. To see bullfights in November or December, Mexico City is the place.

Bibliographical Note

For a list of 2077 books and pamphlets in Spanish dealing with or touching on tauromachia, to the authors of all of which the writer of this book wishes to acknowledge his deep indebtedness and to apologize for his intrusion, the reader who wishes to make a study of the history of the Spanish bullfight is referred to Libros y Folletos de Toros, Bibliografía Taurina, Compuesta Con Vista de la Biblioteca Tauromaca de Don José Luis de Ybarra y Lopez de Calle por Graciano Diaz Arquer and published in Madrid at the Library of Pedro Vindel.

The present volume, *Death in the Afternoon*, is not intended to be either historical or exhaustive. It is intended as an introduction to the modern Spanish bullfight and attempts to explain that spectacle both emotionally and practically. It was written because there was no book which did this in Spanish or in English. The writer asks the indulgence of competent aficionados for his technical explanations. When a volume of controversy may be written on the execution of a single suerte one man's arbitrary explanation is certain to be unacceptable to many.

E. H.

More about Penguins
and Pelicans

Penguinews, which appears every month, contains details of all the new books issued by Penguins as they are published. From time to time it is supplemented by *Penguins in Print*, which is a complete list of all titles available. (There are some five thousand of these.)

A specimen copy of *Penguinews* will be sent to you free on request. For a year's issues (including the complete lists) please send £1.00 if you live in the British Isles, or elsewhere. Just write to Dept EP, Penguin Books Ltd, Harmondsworth, Middlesex, enclosing a cheque or postal order, and your name will be added to the mailing list.

In the U.S.A.: For a complete list of books available from Penguin in the United States write to Dept CS, Penguin Books Inc., 7110 Ambassador Road, Baltimore, Maryland 21207.

In Canada: For a complete list of books available from Penguin in Canada write to Penguin Books Canada Ltd, 41 Steelcase Road West, Markham, Ontario

Hemingway

'He is . . . one of those who, honestly and undauntedly,
reproduces the genuine features of the hard countenance
of the age.'
from the Nobel Prize Citation

Hemingway titles in the Penguin list include:

A Moveable Feast
The Torrents of Spring
Across the River and into the Trees
Green Hills of Africa
The Fifth Column
Men Without Women
The Essential Hemingway
A Farewell to Arms
For Whom The Bell Tolls
The Short Happy Life of Francis Macomber
The Snows of Kilimanjaro
To Have and Have Not
Islands in the Stream